Navigating the Moral Maze

Navigating the Moral Maze is a teaching resource to help students understand and critically engage with the most pressing issues in the world today. From the ruin of Gaza to the climate emergency, from the repeal of Roe v Wade to rising inequality, young people are growing up in a world beset with moral concerns and predicaments. With this book teachers can equip students with the critical skills and conceptual clarity needed to navigate through these issues and reach a clear and articulate understanding of their own views.

Each chapter features numerous lesson ideas with activities, texts and thought experiments that help refine and enrich students' thoughts on the topics while promoting discussion and reflection. Topics covered include:

- Reproduction
- Euthanasia
- Poverty
- Environment
- Borders
- War

Applicable to Religious Studies, Philosophy and Ethics, and touching on topics relevant to PSHE, History and Geography, this will be a valuable resource for secondary teachers wanting to enhance their students' critical writing and thinking skills.

David Birch teaches philosophy and religion at Highgate School, UK. He also works for the Philosophy Foundation, an award-winning charity that brings philosophy to schools and the wider community.

'In this clear and lively guide, David Birch equips both teachers and pupils with the tools needed to tackle some of our most urgent moral problems. The well-chosen questions and activities will stimulate discussion, reflection and genuine understanding – Socrates would approve!'

Angie Hobbs, Professor of the Public Understanding of Philosophy, University of Sheffield

'Imaginatively presented and well-written, David Birch's latest book gives teachers and their pupils useful tools and activities on profoundly challenging topics. I highly recommend this teaching guide as an instrument for helping young people develop their thinking on the issues that affect us all.'

Emma Swinn MBE, Co-director of the UK's National Charity for Philosophical Enquiry

'*Navigating the Moral Maze* contains a multitude of engaging questions, extracts and scenarios that can get even the most disengaged class going. It offers teachers numerous scaffolding tools and activities that they can lift straight off the page to help their pupils think more clearly about the trickiest topics.'

Philip Gaydon, Head of Character Education, St Paul's School

Navigating the Moral Maze

A Teaching Guide to the Problems of Life, Death, Freedom and Justice

David Birch

LONDON AND NEW YORK

Designed cover image: © Getty Images

First published 2025
by Routledge
4 Park Square, Milton Park, Abingdon, Oxon OX14 4RN

and by Routledge
605 Third Avenue, New York, NY 10158

Routledge is an imprint of the Taylor & Francis Group, an informa business

© 2025 David Birch

The right of David Birch to be identified as author of this work has been asserted in accordance with sections 77 and 78 of the Copyright, Designs and Patents Act 1988.

All rights reserved. No part of this book may be reprinted or reproduced or utilised in any form or by any electronic, mechanical, or other means, now known or hereafter invented, including photocopying and recording, or in any information storage or retrieval system, without permission in writing from the publishers.

Trademark notice: Product or corporate names may be trademarks or registered trademarks, and are used only for identification and explanation without intent to infringe.

British Library Cataloguing-in-Publication Data
A catalogue record for this book is available from the British Library

Library of Congress Cataloging-in-Publication Data
Names: Birch, David (Philosopher), author.
Title: Navigating the moral maze : a teaching guide to the problems of life, death, freedom and justice / David Birch.
Description: Abingdon, Oxon ; New York, NY : Routledge, 2025. | Includes bibliographical references.
Identifiers: LCCN 2024029622 (print) | LCCN 2024029623 (ebook) | ISBN 9781032563282 (hardback) | ISBN 9781032563299 (paperback) | ISBN 9781003434979 (ebook)
Subjects: LCSH: Ethics--Textbooks.
Classification: LCC BJ1012 .B533 2025 (print) | LCC BJ1012 (ebook) | DDC 170--dc23/eng/20241016
LC record available at https://lccn.loc.gov/2024029622
LC ebook record available at https://lccn.loc.gov/2024029623

ISBN: 978-1-032-56328-2 (hbk)
ISBN: 978-1-032-56329-9 (pbk)
ISBN: 978-1-003-43497-9 (ebk)

DOI: 10.4324/9781003434979

Typeset in Melior
by KnowledgeWorks Global Ltd.

You do not know what your life is, or what you are doing, or who you are.
                                                                    Euripides

After a certain point there is no turning back. That is the point that must be reached.
                                                                    Franz Kafka

I came not to bring peace, but a sword.
                                                                    Matthew 10:34

Contents

	Acknowledgements	viii
	Introduction	1
1	Reproduction	8
2	Euthanasia	27
3	Animals	48
4	Environment	72
5	War	82
6	Terrorism	102
7	Poverty	111
8	Wealth	126
9	Borders	139
10	Punishment	151
11	The State	172
12	Autonomy and Bodily Integrity	187
	Index	207

Acknowledgements

I am grateful to Eliana Zur-Szpiro for allowing me to draw on both her expertise and library. Clement Boden was a luminous source of ideas. MM McCabe and Andy West helped guide my research. In their energy and intelligence, my 23/24 Y10 class – Luke, Hannah, Ruby, Charlotte, Josh, Maya, James, Amelie, Ava, Sara, Phoebe, Alicia and Gene – have been a constant inspiration. The perspicacity of my Y13 pupils Loukas Arend and Ben Womack has also been much needed when formulating arguments. My deepest thanks belong to Sarah, whose patience and beneficence made this possible.

Introduction

This book is comprised of lesson ideas and materials designed to help pupils understand and critically engage with some of the most pressing issues in the world today. The aim, of course, is not to change pupils' minds or promote any particular agenda, but to afford them an opportunity to discover what they think and to discern the underlying principles behind their views. By entrusting pupils with profoundly serious questions, the wish is to thereby empower them, to awaken them to the responsibilities of life as a moral agent, to the awareness that the world is malleable and that what we do with it and in it matters.

Moral questions often confront adolescents as moments of existential quickening in their lives as emerging adults. In her essay 'A Sketch of the Past', Virginia Woolf (1976) describes several instances from her childhood when 'moments of being' interrupted the stupor of non-being, of the life 'not lived consciously'. One such moment occurred while she was fighting with her brother: 'Just as I raised my fist to hit him, I felt: why hurt another person? I dropped my hand instantly, and stood there, and let him beat me' (p. 71).

Woolf's 'moment of being' took shape in the form of a moral confusion, a sudden incredulity at our norms and attitudes. This rupture in the mundane fabric of experience was occasioned by the bewildering loss of intelligibility, by something familiar no longer making sense. I'd speculate that in this moment Woolf saw the contingency of things, the fact that they needn't be the way they are, that there are alternatives, other possible worlds. This realisation leaves one wondering why our world is as it is. If the architecture of the world is contingent, if reality can be changed, then we ought to be able to provide good reasons for the way we've made it. Woolf discovered, to her great and enlivening dismay, that many of our norms lack reason or justification. Only once this has been noticed can it be changed.

The book's hope is that it will induce in pupils analogous experiences, that in the very process of our presenting pupils with questions on the nature of life and death, freedom and justice, we are showing them that the world can be reconceptualised and restructured, and we thereby create the space for their own particular confrontations with incredulity, their own moments of being. For just as adolescence is the metamorphosis of a child into a new a body with new possibilities of life, it is also their metamorphosis into a new mind, with new powers of thought. The chapters that follow aim to provide the means – an armoury of arresting problems – by which pupils can exercise and experiment with those powers.

Arguments

For the sake of clarity, at various points throughout the book I've used 'argument schematics' and 'argument trees' where the latter are designed to guide pupils through arguments and the former to construct their own. The argument schematics look something like what you see below. While I've endeavoured to make the meanings of the symbols clear whenever they appear, here is a comprehensive breakdown:

~	Similar to
≁	Not similar to
→	Entails that i.e. A → B means 'If A, then B'
↛	Does not entail that
≡	Morally equivalent to
≢	Not morally equivalent to
>	'A > B' means 'A morally supersedes B' i.e. A takes moral priority over B
<	'A < B' means 'B morally supersedes A' i.e. B takes moral priority over A

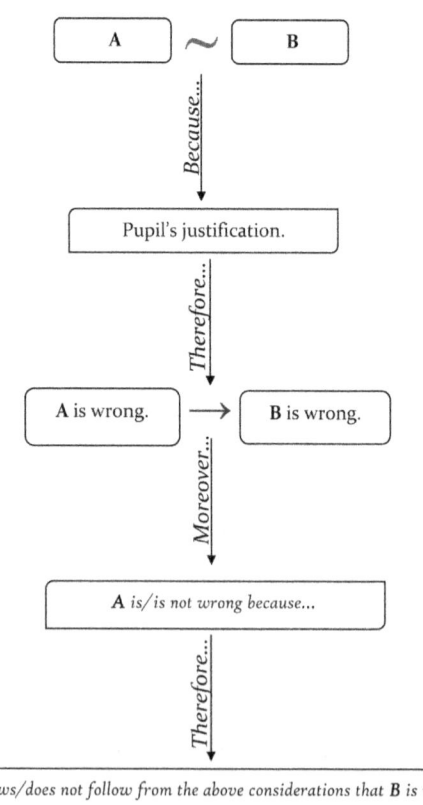

You will find that activities are at times heavily scaffolded. While you should of course feel free to discard these scaffolds, I believe they have genuine value. Firstly, they provide a very direct way of enlarging and enriching pupils' vocabulary and writing styles. More importantly, by obviating the need to think about wording and paragraph structure, it frees pupils to devote their minds to the more significant task of thinking through the philosophical problems.

Skeleton Activities

While the chapters contain various activities to help guide pupils through these issues, below I've presented a series of 'skeleton activities' which can be used to unlock most topics. You should employ these as you see fit.

Moral Barometer

To enable pupils to develop a rich introspective sense of their own minds, becoming alert to their inclinations and fluctuations, you can begin each topic by asking pupils to gauge their pre-reflexive view using something like this:

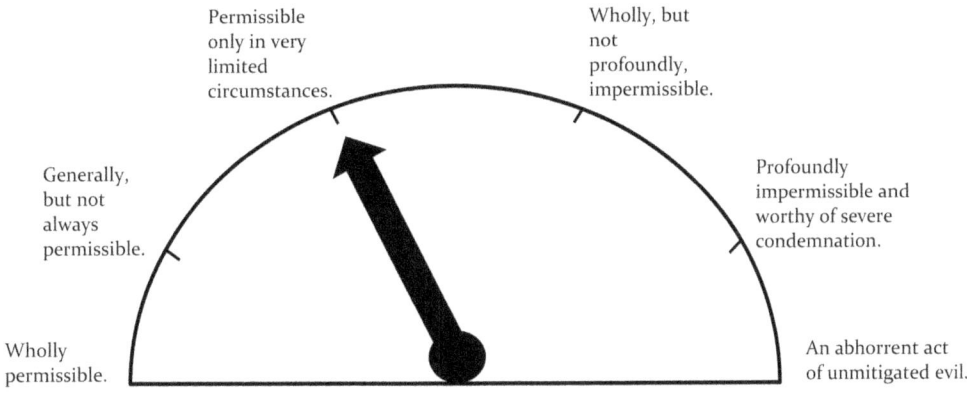

At the end of the topic, give them a fresh dial and repeat. They should then look back at their initial response and see whether there's been a shift. If there has been a shift, the aim is to identify the cause of this. What detail, perspective or concept do they now appreciate that they didn't before?

Moral Detective

This is an activity to complement the use of the moral barometer at the close of topics. The aim is for pupils to try to work out each other's moral stances. This can be done in pairs, or as a class with one person drawing the position of their arrow on the board while the others close their eyes. Before doing this, the class should decide upon four targeted and telling questions e.g. for abortion, these might be 'Do you think the foetus has moral status?', 'Do you think the foetus has a right to life?', 'Do you think killing the foetus involves depriving it of a future like ours?' and 'Do you think the court should have ruled in favour of McFall?' You can then take a blind show of hands to indicate, for each point on the barometer, where they think the arrow falls.

The purpose of this activity, besides fostering a sense of curiosity in each other's views, is to encourage pupils to think through the logical consistency of their positions. It may well be that the class thinks that the arrow should be differently placed given the answers proffered. If so, it's then a matter of talking this through and figuring out the correct logical implications of their answers.

Speed Thinking

This a type of carousel activity to use at the start of topics which, in addition to fostering the aforementioned curiosity in their peers, serves to quickly gather a multitude of different ideas and arguments.

- Ask a closed question on the topic at hand e.g. 'Should the state permit voluntary slavery?'

- With books at the ready and pupils in pairs, each person has 20 seconds to say their thoughts on the question.

- They then have 20 seconds of open discussion.

- They then have 20 seconds to write down either one intriguing, compelling or specious idea they heard.

- Rotate and move onto another person.

Having repeated this five or so times, they then give feedback to the class.

Philosophical Battleships

This is a game to encourage thinking that is both creative and critical. It can be used at the start or end of topics.

- Choose a statement which expresses a clear moral position e.g. 'Capital punishment is immoral.'

- Player 1 (individual or group) writes down three cogent reasons in support of the statement.

- Player 2 (individual or group) tries to anticipate Player 1's reasons.

- One direct hit means that Player 2 wins.

This does require you to act as umpire by checking that Player 1's arguments aren't intentionally fatuous e.g. 'Capital punishment must be immoral because many Americans support it'. Fatuous arguments are void.

Philosophical Tête-a-Tête

In describing his collaboration with the philosopher Gilles Deleuze, Félix Guattari said, '[I]t was less a matter of sharing a common understanding than sharing the sum of our uncertainties … We didn't collaborate like two different people. We were more like two streams coming together to make a third stream … We're doing something together because it works; something greater than ourselves carries us along' (quoted in Dosse, 2011, p. 10).

This image of intermingled deliquescence expresses very well what a philosophy lesson should be. Even when there is disagreement or discord, these form part of a broader collaborative pursuit of generating an abundance of new concepts, theories and arguments. As such, I favour group enquiries and tête-à-têtes over formal class debates. Philosophy is not a field of battle but an experiment in thinking. Having to adhere to and theatrically defend fixed positions is inimical to thought. When there is a substantive disagreement among the class, I find it valuable to foster collaborative thinking, not as a means of dissolving differences or emolliating conflict, but in order to help pupils discern and articulate their presuppositions and moral axioms.

For a tête-à-tête, put disagreeing pupils in pairs. Give each person up to one minute of uninterrupted time to present the reasons for their particular position. Then allow two minutes of open discussion between them. Assign a 'neutral observer' to each pair. Their task is to listen to the tête-à-tête and identify the conflicting principles at play. Following the discussion, ask the neutral observers to share their findings with the two interlocutors.

Group Enquiry

This is simply a class discussion, but one in which you, through facilitating the discussion, try to remain as absent as possible in order to give the pupils space to think. To keep your distance while enabling an effective and inclusive discussion, I suggest using these basic but effective techniques:

- Have one clear task question, which generally will be closed (a closed question, requiring a straightforward yes or no, helps to make the discussion accessible to all pupils).
- Give pupils 30 seconds to discuss the question with their neighbours.

- Follow this by repeating the task question and ask for a show of hands for 'Yes', 'No' or 'Something else'.
- Start to harvest answers. Allow for a period of time in which the focus is on hearing ideas rather than challenging them.
  - If a pupil gives an answer without identifying a supporting reason, ask 'Why do you think that?' or 'Can you say more about that?'
  - If a pupil makes a significant contribution that may serve as a catalyst to the discussion, repeat it using the pupil's own words and frame it as a question: 'Are you saying that such-and-such?'
  - If a pupil presents ideas that don't explicitly address the question, acknowledge their ideas and repeat the task question. This pre-empts digressions that may cause other pupils to feel lost or the discussion to lose shape.
  - If a pupil forgets their thought, repeat the task question and give them 30 seconds to think it through again.
- Once the harvest is complete, start trying to foster dialogues and friction by highlighting specific contributions and asking whether anyone has something to say about them.

It's worth emphasising that a group enquiry is not merely a forum for exchanging different viewpoints but an active vehicle of collective and collaborative thought. The class itself becomes a thinking entity, with pupils emerging from the process with radically different, or at least more vigorously held and understood, ideas than they did upon entering.

Mindprint

The lessons often contain a cornucopia of strange and powerful extracts from various philosophers. While I seek to distil the extracts down to their key arguments, it's valuable to give pupils an opportunity to pause on anything they find particularly evocative, provocative, intriguing, or catalytic. This can be done simply by affording pupils a few minutes at the end of the lesson to look back through the extracts and copy out, thereby introjecting, a sentence or line that leaves an impression on them. They should then write down the questions and thoughts that it elicits.

Extension Material

Several chapters end with an opening to further study. I've provided possible and rather uncooked extension material. If these strike you as interesting avenues of further exploration, I'd suggest drawing on the skeleton activities, argument schematics and argument trees to shape them into lessons.

References

Dosse, F. (2011). *Gilles Deleuze & Félix Guattari: Intersecting Lives* (Trans. D. Glassman). Columbia University Press.

Woolf, V. (1976). A Sketch from the Past. *Moments of Being*. HBJ.

Reproduction

Key Questions

- Does a foetus have moral status?
- Is a foetus a person?
- Is a foetus a human being?
- Were we once foetuses?
- Does the permissibility of abortion entail the permissibility of infanticide?
- Can the rights of a foetus override the rights of the person carrying it?
- Do we have a duty to reproduce? (*Extension*)
- Is it immoral to reproduce? (*Extension*)

Activity 1

Tell pupils that we are working towards determining whether killing a foetus (I'll use the term foetus loosely to cover the whole span of pregnancy) constitutes murder (defined as the intentional killing of an innocent person). The aim is to determine which of the following claims most aligns with their views:

a. *A foetus is not a human being, it has no moral status, and it is not a person.*

b. *A foetus is a human being, but it has no moral status, and is not a person.*

c. *A foetus is a human being, and it has moral status, but it is not a person.*

d. *A foetus is a human being, and it has moral status, and it is a person.*

To start with, present and discuss the following passage from Patrick Lee and Robert George (2005) in which they articulate their view that the fact that the embryo is in a gestational phase of development is not relevant to its status as a human being. Though it is undergoing maturation, this does not mean that it is partial or incomplete, just as a sapling is no less a tree for its immaturity. Lee and George stress that the embryo is not, properly speaking, part of the mother's body. While the mother's body provides the conditions and environment for its growth, it is a distinct and complete being 'internally directing his or her own growth toward full maturity' (p. 14). And so to kill a human embryo is to kill a distinct, unique and complete human being. They write:

> **Fact Check**
>
> In England, Wales and Scotland, abortion remains a criminal offence under the 1861 Offences Against the Person Act. The 1967 Abortion Act stipulates certain exceptions to that general prohibition. To not constitute an offence, the abortion must not take place after the 24th week of the pregnancy, and it must be carried out by a medical practitioner. In 2023, a mother of three in England who terminated her pregnancy at around 32 weeks was convicted under the 1861 Act and sentenced to more than two years in prison (on appeal that sentence was reduced to a 14-month suspended sentence). This was not an isolated case. In 2013, Sarah Catt was sentenced to eight years (reduced to three and a half years on appeal) in prison for terminating her pregnancy one week before the due date.

> [T]he embryo is human: it has the genetic makeup characteristic of human beings ... [It] is a complete or whole organism, though immature ... In abortion, what is killed is a human being, a whole living member of the species homo sapiens, the same kind of entity as you or I, only at an earlier stage of development. (p. 14)

- Enquiry Question: If Lee and George are correct, does this mean that killing a foetus is murder?

Development questions:

- ○ Are Lee and George correct? Is an embryo a human being?
- ○ Are you the 'same kind of entity' as a human embryo?
- ○ Would it make sense to refer to an embryo as a *partial* human being?
- ○ If an embryo is a partial human being, would that mean it only has partial mortal status?

Steer the discussion towards the question of whether our biological kinship with human embryos entails an equivalence in moral status. You could draw on the Universal Declaration of Human Rights[1] to present the idea that having the same biological status doesn't entail possessing the same rights. Presumably, children do not have the rights outlined in the following Articles:

- **Article 13**
  Everyone has the right to freedom of movement and residence within the borders of each state.

- **Article 17**
  Everyone has the right to own property alone as well as in association with others.

- **Article 21**
  Everyone has the right to take part in the government of his country, directly or through freely chosen representatives.

Philosophers often draw a distinction between human beings and persons. Whereas human being is a biological category, person is a metaphysical and moral category that could encompass beings with radically different biological makeups. To be a person is to be possessed of the right of life (Article 3, incidentally), and it is a category of being that Mary Anne Warren (2007) has argued doesn't include foetuses. On the concept of personhood, she writes:

> The presumption that all persons have full and equal basic moral rights may be part of the very concept of a person. If this is so, then the concept of a person is in part a moral one; once we have admitted that X is a person, we have implicitly committed ourselves to recognizing X's right to be treated as a member of the moral community. (p. 131)

In her view, an early foetus is 'a human entity which is not yet a person'. This is for the following reasons:

- It is not sentient.
- It is not capable of emotion.
- It lacks reason (insofar as it cannot solve problems).
- It is incapable of sophisticated communication.
- It is not self-aware.
- It has no moral agency i.e. it cannot regulate itself in order to act in accordance with moral principles or ideals.

To probe Warren's criteria for personhood (she claims that an entity needn't possess all these attributes to be a person, and perhaps no attribute is individually necessary; hers is the modest view that the more criteria that are satisfied by an entity, the more confident we can be in applying the concept of person to it), first ask pupils to list these features from the most to the least important in terms of conferring personhood on a being. Then, in order to determine whether any of these features are necessary (needed) or sufficient (enough) for personhood, ask pupils to imagine two cases: one in which you, the teacher, lose one of these abilities, and another in which the chairs they are sitting on magically acquire one. In each case, is there any particular feature that would change your or the chair's personhood status? Would losing or acquiring any one of these features affect an entity's moral status, including its right to life? Finally, using Warren's criteria, have pupils complete the Venn diagram for the following: foetuses, God, highly intelligent aliens, chimpanzees, Taylor Swift, a brain-dead human, a human corpse, humans with profound and multiple learning disabilities (PMLD), a newborn baby, AI.

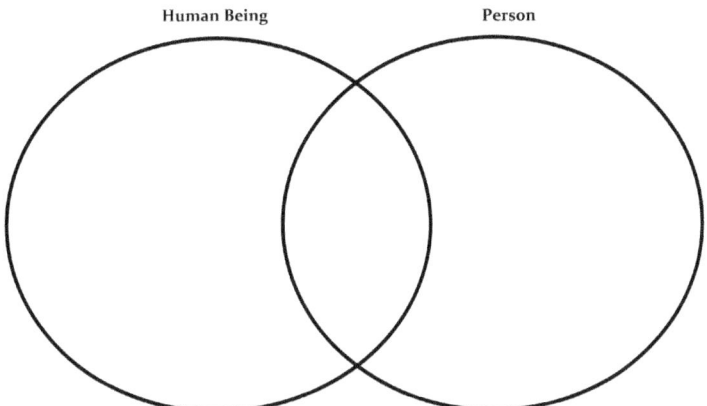

To reiterate, according to Warren, in order to be treated as a member of the moral community and regarded as having complete moral status, one must satisfy the criteria for personhood. Does this raise any problems with respect to those beings who do not fall into the 'person' circle? Is there anything that does seem to have moral status but is not included? By Warren's own admission, her criteria of personhood legitimise infanticide.

> It remains true that, on my view, neither abortion nor the killing of newborns is obviously a form of murder. (p. 135)

Thought Avenue

It is sometimes argued that foetuses have a right to life by virtue of being potential persons. While they do not currently satisfy Warren's criteria, they will at some point and therefore should be treated as such. This argument is often rejected. We wouldn't claim that potential voters should have the actual right to vote or potential smokers the actual right to smoke, so why grant a potential person the actual right to life?

Conduct a discussion to explore the credibility of this view.

- Enquiry Question: Is infanticide murder?

  Development questions:

  ○ Is a newborn baby a person?

  ○ Does a newborn baby have a right to life?

- Does a newborn baby have a higher moral status than a cow?
- Is a newborn baby qualitatively different in abilities and attributes than a foetus?

Activity 2

To further explore the morality of infanticide, consider the argument for its permissibility from Michael Tooley (1986). The core claim of his argument is the following:

> "A has a right to continue to exist as a subject of experiences and other mental states" is roughly synonymous with the statement "A is a subject of experiences and other mental states, A is capable of desiring to continue to exist as a subject of experiences and other mental states … ". (p. 66)

From this, Tooley concludes that a being can only have a right to life if it possesses 'the concept of a self as a continuing subject of experiences and other mental states, and believes that it is itself such a continuing entity'. According to Tooley, however, a newborn baby lacks this concept. Therefore, infanticide that occurs near the time of birth is morally permissible.

Thought Avenue

If a philosophical argument is logically consistent and comprised of credible premises yet delivers a repugnant conclusion, can or should we reject the argument on that basis, or should we abide by reason and relinquish deeply held moral intuitions?

To help pupils make sense of this, have them work through the following argument tree:

(a) Can you desire something you cannot even think about or conceptualise, e.g., can a blind golden mole desire sight?

How?

(b) Do newborn babies have self-awareness? Can they think about or conceptualise their individual on-going existence?

How?

(c) Can you have a right to something (which others are thereby obliged to give you) that you cannot even desire?

 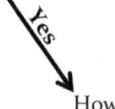

How?

Your view is that newborn babies do not have a right to life, i.e., a right to an individual and on-going existence.

Having worked through the tree, present the class with the argument expressed in standard form.

1. *A only has a right to X if A is able to desire X.*
2. *A can only desire X if A is able to think about and conceptualise X.*
3. *Newborn babies cannot think about or conceptualise their individual on-going existence.*
4. *Therefore, newborn babies cannot desire their individual on-going existence.*
5. *Therefore, newborn babies do not have the right to an individual on-going existence.*
6. *Therefore, it is not wrong to kill newborn babies.*

The next task is to answer the following:

i. Is the argument valid (does the conclusion logically follow from the premises)?

ii. Are premises 1–3 true?

iii. For each erroneous premise, explain the error.

iv. If you do accept the argument, explain the reasons that support premises 1, 2 and 3.

Activity 3

Having seen, then, that Warren and Tooley's criteria for personhood imply that newborn infants do not have a morally significant status, which your pupils may find troubling, let's see whether there is anything troubling about the claim that foetuses do not have significant moral status. Present the following thought experiment:

> In the future it is possible to gestate foetuses ex utero. Like IVF, the embryo is created in a lab, but then, instead of being placed in a biological woman, the embryo is gestated in an artificial womb. Given the ease with which human foetuses can now be harvested, all sorts of new products and markets have emerged. For instance, though there is no actual evidence

Fact Check

Here is an actual illustration of how foetuses have been used *ex utero* for medical research. In an attempt to simulate the functions of the placenta, oxygen was supplied to aborted foetuses. The living foetuses, which were removed by hysterotomy, had tubes placed in their umbilical arteries and veins to pump and remove oxygenated blood. The following extract, quoted by Maggie Scarf (1979), is taken from the investigators' report:

> For the whole 5 hours of life, the fetus did not respire. Irregular gasping

of this, some people believe that ingesting human embryos has youth-preserving benefits. As such, human embryo health products can be purchased, such as human embryo face cream and bath oil, embryo health sweets are available, and even embryo lollipops. In some parts of the world foetal soup has become a delicacy with the severed limbs of the foetus floating in the broth, much like shark fin soup. Many are particularly fond of the ebony-like pigment of foetal eyes and to satisfy this demand various companies have managed to manufacture paint out of them. One final curiosity worth mentioning is the phenomenon of foetal gambling: a number of foetuses, whose neural networks are severed to render them impervious to sensation, are removed from the artificial wombs and left to suffocate, with punters placing bets on which one will expire first.

> movements, twice a minute, occurred in the middle of the experiment but there was no proper respiration. Once the perfusion was stopped, however, the gasping respiratory efforts increased to 8 to 10 per minute. After stopping the circuit, the heart slowed, became irregular and eventually stopped. The fetus was quiet, making occasional stretching limb movements very like the ones reported in other human work. The fetus died 21 minutes after leaving the circuit. (p. 181)

- Enquiry Question: Is this immoral?

Development questions:

- Is disgust a reliable guide to morality? Are all morally abhorrent acts disgusting? Are all disgusting acts morally abhorrent?
- If it seems cannibalistic, does this show that a foetus is a human being?
- If the foetus is a human being, does that mean it has a moral status?
- If it seems immoral, does this show that foetuses have rights which can be violated?
- Even if they are less than persons, might foetuses still be more than mere things?

Have pupils work through the following argument tree:

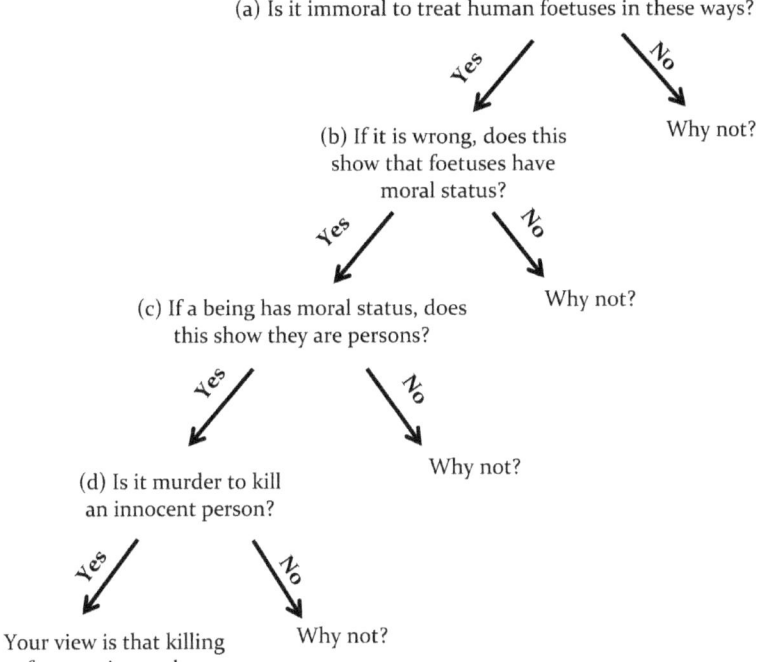

Having worked through the tree, present the class with the argument expressed in standard form.

1. *It is immoral to treat foetuses in the ways described.*
2. *If there are moral rules regulating how we treat foetuses, they must have moral status.*
3. *If a being has moral status, it should be regarded as a person.*
4. *Killing an innocent person is murder.*
5. *Therefore, killing foetuses is murder.*

There are a number of ways this might be challenged. Consider, for instance, premise 3. Does moral status necessitate personhood? One potential avenue for discussion is the question of whether human corpses, though clearly not possessed of the right to life, and presumably not persons, still have a certain moral status. If so, could it be that the moral status of a foetus is somehow analogous to that of a corpse?

Thought Avenue

R. M. Hare (1979) argued that abortion is immoral because it violates the Golden Rule (treat others as you wish to be treated). He wrote: 'The application of this injunction [the Golden Rule] to the problem of abortion is obvious. If we are glad that nobody terminated the pregnancy that resulted in our birth, then we are enjoined not, ceteris paribus, to terminate any pregnancy which will result in the birth of a person having a life like ours' (p. 159). How convincing an argument is this?

Having worked through these arguments, pupils should take stock by completing the following:

> I am/am not necessarily dissatisfied with any criteria of personhood that entails the moral permissibility of infanticide. This is because… As such I do/do not reject, in principle, the conclusions of Warren and Tooley. Warren's views, I believe, are convincing/unconvincing because… My attitude towards Tooely's argument is much the same/different because… With respect to the thought experiment, I believe the actions described there were/were not immoral because… This therefore indicates that foetuses have no/some/significant moral status. My current view is that [insert one of the below]. Killing a foetus, therefore, is/is not murder.
>
> a. *a foetus is not a human being, and it has no moral status, and it is not a person.*
>
> b. *a foetus is a human being, but it has no moral status, and is not a person.*
>
> c. *a foetus is a human being, and it has moral status, but it is not a person.*
>
> d. *a foetus is a human being, and it has moral status, and it is a person.*

Activity 4

Robert George and Patrick Lee (2005) have objected to Warren's and Tooley's accounts of personhood. They believe that being a person is not a matter of the attributes we possess but the kind of thing that we are. If this were not so, it would mean that the body of, say, Taylor Swift came into existence at one time and the person of Taylor Swift at another, and so to look at Taylor Swift perform is to see two entities with different histories: the bodily organism and the person. In explaining why they reject such an implication, George and Lee write the following:

> People may stipulate different meanings for the word "person," but we think it is clear that what we normally mean by the word "person" is that substantial entity that is referred to by personal pronouns – "I," "you," "she," etc. (p. 16)

We can use this to make the following suggestion: x is a person if and only if we can intelligibly refer to x using personal pronouns. If this is correct, and Warren is right that personhood does not emerge till after birth, it follows that you and I (as beings referred to using personal pronouns) were never foetuses. Indeed, you and I were never in fact conceived or born. And that if the foetuses we grew from had been aborted, it would not have been you and I who had been killed. This, at the very least, sounds rather odd.

Let's shape this into an argument in standard form. Present the following to the class:

1. *If we can intelligibly refer to an entity using pronouns 'I', 'you', 'he', 'she', 'they', or 'we' (and their object correlates), then that entity is a person.*
2. *If anyone were to see pictures of an ultrasound of a 12-week-old foetus, they could intelligibly ask, 'Is that me?'*
3. *Therefore, 12-week-old foetuses are persons.*
4. *Persons have significant moral status.*
5. *Therefore, 12-week-old foetuses have significant moral status.*

Premise 2 might accurately reflect what we would say, but is it what we *should* say? To probe premise 1, discuss whether it could ever make sense to use the following sentences:

- 'She is not a person.'
- 'You are not a person.'
- 'I am not a person.'
- 'It is a person.'

> **Thought Avenue**
>
> In John Locke's *An Essay Concerning Human Understanding* (1975), he wrote the following: 'Should the soul of a prince, carrying with it the consciousness of the prince's past life, enter and inform the body of a cobbler, as soon deserted by his own soul, everyone sees he would be the same person as the prince, accountable only for the prince's actions' (II.xxvii.15). We can modify the thought experiment by omitting the complicating reference to souls: if a cobbler presented with the same personality as a prince immediately following the prince's death and had precisely the same memories, knowledge and beliefs as the prince, in addition to the prince's very same desires, and indeed believed he was the prince (the precise reasons for this anomaly may be inexplicable and forever remain a mystery), is the cobbler the same person as the prince? If yes, this suggests that our concept of a person is not inextricably fused with that of a particular physical organism.

On the final statement, you might ask pupils why it is offensive to refer to an individual as 'it' and whether it would be similarly offensive to ask a mother of a foetus 'Why did it kick you?' as it would of a five-year-old. Following this thread, you could also ask whether a foetus can have a name – should we ask of a foetus 'What *is* her/his/its name?' or 'What *will* her/his/its name be?' – or can we only really speak of humans having names once they are born? Importantly, do any of these questions of etiquette and convention reveal anything about the metaphysical and moral status of foetuses?

To return directly to metaphysics, George and Lee's views give rise to a contentious claim about personal identity, namely, that we share a personal identity with the embryos we grew from. Given that we share a personal identity, the embryo must have been a person. Present the class with an image of a human embryo at about 4 weeks of gestation and ask:

- Enquiry Question: Were *you* once *this*?

Development question:

○ Is it more natural to say 'That embryo's me' or 'That's the embryo I grew from'? Which is it right to say?

To help pupils think about this question, have them complete the following table. Given that the reasons offered in the first column target a putative identity criterion, the tenability of that criterion can be tested by considering whether, were we now to lose the named feature, we would remain the same person.

That is not me because…	This implies that I would now stop being me if …	Is this a credible implication?
It doesn't have fingers.		
I have no memory of that time.		
It doesn't have my personality.		
It is not a thinking thing.		

Another way to explore the idea that we were once embryos is to imagine a possible world in which our lives end as they started: as embryos. In this world, at a certain point, we quite rapidly metamorphose from a geriatric adult into a foetus, at which point we enter an artificial womb, and then become an embryo, before eventually dying.

While we can imagine a person in a vegetative state being awarded *in absentia* for some notable achievement that occurred before they entered this state, can you imagine the same for the future embryo of, say, a great chemist, being awarded the Nobel Prize for Chemistry? Would it seem ludicrous to bring the embryo on stage and applaud it? If so, why? Imagine we languished in this embryonic state for decades. At what point would it be appropriate to hold a funeral for someone who had undergone this transformation? Should we regard the embryo as the person or an object which, like the Holy Prepuce or Mary's milk, is more akin to the relic of the person?

Activity 5

We shall explore one more argument for the claim that foetuses have moral status. This argument, from Don Marquis (2007), holds that killing foetuses is immoral, but this is not because they are persons. According to Marquis, what makes killing so egregious is that it deprives an individual of its future. Given that this deprivation can be suffered by both foetuses and adults, it follows that it is similarly wrong to kill both.

Before presenting the passage from Marquis, discuss the following:

- Enquiry Question: Why is killing (innocent people) wrong?

  Development questions:

  ○ Is it simply because it violates and ignores the victim's preference to live?

  ○ Does death necessarily harm or hurt us?

  ○ Is it simply because it causes grief to the victim's family and friends?

  ○ Is it because all life is intrinsically sacred?

Now determine whether any of the reasons that were identified also apply to foetuses. With the groundwork done, present Marquis' account. Having dismissed the idea that killing is wrong due to the loss to family and friends (because it implies that killing hermits is permissible), he writes:

> The loss of one's life deprives one of all the experiences, activities, projects, and enjoyments that would otherwise have constituted one's future ... Inflicting this loss on me is ultimately what makes killing me wrong. (pp. 140–143)

Crucially, this loss is also inflicted on aborted foetuses; they too are deprived of potentially rich future lives. Therefore, it is inconsistent to view killing an innocent adult as impermissible while viewing abortion as permissible; the reason for its wrongness in the former case also applies to the latter.

A notable implication of Marquis' view is that he doesn't seem able to support the intuition, which most anti-abortion advocates have, that it is worse to kill a human adult than a human foetus (in Mississippi, for instance, abortion is punishable by up to 10 years in prison whereas murder is punishable by death). If anything, given that the foetus has more of a future, one could take Marquis' argument to imply that killing a foetus is worse. Whereas Warren and Tooley, in arguing for the permissibility of abortion, were unable to explain why killing infants is wrong, Marquis, in arguing against the permissibility of abortion, is unable to explain why killing adults is more wrong.

To explore their intuitions on this, ask pupils to imagine that they work in a remote hospital, let's say on Ilha da Queimada Grande, where five patients are suffering from snakebites. As it stands, the hospital only holds enough antivenom to save one patient; moreover, the boat that was due to deliver a fresh batch capsized, and while the vials (enough for a single person) have been washing up on shore, this has only been at a rate of one per day. The longer they wait, the more likely it is the patients will die.

The pupils' task is to order the patients into a list, from first to last, of who should receive the antivenom. Once they've placed them in order, their task is to justify their ordering and apply their reasoning to Marquis' argument. Has he accurately articulated the wrongness of killing? Is the killing of an adult no more egregious than the killing of a foetus?

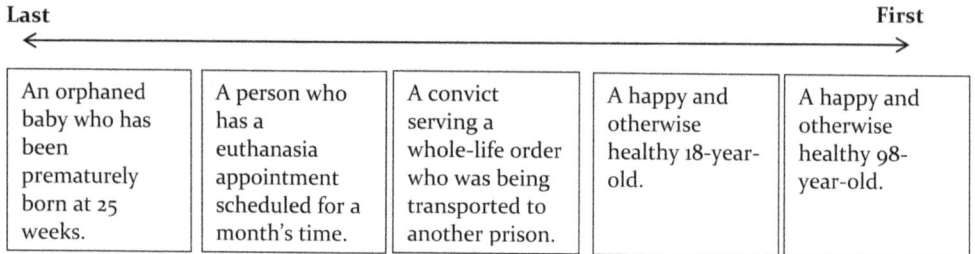

Last				First
An orphaned baby who has been prematurely born at 25 weeks.	A person who has a euthanasia appointment scheduled for a month's time.	A convict serving a whole-life order who was being transported to another prison.	A happy and otherwise healthy 18-year-old.	A happy and otherwise healthy 98-year-old.

To help guide their thinking of this, you could present Jeff McMahan's (2002) view that an infant, and by extension foetus, is 'almost completely severed psychologically from itself as it would have been in the future … It is almost as if the future it loses might just as well have belonged to someone else' (p. 170). On this view, though a future is lost, only tenuously is it the future of the aborted foetus for its psychological connection to that future is virtually non-existent. As such, the foetus is not wronged.

Activity 6

This final argument is for the permissibility of abortion. Judith Jarvis Thomson (2007) argues that the questions of whether a foetus is a person and whether killing deprives it of a future are irrelevant to the morality of abortion. Thomson rejects the claim that 'a person's right to life is stronger and more stringent than the mother's right to decide what happens in and to her body'. She believes that 'no person is morally required to make large sacrifices to sustain the life of another who has no right to demand them' (p. 118).

Thomson's argument works by an analogy. Rather than prefacing the analogy with an explanation of her position, have pupils role-play the scenario, posing the crucial question of whether it would be immoral to unplug, and then ask pupils to decipher the analogy and its implications for the question of the foetus's moral status.

> After getting an early night in the comfort of her own bed, Judith is confused to wake up and find she is in some sort of medical facility. Beside her she sees a pallid man lying unconscious and seemingly connected to her amid a tangle of wires and tubes. A nurse appears. Judith asks why she is here. The nurse explains that the man has a terminal kidney disease and she alone

has right blood type to help; he has been connected to her so that her kidneys can be used to clean his blood. Seeing the distress on Judith's face, the nurse reassures her that the process and will only take nine months after which time Judith can unplug. Nevertheless, if she unplugs at any point before then, he will surely die. When Judith starts to protest at how she has been treated, the nurse objects that her right to bodily autonomy is outweighed by this man's right to life, so Judith has a moral duty to make this sacrifice.

Thomson, writing with the conviction that Judith is under no moral obligation to remain tethered, draws the following conclusions:

> [H]aving a right to life does not guarantee having either a right to be given the use of or a right to be allowed continued use of another person's body – even if one needs it for life itself. So the right to life will not serve the opponents of abortion in the very simple and clear way in which they seem to have thought it would. (p. 121)

- Enquiry Question (a): Would it be wrong for Judith to unplug?

  Development question:

  ○ Is the principle expressed by the nurse – that the right to life outweighs the right to bodily autonomy – absolute? Would it still apply if the required connection time was nine years?

- Enquiry Question (b): If the answer to (a) is yes, does this show that abortion is morally permissible?

When dissecting (b) with the class, there are a number of things to focus on. As an argument from analogy, the strength of the argument depends on the strength of the analogy. Clearly, there are differences between this scenario and pregnancy. The important question is whether these differences are of moral significance. You might draw attention to the following dissimilarities:

1. The woman is unrelated to the man, whereas the foetus is biologically related to the person carrying it.

2. In cases other than rape, the mother chooses to enter into a situation where pregnancy is a known risk. (Why might this matter? David Boonin (2019) expresses it this way: 'If as a foreseeable result of your voluntary act someone will die if you don't assist them, and if they wouldn't need your assistance if you hadn't done the act, then they have a right to your assistance' (p. 69).)

3. In most cases, abortion is not a matter of letting the foetus die but actively killing it (would it affect the morality of the scenario if disconnection required hacking him to pieces?).

4. Sometimes pregnancies are planned, but shifting circumstances mean an abortion is ultimately sought. Had the body donor originally consented to

plugging into the man, would that affect the permissibility of subsequently unplugging?

5. In some respects, pregnancy is worse as it often makes permanent and unwanted changes to one's body.

Thomson's aim is to show that the right to life doesn't entail the right to make non-consensual use of another person's body. This is why she touches on the possibility of remaining attached for one's entire life. She wants to show that one's right to bodily autonomy can override another person's right to life, and so the foetus's status as a person doesn't *ipso facto* mean that it is impermissible to kill it. Despite this, she does also write, 'suppose pregnancy lasted only an hour, and constituted no threat to life or health. And suppose that a woman becomes pregnant as a result of rape ... it might well be said ... that she *ought* to allow it to remain for that hour – that it would be indecent of her to refuse' (2007, p. 123). While she claims one ought to go through with the pregnancy – not doing so would be 'self-centred, callous, indecent' – she nevertheless believes that the foetus doesn't have the right to the use of one's body. Aborting may be wrong, but it is not unjust.

Before moving onto the final activity, have pupils complete the following schematic to express their thoughts on Thomson's argument, using a ~ or ≁ to indicate the accuracy of Thomson's analogy, followed by a → or ↛ to show whether the analogy therefore has implications for the morality of abortion.

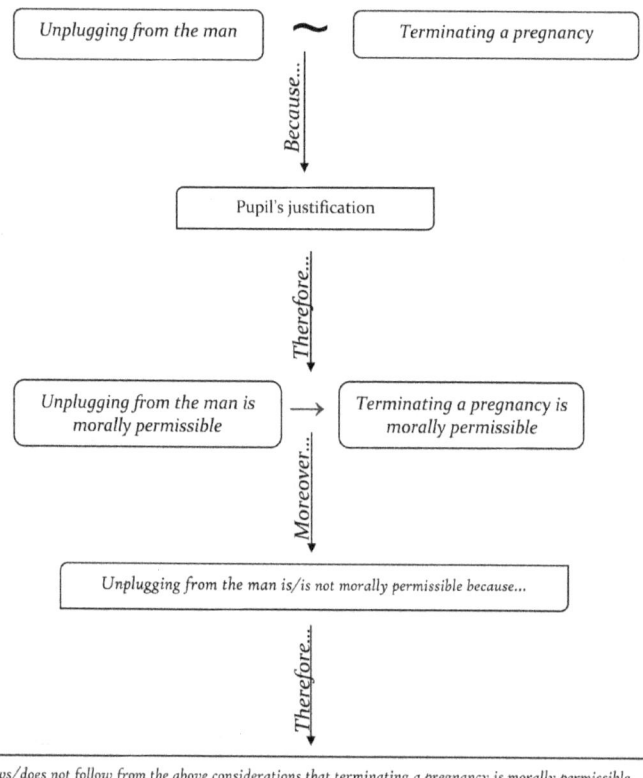

Activity 7

Pupils should collate their views on the various issues by completing the table. Following that, they should now be in a position to write a statement outlining and philosophically justifying their metaphysical and moral views on the status of the human foetus and whether it may permissibly be killed.

	Yes/No	Philosophers whose arguments I agree with on this point.	Philosophers whose arguments I disagree with on this point.
Is the foetus a human being?			
Is the foetus a person?			
Does the foetus have moral status?			
Does the foetus have a right to life?			
Is it morally permissible to kill foetuses?			

CASE STUDY

To explore the legality of abortion, present the Pennsylvania case of *McFall v. Shimp*. In 1978, Robert McFall was diagnosed with a bone marrow disease called aplastic anaemia. To ensure his survival, McFall required a bone marrow transplant. His cousin, David Shimp, was found to be the only compatible donor.

Though an invasive procedure, bone marrow extraction is not risky and is painlessly carried out under general anaesthetic. Nevertheless, Shimp refused to donate his marrow. McFall proceeded to sue him and asked the court to compel Shimp to act as a donor. The court denied the request. This was its ruling:

> Our society, contrary to many others, has as its first principle, the respect for the individual, and that society and government exist to protect the individual from being invaded and hurt by another ... For our law to compel the defendant to submit to an intrusion of his body would change the very concept and principle upon which our society is founded. To do so would defeat the sanctity of the individual and would impose a rule which would know no limits, and one could not imagine where the line would be drawn.
>
> (Quoted in Menikoff, 2001, pp. 469–470)

There are numerous questions to explore in relation to this case, including:

- Do you agree with the court's ruling?
- Are the arguments and principles adduced by the court equally applicable to pregnancy?
- Would it be inconsistent for a state to make this ruling while making abortion illegal?
- Would it be inconsistent for a state to abide by this ruling while imposing a legal time limit (24 weeks in England, Wales and Scotland) on abortion?

Extension Material
Antinatalism

To look at the topic of abortion through a different philosophical lens, you could also consider with your pupils the theory of antinatalism, which claims that procreation is morally impermissible. Given this stance on procreation, an antinatalist might be inclined to argue that abortion is not only permissible but also obligatory. Though there are a variety of arguments for antinatalism, in recent years, it has become most associated with the philosopher David Benatar, which is where we start.

- David Benatar (2013) believes that 'coming into existence is always a serious harm and that procreation is thus always wrong' (p. 121). As such, it is wrong *not* to abort foetuses (in the early stages of pregnancy), and it would be better if humanity became extinct. One of his arguments for this position draws on the apparent asymmetry between pleasure and pain: the absence of pain is good, even if there is no one who experiences this, while the absence of pleasure is only bad if someone has been deprived of it. Consequently, it would have been better if I'd never been born, and thus I was harmed by being brought into existence.

    Imagine two possible worlds, one where I exist and one where I don't. In the first, I experience pleasure, which is good, and pain, which is bad. In the second, I don't experience pain, which is good, and I don't experience pleasure, which is not bad since the absence of pleasure is only bad if there is someone who has been deprived of it, and since I don't exist, I have not been so deprived. As such, the second world (which has good but no bad) is better than the first (which has good *and* bad).

    Independent of and in addition to this argument, Benatar (2017) believes we should not be too wedded to life for it is 'simply much worse than most people think'. He believes that an optimism bias means that most people overestimate the quality of their lives. According to Benatar, there is clearly more good than bad in our lives, and in this, he shares an affinity with Arthur Schopenhauer who in his essay 'On the suffering of the world' claimed that the preponderance of pain in life is exemplified by the disparity between the extreme pain of an animal being devoured and the moderate pleasure of the animal doing the devouring.

- Stuart Rachels' (2014) antinatalism is weaker than Benatar's. His argument against procreation does not derive from metaphysical considerations about the universal nature of suffering but from the practical question of how we can best use our resources to ameliorate the particular suffering of those in the Global South. He does not believe that all people should refrain from procreation, but only those in the Global North who tend to spend hundreds of thousands of dollars on their children.

    Inspired by Peter Singer's argument that we have a moral duty to donate our disposable income to charity because we have a moral duty to prevent the suffering of others whenever doing so will not incur greater or equivalent moral costs (see Chapter 7 on poverty), Rachels argues that we should donate the money we would have spent on our hypothetical children to help alleviate the suffering of destitute children already in existence: '[I]f you wish to help others, then the worst decision you can make is to become a parent, because your child will tie up most of your spare time and resources for the next two decades' (p. 572). He calls his argument 'The Famine Relief Argument Against Having Children'.

- Pronatalists profoundly disagree with antinatalists. They believe that we have a moral duty not to abstain from procreation but to procreate more; childlessness is immoral. The Swedish philosopher Torbjörn Tännsjö (2015), for instance, has outlined a utilitarian account of pronatalism arguing that we ought to procreate in order to maximise the amount of happiness in the world. Disagreeing with Benatar's estimation on the misery of life, he has written:

    > Most people live lives that are, on net, happy. For them to never exist, then, would be to deny them that happiness. And because I think we have a moral duty to maximize the amount of happiness in the world, that means that we all have an obligation to make the world as populated as can be.

    In response, it might be argued that potential individuals don't have rights. On this view, since refraining from procreation harms no actual people, it cannot be immoral. Tännsjö uses a thought experiment to illustrate why he thinks this view is misguided.

    Imagine that the human species began with two individuals, call them Adam and Eve, who didn't want the bother of children and so always used contraception. If this were so, they would've prevented the future existence of billions of people, and all the happiness that those billions would have experienced. To Tännsjö, this would've clearly been wrong of them. Is he right?

Note

1 https://www.un.org/en/about-us/universal-declaration-of-human-rights

References

Benatar, D. (2013). Still Better Never to Have Been: A Reply to (More of) My Critics. *The Journal of Ethics*, 17(1/2), 121–151.

Benatar, D. (2017). *Kids? Just Say No*. Aeon. https://aeon.co/essays/having-children-is-not-life-affirming-its-immoral

Boonin, D. (2019). *Beyond Roe: Why Abortion Should Be Legal – Even If the Fetus Is a Person*. Oxford University Press.

George, R. P. & Lee, P. (2005). The Wrong of Abortion. In A. I. Cohen & C. H. Wellman (Eds.), *Contemporary Debates in Applied Ethics* (pp. 13–27). Blackwell.

Hare, R. M. (1979). Abortion and the Golden Rule. In J. Rachels (Ed.), *Moral Problems* (3rd ed.) (pp. 151–174). Harper and Row.

Locke, J. (1975) [1689]. *An Essay Concerning Human Understanding*, P. H. Nidditch (Ed.), Clarendon Press.

Marquis, D. (2007). An Argument That Abortion Is Wrong. In H. LaFollette (Ed.), *Ethics in Practice* (pp. 148–158). Blackwell.

McMahan, J. (2002). *The Ethics of Killing*. Oxford University Press.

Menikoff, J. (2001). *Law and Bioethics: An Introduction*. Georgetown University Press.

Rachels, S. (2014). The Immorality of Having Children. *Ethical Theory and Moral Practice*, 17(3), 567–582.

Scarf, M. (1979). The Fetus as Guinea Pig. In J. Rachels (Ed.), *Moral Problems* (3rd ed.) (pp. 174–192). Harper and Row.

Tännsjö, T. (2015). *You Should Have Kids*. Leiter Reports. https://leiterreports.typepad.com/blog/2015/08/so-much-for-trying-to-bring-philosophy-to-the-public.html

Thomson, J. J. (2007). A Defense of Abortion. In H. LaFollette (Ed.), *Ethics in Practice* (pp. 117–126). Blackwell.

Tooley, M. (1986). Abortion and Infanticide. In P. Singer (Ed.), *Applied Ethics*. Oxford University Press.

Warren, M. A. (2007). On the Moral and Legal Status of Abortion. In H. LaFollette (Ed.), *Ethics in Practice* (pp. 126–137). Blackwell.

2 Euthanasia

Key Questions

- Can one be better off dead?
- Kant said, 'there is much in the world far more important than life'. Was he right?
- Do we have the right to a quick, clean, non-violent and painless death?
- Do we have a duty to live?
- Is there a moral difference between passive and active euthanasia?
- Do the elderly have a duty to die? (Extension)
- Do infants have a right to life? (Extension)

The notion of living well is readily intelligible, as is the belief, which not everyone holds, that we are all entitled to a good life. But should we also say that there is such a thing as dying well? And if we do think that everyone is entitled to a good life, does consistency demand that we believe the same for a good death?

This chapter addresses the ethics of voluntary euthanasia. While there are concerns about the legal implications of euthanasia, given that it involves the fulfilment of an individual's wish to die, the moral objections to voluntary euthanasia overlap significantly with the moral objections to suicide, which will form part of our focus.

Activity 1

Present the following cases of individuals who wish to die. Ask pupils to decide who they believe is entitled to euthanasia i.e. to a state-sanctioned medically administered (quick, painless, clean, non-violent) death.

She wishes to die –

a. *As a protest against a political injustice.*

b. *To be united with God.**

c. *Because she feels her disability places too much of a burden on her friends and family.*

d. *To enact revenge against a former partner who left her.*

e. *Because she is so profoundly ashamed of her actions.***

f. *To atone for something she did wrong.*

g. *Because she desperately hates herself.*

h. *To escape the unbearable anxiety the climate emergency causes her.*

i. *To escape the profound loneliness of her life.*

j. *To escape the unbearable and unending grief caused by a loss.****

k. *Because she is suffering from a debilitating and painful terminal illness.*

l. *Because she, a 15-year-old, is suffering from a debilitating and painful terminal illness.*

m. *Because she, a medical researcher who is on the verge of making an imminent and world-changing discovery, is suffering from a debilitating and painful terminal illness.*

n. *Because she has been suffering from treatment-resistant depression her entire life.*

o. *Because she recently suffered a spinal injury and is paralysed from the chest down.*

p. *Because she suffers from a painful and debilitating illness. It is expected, however, and she is aware of this, that a cure will become available in four years.*

q. *Because she has reached the age of 80 and feels life has nothing more to offer her.*

r. *Because she has reached the age of 50 and is horrified by the thought of ageing and growing decrepit.*

For illustrative purposes, you might wish to draw on the following ancient examples:

* Cleombrotus (reputed to have fatally thrown himself off a wall immediately after reading Plato's *Phaedo*, in which

Fact Check

Belgium's laws on euthanasia are among the most liberal of any country in the world. Euthanasia may be granted for individuals suffering from a medically it is written (66e) that 'the wisdom which we desire and upon which we profess to have set our hearts will be attainable only when we are dead, and not in our lifetime'), St Paul (who wrote of his 'desire to depart and be with Christ', Philippians 1:23).

** Jocasta (*Oedipus Rex*), Ajax (in Sophocles's *Ajax*).

*** Pyramus and Thisbe (Ovid's *Metamorphoses*).

Having sorted the cases into those that should and should not be sanctioned, the task now is for pupils to extract from this the general criteria they believe ought to be satisfied for access to euthanasia. Approach this as a piece of draft legislation laid out like so:

An individual is entitled to euthanasia if all of the following conditions are satisfied:

futile condition which causes either physical or mental suffering that is constant and unbearable. In Belgium, there are no age restrictions on euthanasia; however, the criteria for children are more stringent: the child must be in a medically futile state of unbearable suffering resulting from a terminal illness that will soon cause death. The child must also be competent of making a request for euthanasia, and both parents must consent.

In the Netherlands, where the euthanasia laws are similarly liberal, the political party Democrats 66 submitted a bill in 2023 that would extend euthanasia to individuals aged 75 and over who wish to die, not because they are suffering from an illness, but because they believe their life is 'complete'. Polling indicates the vast majority of Dutch people are in favour of this legislation.

1. The individual is 18 years of age or older.
2. The individual is suffering from a terminal illness.
3. As a direct result of that illness, the individual's quality of life is profoundly diminished.
4. The individual is unlikely to benefit from a medical advance in relation to that illness during what remains of her life expectancy.
5. The individual has mental capacity to request euthanasia, meaning the individual:
    a. understands the information relevant to the decision,
    b. can use or weigh that information as part of the process of making the decision,
    c. can communicate her decision (whether by talking, using sign language or any other means).

Have pupils put their legislation to the test by applying it to these four real-life cases. If, in light of these cases, they find their legislation either too permissive or too restrictive, they should revise to their satisfaction.

CASE 1

In December 2012, two co-habiting 45-year-old congenitally deaf twin brothers were euthanised together at a hospital in Belgium. A shared genetic condition meant that the pair were both gradually going blind, and they did not wish to reach a point where their only means of communicating with each other would be through touch. They also feared having to live in an institution and losing their autonomy.

CASE 2

In January 2018, Aurelia Brouwers, aged 29, died by assisted suicide at her home in the Netherlands. She did not have a terminal illness and was not in physical pain. She did, however, suffer from severe mental health conditions, including anxiety, depression, eating disorders and psychosis. She had attempted suicide on several occasions and spent a number of years in a psychiatric hospital. This is what she said about her condition: 'I suffer unbearably and hopelessly. Every breath I take is torture. I'm stuck in my own body, my own head, and I just want to be free. I have never been happy - I don't know the concept of happiness. We need to get rid of the taboo that you should always remain in treatment, until the bitter end. For people like me, there isn't always a solution - you can't keep taking medicine, you can't pray indefinitely… At some point you just have to stop' (https://www.bbc.co.uk/news/stories-45117163).

CASE 3

In either 2016 or 2017, a nine-year-old with a brain tumour was euthanised in Belgium. These are the only publicly known details of the child's death, which followed an amendment in 2014 to its euthanasia laws making it available for minors.

CASE 4

In 2008, 23-year-old Daniel James travelled from the UK to Switzerland to receive assisted suicide. Eighteen months earlier, he'd suffered a spinal injury during rugby training, which had paralysed him from the chest down. His mother described his condition as follows: 'He couldn't walk, had no hand function, but constant pain in all of his fingers. He was incontinent, suffered uncontrollable spasms in his legs and upper body and needed 24-hour care.'

Activity 2

The task now is to see whether the pupils' proposed legislation coheres with a doctor's code of ethics. Present the ancient medical pledge known as the Hippocratic Oath (it is unlikely that this was actually penned by Hippocrates) and have the class determine whether the doctor who acts in accordance with their euthanasia criteria violates the Oath.

> I swear by Apollo the physician, and Aesculapius, Hygeia and Panacea and all the gods and goddesses, that, according to my ability and judgement, I will keep this Oath and this covenant ... I will follow that system of regimen which, according to my ability and judgment, I consider for the benefit of my patients, and abstain from whatever is deleterious and mischievous. I will give no deadly medicine to anyone if asked, nor suggest any such counsel; and in like manner I will not give to a woman an abortive remedy. With purity and with holiness I will pass my life and practise my Art ... Into whatever houses I enter, I will go into them for the benefit of the sick, and will abstain from every voluntary act of mischief and corruption; and, further, from the seduction of females or males, of freemen and slaves. Whatever, in connection with my professional practice, or not in connection with it, I see or hear, in the life of men, which ought not to be spoken of abroad, I will not divulge, as reckoning that all such should be kept secret. While I continue to keep this Oath unviolated, may it be granted to me to enjoy life and practice of the Art, respected by all men, in all times. But should I trespass and violate this Oath, may the reverse be my lot.[1]

While the principles of confidentiality and nonmaleficence are regarded as sacrosanct in the medical profession, medical students are not required to take the antiquated Oath. Many medical schools do, nevertheless, include some form of pledge in their graduation ceremonies, with some using the Declaration of Geneva. This was adopted by the World Medical Association in 1948 and has undergone several revisions since. Following a 2017 amendment, this is its current form:

I SOLEMNLY PLEDGE to dedicate my life to the service of humanity;

THE HEALTH AND WELL-BEING OF MY PATIENT will be my first consideration;

I WILL RESPECT the autonomy and dignity of my patient;

I WILL MAINTAIN the utmost respect for human life;

I WILL NOT PERMIT considerations of age, disease or disability, creed, ethnic

Thought Avenue

The Bible contains no explicit or direct condemnation of suicide. In fact, the suicides of Samson (Judges 16:30), Saul (1 Samuel 31:4) and Judas (Matthew 27:5) pass without judgment. Augustine (1871), however, believed that the prohibition of suicide, while not overt, is certainly implied (Samson, he thought, must have been secretly ordered by God to origin, gender, nationality, political affiliation, race, sexual orientation, social standing or any other factor to intervene between my duty and my patient;

I WILL RESPECT the secrets that are confided in me, even after the patient has died;

I WILL PRACTISE my profession with conscience and dignity and in accordance with good medical practice;

I WILL FOSTER the honour and noble traditions of the medical profession;

I WILL GIVE to my teachers, colleagues, and students the respect and gratitude that is their due;

I WILL SHARE my medical knowledge for the benefit of the patient and the advancement of healthcare;

I WILL ATTEND TO my own health, well-being, and abilities in order to provide care of the highest standard;

I WILL NOT USE my medical knowledge to violate human rights and civil liberties, even under threat;

I MAKE THESE PROMISES solemnly, freely, and upon my honour.[2]

> act as he did). He wrote: 'the law, rightly interpreted, even prohibits suicide, where it says, "Thou shall not kill." This is proved especially by the omission of the words "thy neighbour," which are inserted when false witness is forbidden: "Thou shall not bear false witness against thy neighbour" ... [H]ow much greater reason have we to understand that a man may not kill himself, since in the commandment, "Thou shalt not kill," there is no limitation added nor any exception made in favour of any one ...' (p. 31). This is clever and lawyerly. Is it convincing?

Ask the pupils to establish whether this updated version of the Hippocratic Oath is compatible with their legislation. If they prohibit euthanasia on certain grounds, does this, for instance, violate their patients' 'autonomy' and 'dignity'? Contrariwise, if they permit euthanasia on certain grounds, does that evince a lack of respect for human life? Where there are conflicts, they will need to rewrite the relevant pledges to bring them into harmony with their legislation.

Activity 3

With the legal work complete, the philosophical work begins. Pupils need to identify and articulate the philosophical underpinnings of their legal framework. To that end, we shall consider a series of arguments both for and against euthanasia (suicide). As you work through the following three arguments, have pupils refer back to Activity 1 to complete the following table.

	Is the argument persuasive?	Permissible cases	Impermissible cases	Does this align with my own legislation?
Autonomy Argument (Mill)				
Utilitarian Argument				
Rachels' Argument				
Argument from Valour (Seneca)				

The first argument is from autonomy and self-determination. It says nothing about the permissibility of euthanasia as such but addresses the impermissibility of interfering with an individual's free choice to pursue it.

The Universal Declaration of Human Rights (UDHR),[3] while not a treaty, forms the framework for international human rights law (many of the same rights can be found in the legally binding International Covenant on Civil and Political Rights). Much of the UDHR is concerned with human freedom. Present the following Articles and ask whether the legal proscription of euthanasia violates either the *letter* or the *spirit* of the UDHR, and whether, therefore, denying access to euthanasia is a violation of human rights.

- **Article 1**
  All human beings are born free and equal in dignity and rights. They are endowed with reason and conscience and should act towards one another in a spirit of brotherhood.

- **Article 3**
  Everyone has the right to life, liberty and security of person.

- **Article 13**
  Everyone has the right to freedom of movement and residence within the borders of each state.
  Everyone has the right to leave any country, including his own, and to return to his country.

- **Article 18**
  Everyone has the right to freedom of thought, conscience and religion; this right includes freedom to change his religion or belief, and freedom, either alone or

in community with others and in public or private, to manifest his religion or belief in teaching, practice, worship and observance.

- **Article 19**
Everyone has the right to freedom of opinion and expression; this right includes freedom to hold opinions without interference and to seek, receive and impart information and ideas through any media and regardless of frontiers.

- **Article 24**
Everyone has the right to rest and leisure, including reasonable limitation of working hours and periodic holidays with pay.

Even if denying access to euthanasia does not violate any Articles, should it? Should the right to die be a human right? To explore this question, present the following passage from John Stuart Mill (1910):

[T]he only purpose for which power can be rightfully exercised over any member of a civilised community, against his will, is to prevent harm to others. His own good, either physical or moral, is not a sufficient warrant. He cannot rightfully be compelled to do or forbear because it will be better for him to do so, because it will make him happier, because, in the opinions of others, to do so would be wise, or even right. These are good reasons for remonstrating with him, or reasoning with him, or persuading him, or entreating him, but not for compelling him, or visiting him with any evil in case he do otherwise. To justify that, the conduct from which it is desired to deter him must be calculated to produce evil to someone else. The only part of the conduct of any one, for which he is amenable to society, is that which concerns others. In the part which merely concerns himself, his independence is, of right, absolute. Over himself, over his own body and mind, the individual is sovereign. (p. 73)

Fact Check

Oregon was the first state in the United States to legalise assisted suicide when the Death with Dignity Act was enacted in 1997. This allows terminally ill individuals to die by self-administering a lethal dose of medication. The state produces annual reports detailing the end-of-life concerns of patients who died by assisted suicide. In 2023, the most cited concern (91.6%) was losing autonomy, followed by becoming less able to engage in activities that make life enjoyable (88.3%). Issues related to inadequate pain control were reported by 34.3% of patients, and 8.2% were concerned with the financial implications of their treatment. These results are approximately the same every year, with a consistent year-on-year finding that nearly half of patients are concerned about becoming a burden to family and friends/caregivers.

Euthanasia **35**

- Enquiry Question (a): Do Mill's ideas support or oppose euthanasia?

  Development Questions:

  ○ Mill didn't directly address euthanasia, so what is the link between what he does say and euthanasia?

  ○ Is it possible that Mill believes euthanasia is morally impermissible?

  ○ Does the euthanasia of one individual do 'harm to others'?

- Enquiry Question (b): Given that suicide has been legal in England and Wales since 1961, does legally prohibiting euthanasia actually limit our liberty and sovereignty?

  Development Question:

  ○ Present the following analogy: *The state permits you to climb the highest mountain in the country, but it won't let you wear mountaineering boots, which are readily available, nor carry mountaineering equipment, such as ice axes, nor will it let you ascend with an experienced mountaineer as a guide, one who, indeed, may be perfectly willing to help you.* Though you are free to climb the mountain, do the restrictions imposed on how you do it constitute a violation of your liberty and sovereignty? Is this an accurate analogy for euthanasia?

While we can use Mill's claims to support legality of euthanasia, there is more work to be done. To further probe Mill's thinking, use the adjacent argument blocks. While his belief in non-interference rests on the notion of individual sovereignty, what does that notion rest upon? Ask pupils to think about and determine what foundational belief could support the entire argumentative edifice.

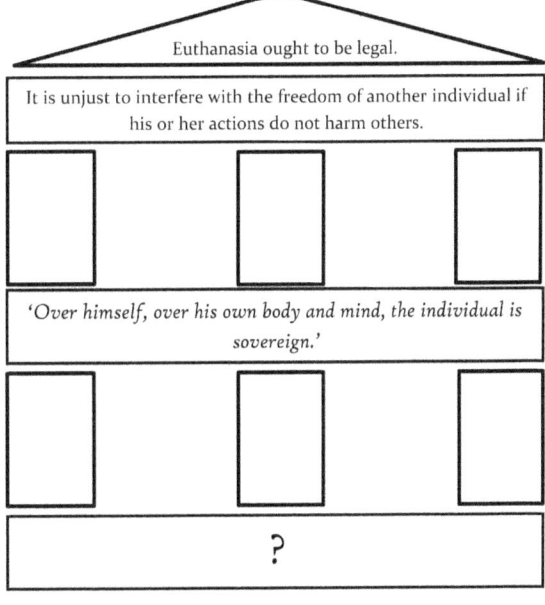

Pupils should now assess whether this Millian argument can viably support their own euthanasia legislation. If they apply the Millian argument to the cases in Activity 1, does it include and exclude all the cases included and excluded by their legislation?

Activity 4

The next argument is a utilitarian one. Drawing again on the work of John Stuart Mill (*ibid.*), apply his Principle of Utility to the cases in Activity 1.

> The creed which accepts as the foundation of morals, Utility, or the Greatest Happiness Principle, holds that actions are right in proportion as they tend to promote happiness, wrong as they tend to produce the reverse of happiness. By happiness is intended pleasure, and the absence of pain; by unhappiness, pain, and the privation of pleasure. (p. x)

Effectively, an action is good to the extent that it tips the world's hedonic scale in favour of pleasure, which can be done by either increasing pleasure or removing pain, and an action is bad to the extent that it tips the scale in favour of pain, which can be done by either increasing pain or removing pleasure.

- Enquiry Question: Does the Principle of Utility support or oppose euthanasia?

  Development Questions:

  ○ Is there a significant moral difference between cases *k* and *m*?

  ○ Would the Principle of Utility permit involuntary euthanasia of an individual who suffers miserably but wishes to cling to life?

  ○ Rather than focus on individual cases, do you think legalising euthanasia would bring an overall net gain to our happiness?

Activity 5

While it is illegal in the UK for doctors to kill their patients at the patients' request, it is legal to withdraw treatment if the patient so wishes (and so long as the patient has capacity). This latter situation is known as passive euthanasia. James Rachels (2016, p. 250), however, has argued that there is no significant moral or metaphysical difference between passive and active euthanasia. That is to say, killing someone and letting someone die are moral equivalents; *passive* euthanasia, moreover, is a misnomer. As such, if passive euthanasia is permissible, the same ought to be true of active euthanasia. He makes his case by presenting an analogous scenario involving Smith and Jones.

> If Smith's six-year-old cousin were to die, he'd be in line to receive a large inheritance. While the cousin is taking a bath one evening, Smith enters the bathroom and drowns him.

> If Jones's six-year-old cousin were to die, he'd be in line to receive a large inheritance. While the cousin is taking a bath one evening, Jones enters the bathroom with the intention of drowning him. Upon entering the bathroom, however, he sees the child slip, crack his head against the side of the bath and fall into the water. Jones waits, prepared to push the boy back down under the water if he regains consciousness. But no such measures are required: the boy remains unconscious and drowns to death.

Rachels then asks whether Jones is any worse than Smith? He thinks not. However, 'If the difference between killing and letting die were in itself a morally important matter, one should say that Jones's behaviour was less reprehensible than Smith's.'

He goes on to argue that one cannot reasonably claim that the difference is that Jones did nothing, or by extension, that a doctor who withdraws treatment is not *doing* anything to their patient:

> [H]e does do one thing that is very important: he lets the patient die. "Letting someone die" is certainly different, in some respects, from other types of action - mainly in that it is a kind of action that one may perform by way of not performing certain other actions … But for any purpose of moral assessment, it is a type of action nonetheless. (p. 251)

- Enquiry Question: If passive euthanasia is legal, should active euthanasia also be legal?

Have pupils complete the following argument schematic to articulate their views on Rachels' claims, using $\equiv$ or $\not\equiv$ to indicate moral equivalence or its lack, and $\to$ or $\not\to$ to show whether these considerations thereby imply an entailment between the permissibility of passive and active euthanasia.

38 Navigating the Moral Maze

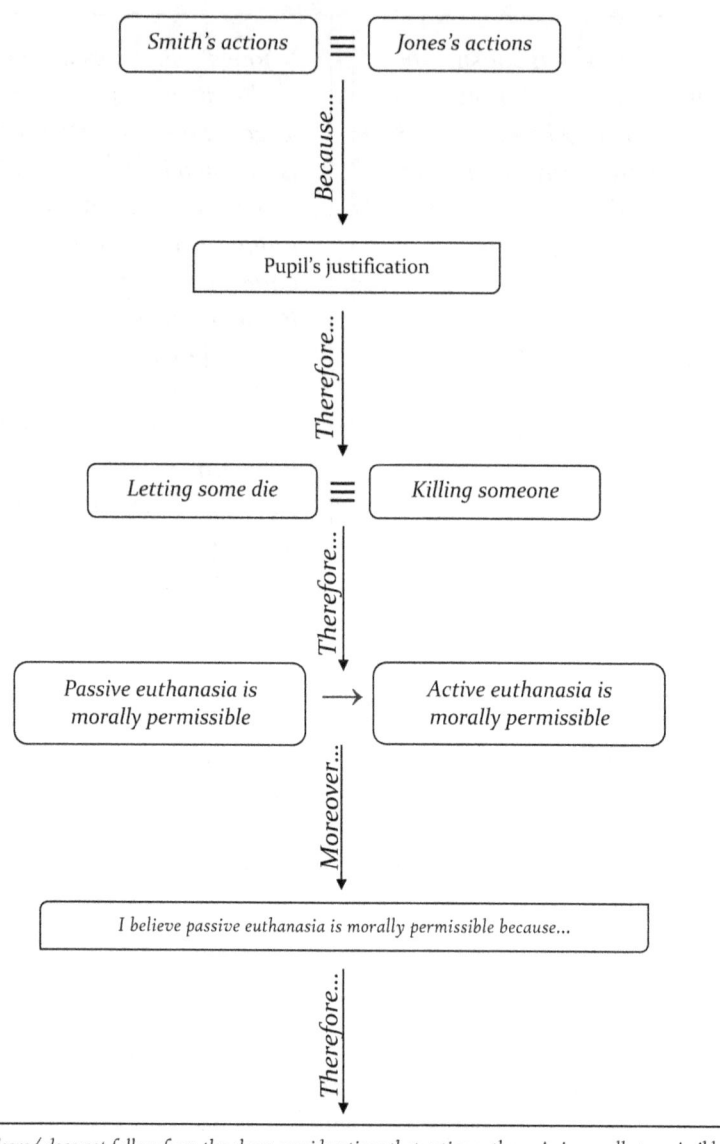

Activity 6

As a prelude to looking at Seneca's views on suicide, present the story of Masada (the details of which are questioned by historians and archaeologists) as told by the Jewish historian Flavius Josephus. In brief:

> *Following the Roman reprisals against Jewish revolt in 70 CE, which included the destruction of Jerusalem and the Second Temple, many families fled Jerusalem to find refuge in Masada, a mountaintop fortress in the Judaean desert where scores of rebels were already ensconced.*

In 72 the Romans laid siege to the fortress and by 73 it was clear that defeat and capture were inevitable, a fate that would expose the captives to the iniquities of rape, murder and slavery.

The rebel leader Eleazar Ben-Yair addressed his followers: 'As we have of old determined, my brave comrades, neither to serve the Romans, nor any other than God—for He alone is the true and just Lord of men—the time has now come which enjoins us to verify by our actions this resolve. Herein then let us not disgrace ourselves ... [T]his hath been granted to us as a favour by God, that we have it in our power to die honourably and in freedom ... Let another day dawn, and assured capture awaits us; but there is still the unfettered choice of a noble death with those dearest to us ... [L]et our wives die undishonoured; our children, ere they know what slavery is; and, when once they are removed, let us confer a noble favour on one another, preserving our freedom as a becoming shroud (Josephus, 1851, pp. 241–242).' Following this the men proceeded to kill their wives and children. They then drew lots to determine who would put whom to death. The sole remaining survivor torched the fortress and fell on his sword.

Thought Avenue

Did Jesus commit suicide? The poet John Donne believed so. In his posthumously published text, Biathanatos, he argued that Jesus ended his own life. The cause of death was not crucifixion but the 'actual emission of his soul', which 'was his own act'. He was not killed by the Romans but by 'his own will'. Donne reminds the reader that Jesus said, 'No one can take my life from me. I sacrifice it voluntarily. For I have the authority to lay it down when I want to ...' (John 10:18). He also points out that Jesus died uncommonly quickly (six hours) and that, unlike a person on the verge of total bodily collapse, immediately prior to his death he possessed sufficient strength to cry out (Mark 15:37). How compelling a case does Donne make? Should a distinction be drawn between self-sacrifice (where death is the incidental means to some greater end) and suicide (where death is the end)? Of course, if 'in him there is no sin' (1 John 3:5), then Donne's interpretation would suggest the moral permissibility of suicide, but under what precise circumstances?

- Enquiry Question: Was the mass suicide at Masada an act of courage or cowardice?

Development Questions:

○ Would the legend be more inspiring if the rebels had fought to the bloody end?

○ Were their actions analogous to any of the cases from Activity 1?

The Roman statesman and philosopher Seneca (1920) believed that to commit suicide to avoid 'living ill' exemplified wisdom, dignity and valour. Read through this extract with the class and ask pupils to decide whether Seneca would have approved of the actions of the Jews at Masada (he died several years before the event).

> [M]ere living is not a good, but living well. Accordingly, the wise man will live as long as he ought, not as long as he can. He will mark in what place, with whom, and how he is to conduct his existence, and what he is about to do. He always reflects concerning the quality, and not the quantity, of his life. As soon as there are many events in his life that give him trouble and disturb his peace of mind, he sets himself free. And this privilege is his, not only when the crisis is upon him, but as soon as Fortune seems to be playing him false; then he looks about carefully and sees whether he ought, or ought not, to end his life on that account. He holds that it makes no difference to him whether his taking-off be natural or self-inflicted, whether it comes later or earlier. He does not regard it with fear, as if it were a great loss; for no man can lose very much when but a driblet remains. It is not a question of dying earlier or later, but of dying well or ill. And dying well means escape from the danger of living ill.
>
> That is why I regard the words of the well-known Rhodian as most unmanly. This person was thrown into a cage by his tyrant, and fed there like some wild animal. And when a certain man advised him to end his life by fasting, he replied: "A man may hope for anything while he has life." This may be true; but life is not to be purchased at any price. No matter how great or how well-assured certain rewards may be, I shall not strive to attain them at the price of a shameful confession of weakness ...
>
> Must I await the cruelty either of disease or of man, when I can depart through the midst of torture, and shake off my troubles? This is the one reason why we cannot complain of life: it keeps no one against his will. (1920, pp. 59–65)

Activity 7

These objections concern the morality rather than legality of euthanasia. It is possible for one to be a Millian liberal on the question of the euthanasia's legality while holding that individuals who pursue euthanasia are acting immorally.

For this activity, pupils are presented with texts and expositions. Their task is to convert those texts into standard form using the following structure:

1. x. [*The argument's central principle*]

2. If x, then it is wrong for us to y.

3. Euthanasia is an instance of y.

4. Therefore, euthanasia is wrong.

For instance, the 'Gift of God' passage would become:

1. Life is a gift from God.

2. If life is a gift from God, then it is wrong for us to dispose of that gift.

3. Euthanasia involves disposing of the gift of life.

4. Therefore, euthanasia is wrong.

Once the arguments are in standard form, pupils should then assess their strength by questioning the truth of the first two premises. This is particularly valuable for atheists who might be inclined to reject 'Gift of God' and 'Possession of God' arguments without actually thinking through them. Evaluating premise 2 allows them to work on the assumption that first premise is correct and then determine the implications of this.

Gift of God

'[I]t is altogether unlawful to kill oneself … because life is God's gift to man, and is subject to the power of Him Who kills and makes to live. Hence whoever takes his own life, sins against God.'

Thomas Aquinas (1918, p. 204)

Possession of God

'I too believe that the gods are our guardians, and that we are a possession of theirs … [I]f one of your own possessions, an ox or an ass, for example, took the liberty of putting himself out of the way when you had given no intimation of your wish that he should die, would you not be angry with him, and would you not punish him if you could?'

Plato (1909, p. 50)

Duty to Others

'[I]t is altogether unlawful to kill oneself … because every part, as such, belongs to the whole. Now every man is part of the community, and so, as such, he belongs to the community. Hence by killing himself he injures the community.'

Thomas Aquinas (1918, p. 204)

Future Self

In *Stay: A History of Suicide and the Philosophies Against It* Jennifer Michael Hecht (2013) makes the point that one's experience of life can vary hugely from one period of time to another, and so the 'you' at any given moment should 'not have the authority to end life for the many yous of many other moments' (2013, p. 177).

Cowardice

'Is it not rather proof of a feeble mind, to be unable to bear either the pains of bodily servitude or the foolish opinion of the vulgar? And is not that to be pronounced the greater mind, which rather faces than flees the ills of life?'

St Augustine (1871, p. 33)

'Another will say that it is noble to destroy oneself. Far from it—but most ignoble! just as I would deem that pilot most dastardly, who dreading a tempest, voluntarily sinks his ship ere the storm sets in.'

Flavius Josephus (1851, p. 34)

'[D]ying to escape from poverty, or the pangs of love, or anything that is simply painful, is the act not of a Brave man but of a coward; because it is mere softness to fly from what is toilsome, and the suicide braves the terrors of death not because it is honourable but to get out of the reach of evil.'

Aristotle (1915, p. 62)

Unnatural

'[E]verything naturally loves itself, the result being that everything naturally keeps itself in being, and resists corruptions so far as it can. Wherefore suicide is contrary to the inclination of nature, and to charity whereby every man should love himself. Hence suicide is always a mortal sin, as being contrary to the natural law and to charity.'

Thomas Aquinas (1918, p. 204)

'[S]uicide is alien to the common nature of all animals … Nor indeed is there any living creature that dies premeditatedly, or by its own act; for nature's law is strong in all—the wish to live.'

Flavius Josephus (1851, p. 34)

Thought Avenue

On January 10th 1917, during a period in which he was fighting for the Austro-Hungarian Army on the Russian Front, Ludwig Wittgenstein wrote in his notebooks that suicide is the 'elementary sin' because 'if suicide is allowed then everything is allowed' (1961, p. 91). Wittgenstein didn't elaborate on these remarks, and we cannot be certain why he regarded suicide as a qualitatively distinct and foundational wrong. As an exegetical exercise, ask pupils to determine what he may have meant by these cryptic claims.

A possible interpretative aid, present the following extract from G. K. Chesterton (1909) to see whether this might shed any light on Wittgenstein's meaning:

> Not only is suicide a sin, it is the sin. It is the ultimate and absolute evil, the refusal to take an interest in existence; the refusal to take the oath of loyalty to life. The man who kills a man, kills a man. The man who kills himself, kills all men; as far as he is concerned he wipes out the world … [The suicide] defiles every flower by refusing to live for its sake. There is not a tiny creature in the cosmos at whom his death is not a sneer … spiritually, he destroys the universe.
>
> G. K. Chesterton (1909, p. 129–130)

Activity 8

In light of the arguments considered, pupils may wish to go back and revise their legislation. The final task is to draw on these arguments to articulate the philosophical underpinnings of their views. The two requirements are to justify their legal (under what circumstances, if any, it ought to be legal) and moral (under what circumstance, if any, it is morally permissible) views on euthanasia.

> **Thought Avenue**
>
> Christianity is commonly associated with the belief in the sanctity of life. The *Catechism of the Catholic Church*, for instance, states that 'human life is sacred'. *Prima facie*, there is an incompatibility between this teaching and the views expressed in scripture and by early theologians. Consider the case of the bishop Ignatius of Antioch (1987), who was executed for his faith in the 2nd century. During his fateful transportation from Antioch to Rome, he wrote to his fellow Christians in Rome expressing a morbid desire for martyrdom and imploring them not to intervene in his execution. He described his wish to be ground down by the teeth of lions into wheat for God, explaining: 'I am yearning for death with all the passion of a lover. Earthly longings have been crucified; in me there is left no spark of desire for mundane things, but only a murmur of living water that whispers within me, "Come to the Father"' (1987, pp. 77–78).
>
> Is there a genuine dissonance here with the notion that life is sacred, or can this sentiment and those expressed in the verses below be regarded as consonant with life's holiness?
>
> *If anyone comes to me and does not hate father and mother, wife and children, brothers and sisters—yes, even their own life—such a person cannot be my disciple.*
> Luke 14:26
>
> *The good shepherd lays down his life for his sheep.*
> John 10:11
>
> *Anyone who loves their life will lose it, while anyone who hates their life in this world will keep it for eternal life.*
> John 12:25
>
> *There is no greater love than to lay down one's life for one's friends.*
> John 15:13
>
> *Do not love the world or anything in the world.*
> 1 John 2:15
>
> *For we know that if the earthly tent we live in is destroyed, we have a building from God, an eternal house in heaven, not built by human hands. Meanwhile we groan, longing*

> to be clothed instead with our heavenly dwelling ... Therefore we are always confident and know that as long as we are at home in the body we are away from the Lord ... We are confident, I say, and would prefer to be away from the body and at home with the Lord.
>
> 2 Corinthians 5:1–8
>
> If I am to go on living in the body, this will mean fruitful labour for me. Yet what shall I choose? I do not know! I am torn between the two: I desire to depart and be with Christ, which is better by far.
>
> Philippians 1:22–23

Extension Material

These extension materials approach the issues of whether the very old have duty to choose euthanasia and whether it is morally permissible to euthanise the very young, even in cases where the infant is not suffering. Could it be the case that there is something about those who exist at the margins of life that renders their lives more disposable?

Senicide

- An early expression of the view that the elderly effectively outstay their welcome comes from Iphis in Euripides' play *The Suppliant Women:*

  > I hate the men who would prolong their lives
  > By foods and drinks and charms of magic art
  > Perverting nature's course to keep off death
  > They ought when they no longer serve the land
  > To quit this life and clear the way for youth.
  >   (Quoted by Plutarch, 1928, p. 153)

- Friedrich Nietzsche (1927) was no less damning of the sick, and by extension, the sickly old. The irony, however, is that Nietzsche himself experienced profound cognitive decline from 1889 and spent the final years of his life in the care of his sister till his death in 1900.

  > The sick man is a parasite of society. In certain cases it is indecent to go on living. To continue to vegetate in a state of cowardly dependence upon doctors and special treatments, once the meaning of life, the right to life, has been lost, ought to be regarded with the greatest contempt by society ... One should die proudly when it is no longer possible to live proudly. Death should be chosen freely,—death at the right time, faced clearly and joyfully and embraced while one is surrounded by one's children and other witnesses. It should be

affected in such a way that a proper farewell is still possible, that he who is about to take leave of us is still *himself*, and really capable not only of valuing what he has achieved and willed in life, but also of *summing-up* the value of life itself. (1927, p. 88)

- More recently in her 'Apologia for suicide', the barrister Mary Rose Barrington (2015), who was a chairman of the Voluntary Euthanasia Society (subsequently renamed Dignity in Dying), and who died in 2020, modified Horace's famous line, 'dulce et decorum est pro patria mori' ('It is sweet and right to die for one's country') to read 'dulce et decorum est pro familia mori' ('It is sweet and right to die for one's family'). She hoped that striving to live for the maximum number of years despite one's growing dependence on our family, friends, and society, would come to be seen as contemptibly egoistic.
- In his 1997 essay, 'Dying at the Right Time: Reflections on (Un)assisted Suicide philosopher' the philosopher John Hardwig (2020) similarly argued that there is, for the elderly, a duty to die. Caring for an elderly relative can take a profound emotional and financial toll on a family while also derailing their life plans. In many cases, this will drastically diminish the family's quality of life. But sacrificial duties ought to be reciprocal, and just as younger family members should be expected to make some sacrifices in order to help older relatives, likewise those older relatives should be prepared, at a certain point, to be willing to sacrifice their lives for the good of others.

Infanticide

- In *The Ethics of Killing,* Jeff McMahan (2002) argues that infanticide is morally permissible. While we may have powerful emotive resistance to such claims, McMahan believes that our sentiments are unreliable in determining a being's moral status. Moreover, our confidence in the moral intuition that infanticide is just as wrong as killing adults should be tempered by the fact that infanticide has occurred through most of human history (in Sparta, for instance, it was a legal requirement to euthanise disabled infants).

  McMahan also argues that it is inconsistent to permit the death of the foetus but not the premature infant (we permit abortions up to 24 weeks and the chance of survival of a baby born prematurely at 23 weeks is now about 50:50). The only difference between the premature baby and the foetus is their location, which is not morally relevant. Moreover, the Abortion Act 1967 permits abortions up to the point of birth, if there is a risk the baby will be 'handicapped', a term that includes Down's syndrome. If its life may be ended up to the point of birth, why not the day after birth?

Irrespective of consistency, McMahan also thinks that infants are not significantly harmed by death. This is because the infant has weak 'time-relative interests'. While the infant may have a whole life ahead of it, and so, seemingly, much to lose, its psychological connection to and investment in that life are weak 'because it would be only weakly psychologically related to itself in the future' (2002, p. 346). Since its time-relative interests are not thwarted by death, its death does not constitute harm. One potential strength of McMahan's account is that it is able to explain the common intuition that the death of a 10-year-old is a greater tragedy than the death of a 10-day-old (as a cognisant individual with a sense of a persisting self, the 10-year-old has far stronger time-relative interests).

- Peter Singer (2011) has argued that killing disabled infants is morally permissible if it enables the parents to have another child in its stead (i.e. to 'replace' the disabled infant) who would be happier. While we may recoil from the idea of 'replacing' a disabled infant with an able-bodied one, he believes we should not morally recoil from the notion of infanticide because, according to him, infants lack self-awareness and a sense of themselves as distinct individuals. It is these cognitive limitations that help explain why 'it is only for newborn infants, or for still earlier stages of human life, that replaceability should be considered to be an ethically acceptable option' (p. 165).
- See the 'Reproduction' chapter for Michael Tooley's argument for the permissibility of infanticide.

Notes

1 https://www.britannica.com/topic/Hippocratic-oath
2 https://www.wma.net/policies-post/wma-declaration-of-geneva/
3 https://www.un.org/en/about-us/universal-declaration-of-human-rights

References

Aquinas, T. (1918) [1272]. *Summa Theologica* (English Dominican Fathers, Trans.). Burns, Oates and Washburne.

Aristotle. (1915) [c. 330 BCE]. *The Nicomachean Ethics* (D. P. Chase, Trans.). J. M. Dent & Sons.

Augustine. (1871) [c. 426 CE]. *City of God* (Rev. Marcus Dods, Trans.). T & T Clark.

Barrington, M. R. (2015). Apologia for Suicide. In M. P. Battin (Ed.), *The Ethics of Suicide* (pp. 702–706). Oxford University Press.

Chesterton, G. K. (1909). *Orthodoxy*. The Bodley Head.

Hardwig, J. (2020). Dying at the Right Time: Reflections on (Un)assisted Suicide. In H. Lafollette (Ed.), *Ethics in Practice: An Anthology* (5th ed.) (pp. 106–118). John Wiley & Sons.

Hecht, J. M. (2013). *Stay: A History of Suicide and the Philosophies Against It*. Yale University Press.

Ignatius of Antioch. (1987) [c. 130 CE]. The Epistle to the Romans. In M. Stainforth & A. Louth (Trans.), *Early Christian Writings: The Apostlic Fathers*. Penguin Classics.

Josephus. (1851) [c. 75 CE]. *The Jewish War Vol. II* (I. Taylor, Ed., R. Traill, Trans.). Houlston and Stoneman.

Kant, I. (1991) [1797]. *The Metaphysics of Morals* (M. Gregor, Trans.). Cambridge University Press.

McMahan, J. (2002). *The Ethics of Killing*. Oxford University Press.

Mill, J. S. (1910). *Utilitarianism, Liberty and Representative Government*. J. M. Dent & Sons.

Nietzsche, F. (1927) [1889]. Twilight of the Idols. In O. Levy (A. Ludovici, Trans.), *The Complete Works of Friedrich Nietzsche Vol. XVI*. George Allen & Unwin.

Plato. (1909) [c. 380 BCE]. Phaedo. *The Apology, Phaedo and Crito of Plato* (B. Jowett, Trans.). PF Collier & Son.

Plutarch. (1928). A Letter of Condolence to Apollonius. In F. C. Babbitt (Trans.), *Moralia*. Harvard University Press.

Rachels, J. (2016). Active and Passive Euthanasia. In H. Kuhse, U. Schüklenk and P. Singer (Eds.), *Bioethics: An Anthology* (3rd ed.) (pp. 248–252). John Wiley & Sons.

Seneca. (1920) [c. 65 CE]. *Ad Lucilium Epistulae Morales* (R. M. Gummere, Trans.). G. P. Putnam's Sons.

Singer, P. (2011). *Practical Ethics* (3rd ed.) Cambridge University Press.

Wittgenstein, L. (1961). *Notebooks, 1914–1916* (G. H. von Wright & G. E. M. Anscombe, Eds., G. E. M. Anscombe, Trans.). Basil Blackwell.

3 Animals

> **Key Questions**
>
> - Can non-human animals be wronged?
> - Do they have moral status?
> - Do they have a right to a good life?
> - Do they have a right to life?
> - Is predation a moral tragedy?

This chapter is focused on the moral status of non-human animals. It questions the extent to which animals are capable of having good lives and, correlatively, bad lives, and thereby whether it is possible to wrong them. If animals can be wronged, to what extent do we have moral duties to them? Is it permissible to abuse them? Use them? Kill them? These questions are explored in relation to both intensive and extensive farming practices. We finally consider the rather surprising philosophical problem of predation: if animals do have moral status, are we thereby obliged to prevent predators from killing them?

PART I: INTENSIVE FARMING

Activity 1

Start by considering the question of whether animals can have good lives and, correlatively, bad lives, and therefore whether it is possible to wrong an animal. Once it is established that it is possible to wrong an animal, if it is, then the challenge is to determine the extent of our duties to them.

Start by asking pupils to complete the table on the extent to which animals and humans can suffer in similar ways.

Forms of human suffering	Shared by pigs?
Loneliness	
Boredom	
Fear	
Physical pain	
Stress	
Ill-health	
Depression	
Anxiety	
Frustration	
Despair	
Hunger	
Thirst	
Excessive cold	
Excessive heat	
Confinement/Absence of liberty	
Shame	
Humiliation	
Grief	

Drawing on the above, now ask pupils to think of five necessary criteria for a good life of a pig and then five correlative features of a bad life. For instance:

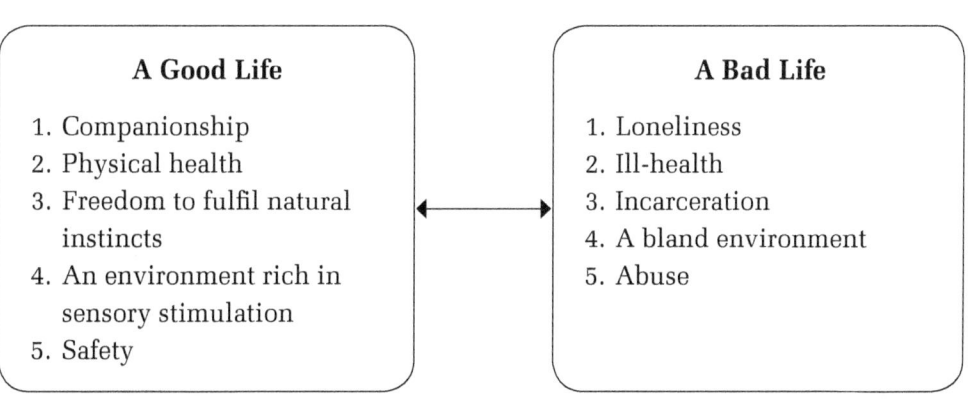

A Good Life
1. Companionship
2. Physical health
3. Freedom to fulfil natural instincts
4. An environment rich in sensory stimulation
5. Safety

A Bad Life
1. Loneliness
2. Ill-health
3. Incarceration
4. A bland environment
5. Abuse

- Enquiry Question: Is it possible to wrong an animal?

    Development Questions:

    ○ If animals can be wronged, does it follow that they have rights?

    ○ Does the fact that a being can be wronged automatically mean that we have duties towards that being?

    ○ Could it ever be right to wrong an animal?

    ○ If animals can have bad lives, does that mean inflicting such lives on them is bad?

    ○ Can animals be wronged to the same extent that humans can be wronged?

Activity 2

The task now is to consider whether the suffering animals endure when intensively farmed constitutes a wrong and whether that wrong is justifiable. Intensive farming, also known as industrial or factory farming, involves producing meat, dairy products and eggs as cheaply as the law will permit. The precise legal bounds of this vary from country to country. Below is an outline of intensive pig-farming practices in the UK. To give pupils a clear and graphic understanding of intensive farming, there are a number of documentaries you might watch, including *Earthlings* (2005), *Lucent* (2014) and *Dominion* (2018). The documentary *Pignorant* (2024) exposes the experiences of pigs as they are gassed, and while this method of slaughter isn't exclusive to intensively farmed pigs, it is indicative of the general experiences of the lives of intensively farmed pigs. These films can be extremely graphic and upsetting, so you might opt to simply present the information below.

An Outline of Intensive Pig Farming Practices in the UK (as of 2024).

Pigs

- Approximately 10 million pigs are slaughtered in the UK every year.

- Most pigs remain indoors their entire life.

- The majority of sows are placed in farrowing crates up to a week before they are expected to give birth. These cages prevent the sow from turning around. They also prevent the sow

Thought Avenue

Timothy Pachirat's *Every Twelve Seconds: Industrialized Slaughter and the Politics of Sight* (2011) sheds light on the affect intensive farms have on those who operate them. The book documents his experience going undercover – Pachirat is a political scientist – to work in an from carrying out her natural instinct to build a nest. She cannot interact with the piglets who suckle her from a small area known as a 'creep' from the other side of the crate. The sow will remain in the crate until the piglets are weaned at approximately 28 days of age. (Feral piglets do not wean till at least twice this age.)

- Following the removal of her piglets, the sow will be impregnated again within a matter of days.

- Many piglets have their tails docked and teeth clipped. These procedures can be carried out without anaesthetic before the piglet is 7 days old.

- These procedures reduce the risk of pigs biting each other's tails. It is believed that this behaviour is caused by their cramped and insufficiently stimulating pens. In these environments they are unable to fulfil their instincts to root and forage.

> abattoir. During this period he drove over six thousand cattle down chutes to be slaughtered and witnessed many of them getting shot through the skull with a captive bolt. Asking one of his colleagues what it would be like to be a knocker (the person who fires the captive bolts) he was told, 'Man, that's killing … that shit will fuck you up for real' (p. 158). Though he only worked in the chute, these words resonated deeply: '"Fucked up" is exactly how I feel; it is how I would describe many of the chute workers' (ibid).
>
> One question to consider in relation to this account is whether those who purchase and consume intensively farmed meat are culpable for the adverse consequences such work has on the state of mind and well-being of those who are (poorly) paid to produce it.

- Though castration without anaesthetic is legal for male pigs within the first week of their lives, this is not a common practice in the UK.

- Pigs for small joints or fresh meat are slaughtered at 15–16 weeks of age. Bacon pigs are slaughtered at 22 weeks of age. Those selected for breeding will give birth twice a year before being slaughtered at around 5 years old. (Feral pigs can live up to 8 years. A domestic pig can live as long as 25 years.)

- Most pigs are crowded into cramped cages and gassed with carbon dioxide prior to having their throats slit. Carbon dioxide poisoning causes pain, respiratory distress and fear in the animals.

Present the following responses and ask your pupils to identify the one that best expresses their views. Ask pupils to then justify their particular responses. This will serve as a provisional and preliminary articulation of their moral stance, which we shall subsequently seek to refine.

1	2	3	4	5
This is morally permissible, and it is frankly ridiculous that anyone would think otherwise.	*This is morally permissible, though I can understand why others might think it's wrong.*	*I'm uncertain about the morality of this.*	*This is morally impermissible, but the state should not intervene. It is for corporations and individuals to decide whether they want to produce and consume this.*	*Not only is this morally impermissible it should be illegal.*

Activity 3

We now turn to an argument against eating intensively farmed animals by Alastair Norcross (2004). This is an argument from analogy: since one type of action is immoral, then another type of action that significantly resembles this action must also be immoral. Norcross formulates the analogy using the following story:

> Fred's neighbours, concerned by the strange noises coming his basement, have contacted the police. The police arrive and are taken by Fred down to the basement where they are horrified to see over a dozen howling and whimpering puppies locked in cramped cages. It is clear that they have all been mutilated in various ways: some are missing tails, some teeth, others their genitals. Fred says that the puppies are kept down here for twenty-six weeks before he slaughters them. He calmly explains that he needs to inflict severe stress and suffering on the puppies in order to harvest the cocoamone from their godiva glands.
>
> Cocoamone is the hormone responsible for the experience of chocolate. A few years ago following a car accident Fred damaged his godiva gland and was no longer able to experience the pleasures of chocolate. Fortunately for Fred, a veterinary surgeon discovered that if subjected to intense suffering, puppies produce cocoamone. And so Fred set up this makeshift farm in his basement in order to continue enjoying chocolate.

The first task is to determine and articulate the morality of Fred's actions. Have pupils complete the following schematic, using either < > to show which state of affairs is more important than, and thereby morally supersedes, the other, such that when the two are mutually exclusive we know which we ought to prioritise.

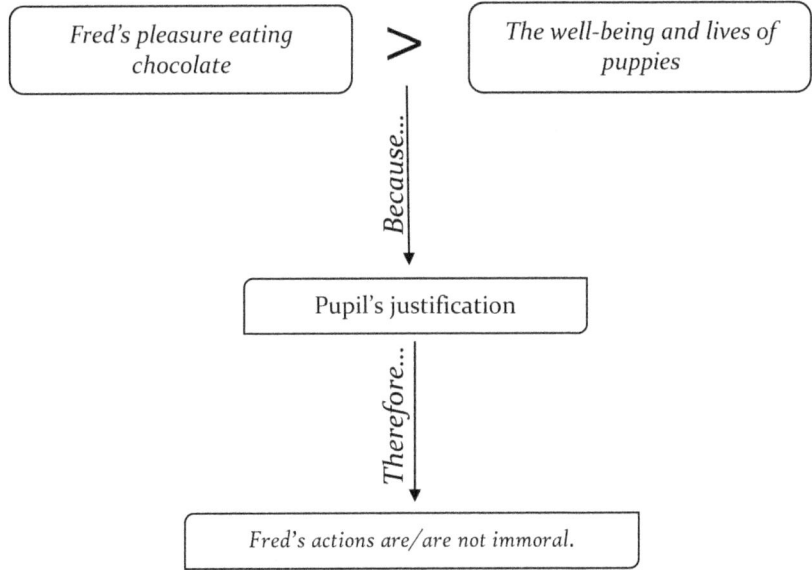

Norcross notes that the conditions involved in intensive farming resemble those in the story, with many animals, particularly in the US, living in cramped, stressful confinement and enduring unanaesthetised mutilations. Just like Fred and chocolate, the vast majority of people could live a healthy life without meat. He goes on to issue this challenge:

> If we are prepared to condemn Fred for torturing puppies merely to enhance his gustatory experiences, shouldn't we similarly condemn the millions who purchase and consume factory-raised meat? Are there any morally significant differences between Fred's behaviour and their behavior? … If morality demands that we not torture puppies merely to enhance our own eating pleasure, morality also demands that we not support factory farming by purchasing factory-raised meat. (pp. 231, 236)

- Enquiry Question: Are those who buy intensively farmed meat acting like Fred?

Development Questions:

- Is it a morally significant difference that Fred tortures the puppies himself while meat-eaters consume animals that have been tortured by others?
- Is it a morally significant difference that abstaining from eating intensively farmed meat does not prevent any animals suffering, whereas Fred can stop the puppies suffering?

On the question of the moral culpability of the consumer, the views of David DeGrazia (2016) may serve as a catalyst. He advocates the following moral rule: we should endeavour to not financially support institutions that cause profound and unnecessary harm. He writes:

> But what about the consumer? She isn't harming animals; she's just eating the products of factory farming. Well, imagine someone who says, "I'm not kicking dogs to death. I'm just paying someone else to do it." We would judge this person to act wrongly for encouraging and commissioning acts of cruelty ... [T]he purchase of factory-farmed meat directly encourages and makes possible the associated cruelties – so the consumer is significantly responsible. (p. 248)

Having discussed the strength of the analogy, pupils should complete the following schematic using ~ or ≁ to indicate whether the two actions are similar, and therefore, shown by either → or ↛, whether the wrongness of one entails the wrongness of the other. For pupils who concluded that Fred's enjoyment of chocolate does morally supersede the well-being of puppies, even if Fred's actions and the actions of meat-eaters are similar, we cannot conclude from this that the latter is wrong. There may also be pupils who believe that it is wrong to eat or purchase intensively farmed meat, but not for the reasons presented by Norcross.

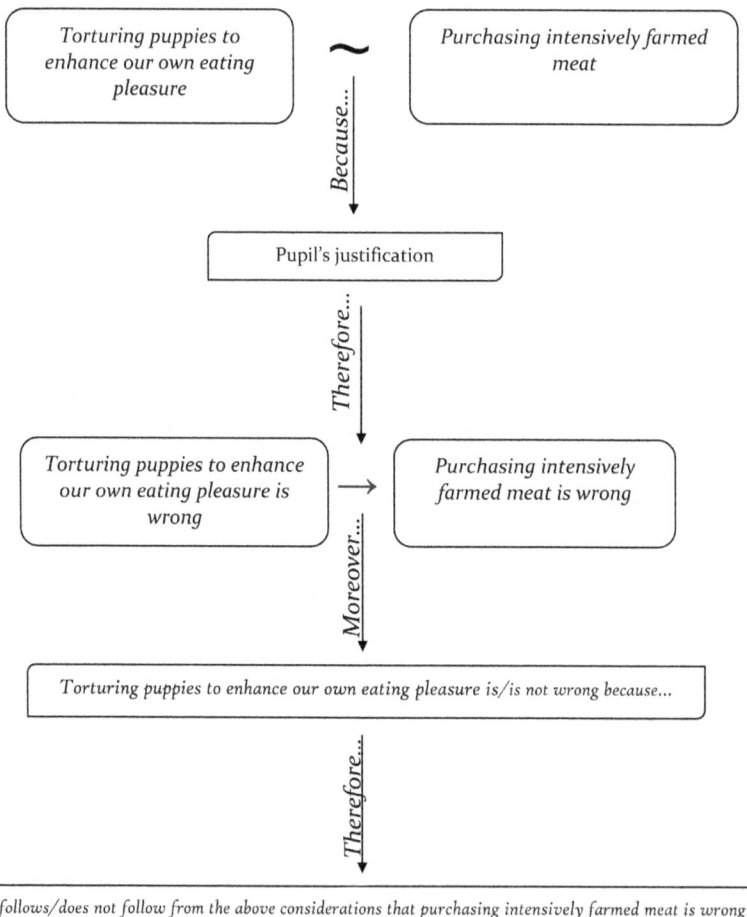

Activity 4

What Norcross doesn't do in the extracts above is articulate why exactly it is wrong to treat puppies as Fred does. So let's now turn to three theories on what precisely it means to wrong an animal. For each philosopher, have pupils summarise the reasons why they would oppose intensive farming (and Fred's behaviour).

- **Martha Nussbaum's** approach to animal ethics is known as the Capabilities Approach. She believes that we should not use pleasure and pain as the primary metric of our moral evaluations. While an elephant born in captivity and held in a zoo may be treated well and not suffer any particular pain or dissatisfaction at its lack of free movement and social company, its incarceration is nevertheless wrong. This is because, according to Nussbaum, it is unable to fulfil its characteristic set of capabilities as an elephant and therefore cannot lead a flourishing life, which every striving creature is entitled to.

  Capabilities are core entitlements that include bodily integrity, enjoying good health, enjoying the use of one's senses and imagination, social interaction and control over one's environment. While each striving species has a distinct form of life and so will pursue these capabilities in unique ways, all such species cannot flourish when these capabilities are thwarted. In her own words:

  > 'Each form life is worthy of respect and it is problem of justice when a creature does not have the opportunity to unfold its (valuable) power, to flourish in its own way, and to lead a life with dignity. The fact that so many animals never to get to move around, enjoy the air, exchange affection with other members of their own kind – all that is a waste and a tragedy, and it is not a life in keeping with the dignity of such creatures.'
  > Nussbaum (2007, p. 33)

- In *The Case for Animal Rights* **Tom Regan** (2004) presents his view that any creature that satisfies the criterion of being a 'subject-of-a-life' thereby has 'inherent value' and with it a host of rights to protect that value. A being can be considered a subject-of-a-life when it has, among other attributes, 'beliefs and desires; perception, memory, and a sense of the future, including their own future; an emotional life together with feelings of pleasure and pain; preference and welfare interests; the ability to initiate action in pursuit of their desires and goals; a psychophysical identity over time; and an individual welfare in the sense that their experiential life fares well or ill for them independently of their utility for others and logically independent of their being the object of anyone else's interest' (p. 243).

  The being who satisfies these criteria has a right to respectful treatment and should not be used as a mere resource for others, as a mere means to someone else's ends. And so any harm done to this being cannot be justified on the grounds that others may derive a benefit from such harm.

- According to **Peter Singer**, a being's capacity to suffer is what determines whether it can have interests, and so whether we have any moral obligations towards it. A stone, for instance, is not sentient and cannot suffer. It therefore makes no sense to say that a stone has an interest in not being kicked. As such, we have no moral obligations towards stones. However, for beings with the capacity to suffer, 'there can be no moral justification for refusing to take that suffering into consideration' (2016, p. 533). To disregard the suffering of a being on the basis of a morally insignificant trait – say, its race, sex or species – would violate the principle of equality, which requires that a being's suffering 'be counted equally with the like suffering – in so far as rough comparisons can be made – of any other being' (ibid). To dismiss the suffering of a non-human animal simply because it is not human is speciesist.

It would constitute a clear violation of the principle of equality if we were to sacrifice the most important interests of a being – its interests not to suffer, not to subsist in misery and squalor – in order to satisfy our own comparatively trivial interests, such as the wish to experience certain edacious pleasures. We are therefore morally obliged not to participate in or support practices that involve such sacrifices.

Using their own provisional principles extracted from the schematic above,

Concept Check

Peter Singer makes reference to **speciesism**, a concept he did much to popularise. It refers to discriminatory behaviour or attitudes on the basis of species alone. He contends that humans and animals are morally relevant insofar as we are sentient and thereby capable of experiencing suffering and happiness. Therefore, to inflict levels of suffering on animals that we wouldn't on humans is speciesist and exemplifies a type of discrimination analogous to racism:

> The racist violates the principle of equality by giving greater weight to the interests of members of his own race, when there is a clash between their interests and the interests of another race. Similarly the speciesist allows the interests of his own species to override the greater interests of members of another species. The pattern is the same in each case. (2016, pp. 533–534)

The disability scholar and activist Sunaura Taylor (2017) has elaborated on the concept by stating that speciesism is predicated on ableism. The billions of dollars in profit made from the slaughter of animals is facilitated by the 'dependency, vulnerability, and presumed lack of emotional awareness or intellectual capacity of animals' (p. 60). And so, 'the very norms and institutions that perpetuate animal suffering and exploitation are supported by ableism' (ibid.).

while also drawing on the above extracts, citing similarities and differences, the task is to write a paragraph outlining the nature of intensive farming and their views on the morality of it. This might look something like this –

> **Thought Avenue**
>
> Judith Jarvis Thomson (1990) argued that it is worse to cause an animal pain than to cause an adult human pain. This is because an adult human can 'think his or her way around the pain to what lies beyond it in the future' (p. 292). An animal, however, is not able to do this, which leaves them trapped inside raw and undiluted pain. Is it worse, then, to forcibly teeth clip a piglet than an adult human?

Intensive farming refers to agricultural practices that aim to minimise the cost, thereby maximising the profit, of producing meat, dairy and eggs. With respect to pig farming in the UK, I believe that the dominant practices are morally impermissible and ought to be illegal. For example, while the law permits pigs to have their tails docked without anaesthetic within the first 7 days of the animal's life, this is impermissible because we should not inflict unnecessary pain on a sentient being. Moreover, the fact that this procedure exists to prevent tail biting points to another moral infraction: preventing a living being from fulfilling its natural instincts. This point somewhat aligns with Martha Nussbaum's 'Capability Approach' to animal welfare. She argues that… However, I am not in total agreement with her because…

Pupils may find the philosophical tendency to use impassive phrases like 'morally impermissible' somewhat dissociating. To ensure they are able to articulate their views accurately, offer an array of other words they might prefer to use, such as, *heinous, abhorrent, barbaric, brutal, contemptible, disgusting, evil, obscene.*

Activity 5

In my experience, most pupils oppose intensive farming practices. To help sharpen their views on the moral status of animals, it would, however, be worth examining possible justifications for intensive agricultural practices. While the two philosophers below don't necessarily agree with intensive farming, their arguments can be used to support the industry. Whether this can be done successfully is for your pupils to determine.

Peter Carruthers

According to the philosopher Peter Carruthers (2011) animals have no moral standing because they are unable to think about their obligations and duties to other beings. He subscribes to moral contractualism, which holds that morality is constituted by agreements made between individuals within a community on the appropriate rules of behaviour. In other words, moral rules are constructions rather than objective truths. As such, a being who cannot enter into such a contract does not have moral standing. To have moral standing an individual must be capable of evaluating rules by thinking about their costs and benefits, while also having the ability to consciously follow such rules. Animals, he contends, are unable to think in these terms. A pig cannot think, 'I ought to share my excess food because there exists a rule, the necessity of which I accept, that says I ought to share my excess resources'. He writes:

> What does it take to qualify as a rational agent from the perspective of contractualist moral theory? A rational agent is a potential contractor, which means that such a person should be capable of proposing and examining normative rules, as well as reasoning about the consequences of their adoption ... [T]here is no reason to believe that apes are capable of thinking in terms of normative rules, or that they would be motivated to comply with such rules if they could. (p. 391)

Thought Avenue

Peter Carruthers (1992) believes that the concern with animal rights in our culture is a 'reflection of moral decadence' (p. xi). He likens those who are preoccupied by the welfare of animals while human beings are starved and enslaved to Nero, who is apocryphally said to have fiddled while Rome burned.

Accepting the implication that animals have a lower moral standing than humans, how might one respond to this? Is animal welfare a distraction from worthier issues? Is it even worth expending lesson time on these matters?

R. G. Frey

According to Frey (1979) animals cannot have desires because they cannot have beliefs. And they cannot have beliefs because they do not have language. Therefore, they have no interests. We cannot truthfully say it is not in the animal's interest to be harmed. Statements such as 'The piglet doesn't want its tail docked' or 'The sow wants more space' are specious. This is because we can only attribute desires to beings that are capable of belief. For instance, to say that the pig desires water implies that the pig believes that having water will sate its thirst. According to Frey, however, a pig cannot have such beliefs because this requires linguistic ability. Specifically, believing that the water will sate my thirst means believing that the sentence 'The water will sate my thirst' is true.

> [I]f someone were to say, e.g., "The cat believes that the door is locked," then that person is holding, as I see it, that the cat holds the declarative sentence "The door is locked" to be true; and I can see no reason whatever for crediting the cat or any other

creature which lacks language, including human infants, with entertaining declarative sentences and holding certain declarative sentences to be true ... [N]o creature which lacks language can have beliefs; and without beliefs, a creature cannot have desires. (pp. 235–236)

Before evaluating the two positions, pupils should start by applying them: how could these views of animal nature be used to justify intensive farming? In evaluating the theories, there are two main questions to consider:

- What is the moral implication of this view of animal nature for our treatment of animals? Does it sanction intensive farming?
- Is that view of animal nature accurate?

PART II: EXTENSIVE FARMING

Having considered the morality of intensive farming practices, we now turn to the question of whether it is immoral to slaughter animals who have been afforded a good life. Extensive farming refers to a system that provides more space for animals, typically outdoor space where animals can range over a large area. Organic animal farming, for instance, is an extensive system with high welfare standards. Pigs on organic farms spend their lives outdoors (with access to shelter) in family groups and are able to express many of their natural instincts. They do not undergo mutilations such as tail docking and teeth clipping. Sows are not placed in farrow crates and are free to build their own nests. Piglets are weaned at a later point than on intensive farms (despite these higher welfare standards, organic pigs can still be gassed with carbon dioxide prior to their slaughter).

Activity 1

While it might seem self-evidently wrong to needlessly kill an innocent person, in order to think about the morality of killing animals, it would help to start by exploring the type of wrong that it is to kill. We'll approach this with a sorting exercise using legal punishments as a way to quantify the wrongness of an action. First, pupils should try to match the offence with the correct corresponding sentence (the answers, in order of severity of punishment, are as follows: Thomas Mair, Roshonara Choudhry, Perrty Sutcliffe-Keenan, Morgan Trowland and Harry Finn-Conway). The next task is to determine the punishment they believe would be appropriate for each offence.

In 2010, Roshonara Choudhry stabbed MP Stephen Timms twice in the abdomen. He survived the attack.	A whole life order, meaning the individual will never be released from prison.
In 2016, Thomas Mair murdered MP Jo Cox by repeatedly stabbing and shooting her.	A life sentence with a minimum prison term of 15 years.
The graffiti artist Harry Finn-Conway, who tagged under the alias Zerx, was convicted for 13 counts of criminal damage to property.	A custodial sentence of 12 months.
During the 2011 UK riots, Perry Sutcliffe-Keenan drunkenly set up a Facebook page inviting others to riot in his hometown of Warrington. The next morning he deleted the page. There was no rioting in Warrington.	A custodial sentence of 4 years.
In 2022, Morgan Trowland, a Just Stop Oil protester, scaled the Queen Elizabeth II Bridge causing it to close for two days.	A custodial sentence of 3 years.

Having thought through these particular cases, pupils should be well placed to complete the following sentences:

It is wrong to kill an innocent person for no significant reason because... Arguably, this is a greater wrong than merely harming an innocent person because...

Now, to apply these ideas to animals, with those opposed to killing animals playing devil's advocate:

Arguably, the immorality of killing a person for no significant reason doesn't apply to non-human animals because...

> **Thought Avenue**
>
> Are humans, as Hamlet described, truly the 'paragon of animals'? Paul Taylor (1986) is wary of the chauvinistic character of such pronouncements. Unquestionably, human beings are on the whole better at mathematics than monkeys. But monkeys are on the whole better at climbing trees. According to Taylor, our belief that mathematics is more valuable than arboreal gymnastics is simply because 'our conception of civilized life makes the development of mathematical ability more desirable than the ability to climb trees' (p. 130). Is he right to claim that there are no objective standards by which we can judge the abilities and attributes of animals? Is there no justification for the claim that humans are superior to other animals?

Activity 2

The next three activities involve straightforward argument analysis, with two arguments that support killing animals and one that opposes. We start with the opposing argument, known as the argument from marginal cases.

As we have touched upon, some philosophers argue that animals lack moral status due to their supposed deficiencies in certain areas, including reason, language and thought. However, there are many humans who fail to satisfy these criteria. This is either because they don't yet possess these abilities (such as infants), or they've lost them (such as the elderly), or they will never possess them (such as those with profound learning disabilities). Arguably, then, it is not possible to cast a net over those animals it is morally permissible to kill without also catching these so-called marginal, or atypical, human cases.

As a way into the argument, ask your class to try to establish the necessary and sufficient conditions for what constitutes a human. A necessary condition is one that *all* humans satisfy, and a sufficient condition is one that *only* humans satisfy. The challenge then is to complete the following:

All humans, and only humans, have/do...

While it may be true that only humans write sonnets, it's not true that all humans do or are capable of doing so. And while it's also true that all humans are mortal, this is not true for only humans. As such, writing sonnets and being mortal are not viable grounds for establishing a moral divide between those beings it is permissible and impermissible to kill. The argument from marginal cases works on the basis that it is not possible to establish the required necessary and sufficient conditions. (You might introduce the challenge by recounting the story of Diogenes interrupting Plato's lecture swinging a plucked chicken and yelling that he'd brought him a human as a counterexample to Plato's definition of a human as a featherless biped.) The difficulty particularly arises with marginal cases.

First, present the argument as an argument tree. If they fall out of the tree with a 'no', they need to explain why this is. If they climb the entire way to the final fruit, they need to outline whether it does reflect their views, and if not, to find the fault with the tree.

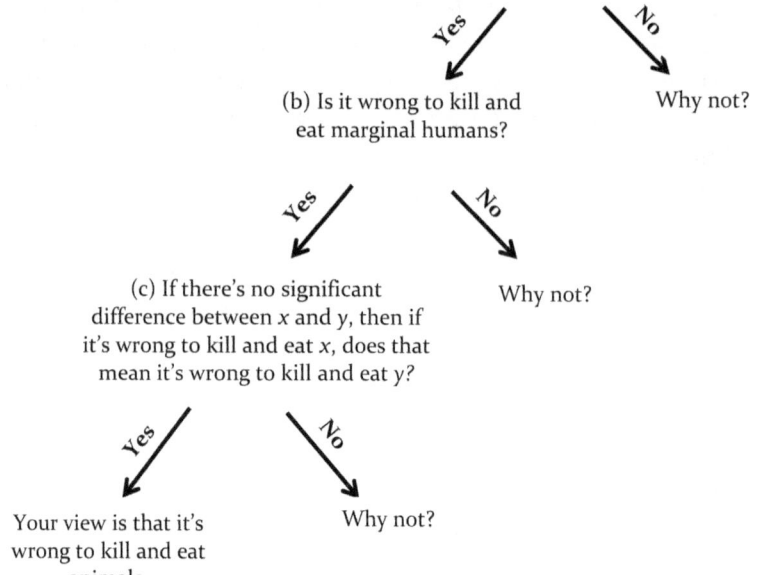

Having worked through the tree, present the class with the argument stated in premise/conclusion format:

1. *There is no significant difference between animals and marginal humans.*

2. *If there is no significant difference between x and y, and it is wrong to φ x, then it is also wrong to φ y.*

3. *It is wrong to kill and eat marginal humans.*

4. *Therefore, it is wrong to kill and eat animals.*

The next task is to answer the following:

i. Is the argument valid (does the conclusion logically follow from the premises)?

ii. Are premises 1–3 true?

iii. For each erroneous premise, explain the error.

iv. If you do accept the argument, explain the reasons that support premises 1, 2 and 3.

Activity 3

Peter Singer has offered a justification for eating extensively farmed meat known as the replaceability argument. The basic idea is that killing an animal (one that is not self-conscious and therefore has no capacity to desire continued life) is morally neutral if we ensure that in its stead another animal is born and leads an equally fulfilling life. Letting the happy animal live or killing and replacing it with another happy animal are morally indistinguishable options.

1. *An action is only wrong if it leads to a reduction in the overall amount of pleasure in the world.*
2. *If a painlessly killed animal is replaced by another animal that leads an equally pleasurable life, then there is no reduction in the overall pleasure in the world.*
3. *Therefore, it is not wrong to painlessly kill an animal so long as it is replaced by an animal with an equally pleasurable life.*

The next task is to answer the following:

i. Is the argument valid (does the conclusion logically follow from the premises)?

ii. Are premises 1–2 true?

iii. For each erroneous premise, explain the error.

iv. If you do accept the argument, explain the reasons that support premises 1 and 2.

Activity 4

Roger Crisp (1989) has taken the thinking behind Singer's argument a step further by arguing that it is in fact wrong *not* to kill and eat extensively farmed animals. This industry brings pleasure to both the animals (who would not have otherwise existed) and their consumers. Crisp writes:

> Most non-intensively-reared animals lead worthwhile lives, and we enjoy eating them ... And if we were not to eat them, both of these sources of utility [pleasure] would disappear ... [Thus] one is morally required both to abstain from the flesh of intensively reared animals and to eat the flesh of certain non-intensively-reared animals. (pp. 41, 44)

In standard form:

1. *The practice of rearing and eating extensively farmed animals adds to the overall amount of pleasure in the world.*

2. *You should always support practices that contribute to the overall pleasure in the world.*

3. *Therefore, you should support the practice of eating and rearing extensively farmed animals by eating or purchasing extensively farmed meat.*

The next task is to answer the following:

i. Is the argument valid (does the conclusion logically follow from the premises)?

ii. Are premises 1–2 true?

iii. For each erroneous premise, explain the error.

iv. If you do accept the argument, explain the reasons that support premises 1 and 2.

PART III: PREDATION

The American lawyer Clarence Darrow (1996) made the following observation in his autobiography *The Story of My Life:* 'There is no place in the woods or air or sea where all life is not a carnage of death in terror and agony … No landscape is so beautiful or day so balmy but the cry of suffering and sacrifice rends the air. When night settles down over the earth the slaughter is not abated … Almost all animals meet death by violence and through the most agonizing pain' (pp. 392–393).

If, as many philosophers have argued, it is wrong to kill and eat animals, ostensibly Darrow's depiction of nature should be deemed morally intolerable. For such philosophers, the fact of animal predation is seemingly a tragic one. If an animal has the right to life, it's not immediately obvious why this right should not protect it against both slaughterhouse workers and apex predators. Is it not inconsistent to both prevent a poacher from killing an antelope while permitting lions to do the same? On this question, Martha Nussbaum (2022) has written, 'It's important to keep pointing out that antelopes were not made to be food; they were made to live antelope lives … To say that it is the destiny of antelopes to be torn apart by predators is like saying that it is the destiny of women to be raped.'

Activity 1

To question whether predation is a lamentable fact of the world, begin by asking the class to outline what a perfect world might be like. Do this by focusing on what the world would lack, for example –

- Poverty
- Murder

- Extreme pain
- Violence
- Racism
- Exploitation
- Subjugation
- …

> **Thought Avenue**
>
> The transhumanist philosopher David Pearce believes that as a species we ought to pursue a project of 'paradise engineering', which involves eliminating all suffering from sentient life. He believes that advances in neurosurgery, pharmacology, genetic engineering and nanotechnology could help us achieve this goal. Eliminating or limiting predation is a vital part of this endeavour. Pearce claims this could be achieved by either preventing predators from procreating or through 'reprogramming' their behaviour. Where the ancient Greek philosopher Pythagoras is reputed to have used the power of persuasion to convince a bear to become vegetarian, Pearce anticipates the use of 'computer control' as a potential means of determining the behaviour of predators.

Following this, present the following two Old Testament visions of a perfect world – the latter of a past perfection, the former of a perfection yet to come – and ask pupils to identify the core similarity between these utopian visions.

> *The wolf will live with the lamb,*
> *and the leopard will lie down with the young goat,*
> *the calf, the young lion, and the fattened calf together;*
> *and a little child will lead them.*
> *The cow and the bear will graze.*
> *Their young ones will lie down together.*
> *The lion will eat straw like the ox.*
> *The nursing child will play near a cobra's hole,*
> *and the weaned child will put his hand on the viper's den.*
> *They will not hurt nor destroy in all my holy mountain;*
> *for the earth will be full of the knowledge of the Lord, as the waters cover*
>   *the sea.*
>
> Isaiah 11:6–9

God created man in his own image. In God's image he created him; male and female he created them. God blessed them. God said to them, "Be fruitful, multiply, fill the earth, and subdue it. Have dominion over the fish of the sea, over the birds of the sky, and over every living thing that moves on the earth." God said, "Behold, I have given you every herb yielding seed, which is on the surface of all the earth, and every tree, which bears fruit yielding seed. It will be your food. To every animal of the earth, and to every bird of the sky, and to everything that creeps on the earth, in which there is life, I have given every green herb for food;" and it was so. God saw everything that he had made, and, behold, it was very good. There was evening and there was morning, a sixth day.

Genesis 1:27–31

Note whether and why the pupils' perfect worlds didn't explicitly abolish predation. Then consider whether the abolition of murder and unbearable pain entails the abolition of predation. If, in a perfect world, humans wouldn't suffer in such ways, is there a good reason to not extend this mercy to animals? The key question is this –

- Enquiry question: Would violent predation exist in a perfect world?

  Development Questions:

  ○ If the elimination of animal predation didn't feature in your perfect world, why not? Is it a relatively minor improvement to our world? If so, why?

  ○ Would you rather live in a world where our appetites are satisfied without the need to kill or harm conscious beings?

  ○ Is the suffering inflicted by humans on animals a greater evil than the suffering inflicted by animals on animals?

  ○ Is extreme suffering compatible with a perfect world?

  ○ Is predation a moral tragedy?

  ○ If violent predation wouldn't exist in a perfect world, should we endeavour to end it? Should we strive for perfection?

Activity 2

To make the preceding activity more concrete, present the following thought experiments.

A

Hiking along a train track you see two lambs bleating with their distressed mother standing helplessly by their sides. The hind legs of each lamb are trapped in the track fastenings. You hear the sound of an approaching train. You have time to free the lambs without any danger to your own life.

- Enquiry Question (a): Should you free the lambs?

B

Hiking along the bank of a river you pass a ford where you see two lambs bleating with their distressed mother standing helplessly by their sides. The hind legs of each lamb are trapped between a cluster of rocks. On the other bank you see a pack of wolves, one of which is carrying in its mouth the fresh carcass from another kill, stealthily approaching the water, their eyes locked on the lambs. In your bag is a rescue whistle. With one forceful blow of the whistle the wolves will retreat and the lambs will live.

- Enquiry Question (b): Should you blow on the whistle to save the lamb?

Now present this thought experiment:

C

You have inexplicably become omnipotent. It is now within your power to ensure that no lamb is ever torn to shreds by hungry wolves. With a click of the finger, you can make every animal a herbivore, and with a second click of the finger, you can ensure that this causes no ecological damage and brings no greater harm to any creature.

- Enquiry Question (c): Should you enact these changes?

Having discussed these scenarios, ask pupils to evaluate the following statement:

If you say 'Yes' to A, then you ought to say 'Yes' B, and if you say 'Yes' B, then you ought to say 'Yes' to C, and if you say 'Yes' to C, you clearly believe that predation is a morally regrettable fact of the world. So, if you say 'Yes' to A, you are, in principle, morally opposed to predation.

Activity 3

Let's look at how the philosopher Jeff McMahan (2015) has expressed his opposition to predation.

> It would be good to prevent the vast suffering and countless violent deaths caused by predation. There is therefore one reason to think that it would be instrumentally good if predatory animal species were to become extinct and be replaced by new herbivorous species, provided that this could occur without ecological upheaval involving more harm than would be prevented by the end of predation ... I am therefore inclined to embrace the heretical conclusion that we have reason to desire the extinction of all carnivorous species.

Having discussed passage, present this attempted formulation of it and have pupils evaluate the argument.

1. *The world would be significantly improved without extreme suffering.*
2. *Predation is a cause of extreme suffering.*
3. *We ought to significantly improve the world, if we are able to do so.*
4. *Therefore, if it were possible to eliminate predation (carnivores) without this leading to even greater suffering, it would be our duty to do so.*

   i. Is the argument valid (does the conclusion logically follow from the premises)?

   ii. Are premises 1–3 true?

   iii. For each erroneous premise, explain the error.

   iv. If you do accept the argument, explain the reasons that support premises 1, 2 and 3.

Activity 4

To bring their thoughts together on this matter, have pupils complete the following:

Predation is a cause of constant and extreme suffering. And/But I believe that the suffering of preyed upon animals does/does not matter because… Therefore, predation is/is not a morally regrettable aspect of the world. Unquestionably, it is/is not a moral tragedy. As such, if I were an omnipotent being and I could eliminate predation without this causing even greater harm, then I would/would not.

Extension Material
Animal Nature

The points below touch on a number of ways philosophers have conceived of the differences between human and animal nature throughout the history of Western ideas.

- There is a venerable tradition of vegetarianism in western philosophy with figures such as Pythagoras, Empedocles, Plutarch and Plotinus all morally opposed to the killing and eating of animals. Writing in the late 1st and early 2nd centuries, Plutarch (1957) expressed his belief that the barbarity of the practice was self-evident, thus placing the burden of proof on omnivores. He was incredulous at how anyone could have first thought to feed on flesh. Who was this first man who 'made contact with the sores of others and sucked juices and serums from mortal wounds', who 'touched his mouth to gore and brought his lips to the flesh of a dead creature', who called food the carcasses that before their place on one's plate had 'bellowed and cried, moved and lived'? (pp. 541–544).

Plutarch even gave voice to the view that animals are morally superior to human beings. In his dialogue 'Gryllus' he reimagines book 10 of Homer's *Odyssey*, where Odysseus's crewmen are drugged and turned into swine by the enchantress Circe. According to the original poem, Odysseus managed to have the spell reversed, but in Plutarch's version, Odysseus is shocked to learn that his crewmen wish to remain in their bestial state. This is because animals are more courageous and more valiant. Plutarch notes that when we wish to praise a warrior we describe them as animals, calling them, for instance, lion-hearted. We do not, however, furnish praise on animals by describing them as 'man-hearted'. Animals, moreover, show neither gluttony nor avarice. Their desires are bound by their natural needs. They do not crave to excess.

- A number of Christian writers have shared Pythagoras's and Empedocles's view that animals possess immortal souls. The Puritan Richard Overton (1644) claimed 'all other Creatures as well as man shall be raised and delivered from death at the resurrection' (pp. 38–39), and Bishop Butler also held this view. (Despite Eusebius's claim that Jesus's brother James was a vegetarian, this was not owing to any particular metaphysical or moral beliefs about the status of animals but was entirely for ascetic reasons – he also didn't take baths.)
- In contrast to these theologians and philosophers, there is a parallel tradition in philosophy (continued by the likes of Carruthers and Frey) of those who believe there are qualitative differences between humans and animals such that humans have far greater moral value. René Descartes (1970), for instance, believed that animals lack thought. Though animals use sound and movement to communicate a variety of mental states, such as anger, hunger and fear, these are mere expressions of natural impulses and not expressions of thought. No animal has developed the means of communication – 'real speech' – to express thought, yet 'such speech is the only certain sign of thought hidden in a body' (p. 245). The best explanation for their silent tongues is that they have silent minds.

Below are three extracts that further expound these putative differences between animals and humans.

> It is clear that the rule of the soul over the body, and of the mind and the rational element over the passionate, is natural and expedient; whereas the equality of the two or the rule of the inferior is always hurtful. The same holds good of animals in relation to men; for tame animals have a better nature than wild, and all tame animals are better off when they are ruled by man ... Where

then there is such a difference as that between soul and body, or between men and animals, (as is the case of those whose business is to use their body, and who can do nothing better), the lower sort are by nature slaves, and it is better for them as for all inferiors that they should be under the rule of a master.

Aristotle (1885, p. 8)

Now the order of things is such that the imperfect are for the perfect, even as in the process of generation nature proceeds from imperfection to perfection. Hence it is that just as in the generation of a man there is first a living thing, then an animal, and lastly a man, so too things, like the plants, which merely have life, are all alike for animals, and all animals are for man. Wherefore it is not unlawful if man use plants for the good of animals, and animals for the good of man, as the Philosopher [Aristotle] states ... Dumb animals and plants are devoid of the life of reason whereby to set themselves in motion; they are moved, as it were by another, by a kind of natural impulse ... [W]hile properly speaking, we cannot wish good things to an irrational creature, because it is not competent, properly speaking, to possess good, this being proper to the rational creature which, through its free will, is the master of its disposal of the good it possesses. Hence the Philosopher says that we do not speak of good or evil befalling suchlike things, except metaphorically.

Thomas Aquinas (1918, pp. 62, 196–197).

So far as animals are concerned, we have no direct duties. Animals are not self-conscious and are there merely as a means to an end. That end is man.

Immanuel Kant (1930, p. 239)

References

Aquinas, T. (1918) [1272]. *Summa Theologica* (English Dominican Fathers, Trans.). Burns, Oates and Washburne.
Aristotle. (1885) [c. 330 BCE]. *Politics* (B. Jowett, Trans.). Clarendon Press.
Carruthers, P. (1992). *The Animals Issue: Moral Theory in Practice*. Cambridge University Press.
Carruthers, P. (2011). Animal Mentality: Its Character, Extent, and Moral Significance. In R. G. Frey & T. L. Beauchamp (Eds.), *The Oxford Handbook of Animal Ethics* (pp. 373–407). Oxford University Press.
Crisp, R. (1989). Utilitarianism and Vegetarianism. *International Journal of Applied Philosophy*, 4, 41–47.
Darrow, C. (1996). *The Story of My Life*. Da Capo Press.
DeGrazia, D. (2016). Meat Eating. In S. J. Armstrong & R. G. Botzler (Eds.), *The Animal Ethics Reader* (pp. 245–251) (3rd ed.). Routledge.
Descartes, R. (1970) [1649]. Letter to Henry More. In A. Kenny (Ed. & Trans.), *Descartes: Philosophical Letters*. Oxford University Press.
Frey, R. G. (1979). Rights, Interests, Desires, and Beliefs. *American Philosophical Quarterly*, 16(3), 233–239.
Kant, I. (1930). *Lectures on Ethics* (L. Infield, Trans.). Methuen & Co.

McMahan, J. (2015). *The Meat Eaters*. The New York Times. https://archive.nytimes.com/opinionator.blogs.nytimes.com/2010/09/19/the-meat-eaters/

Norcross, A. (2004). Puppies, Pigs, and People: Eating Meat and Marginal Cases. *Philosophical Perspectives*, 18(1), 229–245.

Nussbaum, M. (2007). The Moral Status of Animals. In L. Kalof and A. Fitzgerald (Eds.), *The Animals Reader: The Essential Classic and Contemporary Writings*. Routledge.

Nussbaum, M. (2022). *A Peopled Wilderness*. The New York Review. https://www.nybooks.com/articles/2022/12/08/a-peopled-wilderness-martha-c-nussbaum/

Overton, R. (1644). *Mans Mortalitie*. Amsterdam.

Pachirat, T. (2011). *Every Twelve Seconds: Industrialized Slaughter and the Politics of Sight*. Yale University Press.

Plutarch (1957). *Moralia Volume XII* (H. Cherniss & W. C. Helmbold, Trans.). Harvard University Press.

Regan, T. (2004). *The Case for Animal Rights*. University of California Press.

Singer, P. (2016). All Animals Are Equal. In H. Kuhse, U. Schüklenk and P. Singer (Eds.), *Bioethics: An Anthology* (3rd ed.) (pp. 530–540). John Wiley & Sons.

Taylor, P. (1986). *Respect for Nature*. Princeton University Press.

Taylor, S. (2017). *Beasts of Burden: Animal and Disability Liberation*. The New Press.

Thomson, J. J. (1990). *The Realm of Rights*. Harvard University Press.

4 Environment

> **Key Questions**
>
> - Do humans have a right to destroy the environment?
> - If we have a right to kill animals, why do we not also have a right to destroy ecosystems?
> - To what extent can nature be wronged?
> - Do only humans have intrinsic moral value?
> - Do all sentient beings have intrinsic moral value?
> - Do all living things have intrinsic moral value?
> - Do ecosystems have intrinsic moral value?

Activity 1

In order to challenge anthropocentrism, Richard Routley devised the 'last man' thought experiment. He asks whether it would be morally permissible for the last surviving member of the human species to destroy the planet. If anthropocentrism is correct and only humans have intrinsic worth, then there would be nothing wrong in doing so.

Our central activity is a variation on Routley's thought experiment. It aims to help pupils distinguish between a variety of positions: the views that value ultimately resides in humans (anthropocentrism), sentient beings (sentiocentrism) or living beings (biocentrism).

> *In the future a weapon capable of planetary destruction has been developed. While AI can accurately test the effectiveness of the weapon, there is a wish to see it in action. Several*

exoplanets have been identified as possible targets. These isolated planets, which are mere grains of sand within the context of the universe, are at such a distance from earth that no human will ever be able to visit them. They include:

Planet α	Planet β	Planet γ
A planet much like earth, populated with mammals, reptiles, birds etc. though without any organisms of comparable intelligence to humans.	This planet is rich in vegetation and teeming with plant life, from mile-high trees to vast plains of flowers. There is, however, no animal life.	An uninhabitable planet of rock and dust that is devoid of life. From the depths of its canyons to the peaks of its mountains, not a single living entity exists.

For each of the judgments below, have pupils outline a possible reason that would justify it.

Judgment 1

Earth — Destruction: Morally Impermissible

α, β, γ — Destruction: Morally Permissible

Judgment 2

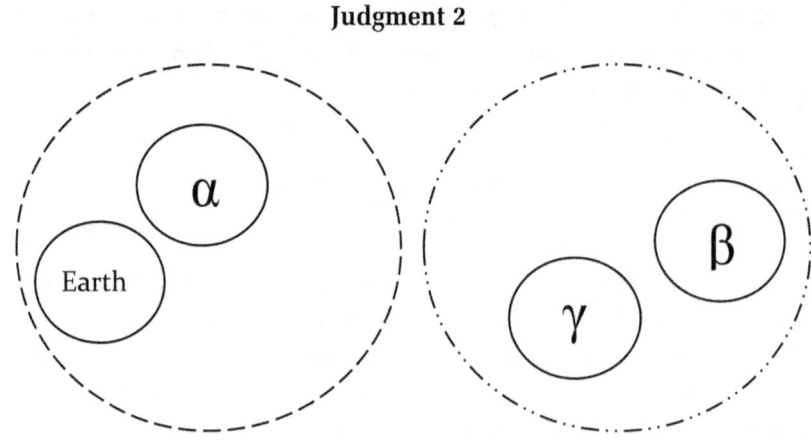

Destruction: Morally Impermissible   Destruction: Morally Permissible

Judgment 3

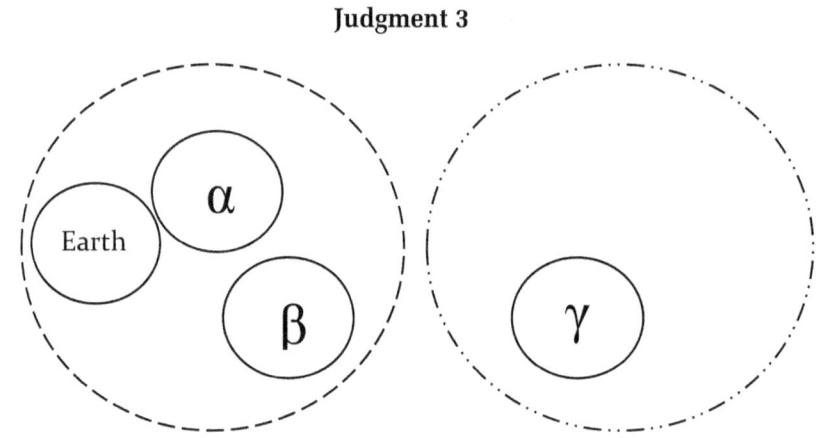

Destruction: Morally Impermissible   Destruction: Morally Permissible

Judgment 4

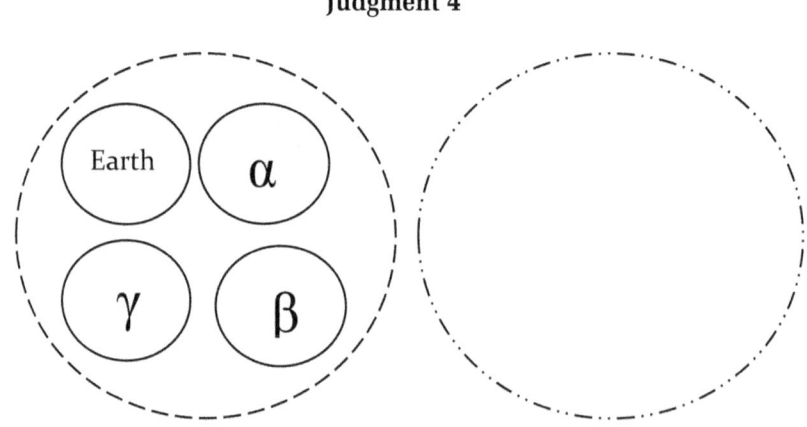

Destruction: Morally Impermissible   Destruction: Morally Permissible

Following that, ask the class to determine which judgment the philosophers, theologians and poets below would support.

- In the Ten Commandments, God issued the following injunction: 'You shall not kill' (Exodus 20:13). What is the scope of this injunction? Does it apply to all life? The theologian **St Augustine** (2003) thought not. He believed that God was not referring to 'bushes, which have no feelings, nor to irrational creatures, flying, swimming, walking, or crawling, since they have no rational association with us, not having been endowed with reason as we are' (pp. 31–32). Given that goldfinches, chestnut trees, adders, and the like, lack reason, they exist simply to serve us, 'their life and death is subordinated to our needs' (ibid.).

- Winner of the 1952 Nobel Peace Prize, **Albert Schweitzer** (2009) believed that we ought to act in the world with a 'reverence of life'. Doing so is not simply one aspect of acting ethically, it is the foundation and essence of an ethical life: 'Ethics is none other than reverence for life. Good consists in maintaining, assisting and enhancing life, and to destroy, to harm or to hinder life is evil' (p. 147).

- What determines whether a given entity has moral status? Whereas St Augustine believed that that reason was crucial, **Jeremy Bentham** (1879) believed this would unacceptably entail the moral worthlessness of human infants. For Bentham, moral status is not a matter of what we can do, the cognitive abilities we possess, but the extent to which we can feel. He wrote: 'The French have already discovered that the blackness of the skin is no reason why a human being should be abandoned without redress to the caprice of a tormentor. It may come one day to be recognized, that the number of the legs, the villosity of the skin, or the termination of the os sacrum, are reasons equally insufficient for abandoning a sensitive being to the same fate. What else is it that should trace the insuperable line? Is it the faculty of reason, or, perhaps, the faculty of discourse?

> **Concept Check**
>
> Typified by Immanuel Kant's (1987) claim that 'Man is indeed the only being on earth that has understanding and hence an ability to set himself purposes of his own choice, and in this respect he holds the title of lord of nature,' (p. 318) **anthropocentrism** (see Augustine) is the view that only humans have rights for they are the only source of value on earth. As such, environmental destruction is only wrong if it harms humans; that is to say, the natural world only holds extrinsic value. **Sentiocentrism** (see Bentham) widens the circle of intrinsic moral value to encompass all sentient beings capable of pain or pleasure. This comes in two forms: inegalitarian and egalitarian sentiocentrism, where the former claims that some sentient beings are more valuable than others, while the latter regards all sentient beings as equally valuable. **Biocentrism** (see Schweitzer) goes further by holding that all life forms have intrinsic value. This also comes in inegalitarian and egalitarian forms. According to **ecocentrism** (see Leopold), ecosystems as such are the primary sources of moral value.

But a full-grown horse or dog is beyond comparison a more rational, as well as a more conversable animal, than an infant of a day, or a week, or even a month, old. But suppose the case were otherwise, what would it avail? the question is not, Can they reason? nor, Can they talk? but, Can they suffer?' (p. 311).

- To attain spiritual growth, or 'unfolding', the deep ecologists **Bill Devall** and **George Sessions** (1985) believed it was necessary to undo the misconception that we are 'isolated and narrow competing egos' (p. 67). Spiritual maturity requires us to form bonds of identification that reach beyond the human world. To achieve this 'unfolding of the self' we need to embrace the view that 'No one is saved until we are all saved', where this encompasses 'all humans, whales, grizzly bears, whole rain forest ecosystems, mountains and rivers, the tiniest microbes in the soil, and so on' (ibid.).

- The feminist philosopher of religion **Grace Jantzen** (1984) believed that pantheism can help overturn the hierarchical dualisms of spirit and matter, reason and body, that have been used to justify a relationship of domination between humans and the environment. She advocated conceptualising the universe as 'God's body' for this 'helps to do justice to the beauty and value of nature, the importance of conservation and ecological responsibility …' (p. 156). If we were to see the universe as the 'embodiment and self-manifestation of God', then we'd be unlikely 'to continue to treat it in a cavalier way or feel it utterly alien or devoid of intrinsic significance and worth' (p. 157).

> **Concept Check**
>
> **Deep ecology** is the view that we can and should identify with the natural world. In the words of Arne Naess (1995), who spoke of seeing himself in a dying flea, 'The destruction of nature (and our place) threatens us in our innermost self' (p. 232). Through identification with nature, we can overcome the anthropocentric division of man and earth. **Ecofeminism** has a similar project; however, it sees androcentrism as the central problem. This requires not merely a spiritual but a political solution. As described by Karen J. Warren (1996), ecofeminism is 'the view that there are important connections between the domination of women (and other human subordinates) and the domination of nature' (p. x). The 'logic of domination' manifests in the oppression of both women and nature. Both forms of oppression are predicated on a dualism of mind and body, where men are identified with the elevated mental faculty of reason, while women are seen, like the earth, in terms of instinct and the body. This hierarchical vision of the world justifies subjugation. As such, ecofeminism regards environmentalism as part of a broader political agenda to overcome oppression in all its forms.

- In his influential book *Sand County Almanac and Sketches Here and There* **Aldo Leopold** (1949) expressed his view that we should move away from an atomised view of moral action where we consider how our actions might affect particular beings. He instead advocated a 'land ethic' in which we regard environmental communities themselves as the units of moral value. Humans are not distinct from or outside of these communities; the land is a 'community to which we belong', which we should therefore use with 'love and respect' (p. viii). He succinctly outlined his land ethic thus: 'A thing is right when it tends to preserve the integrity, stability and beauty of the biotic community. It is wrong when it tends otherwise' (pp. 224–225).

- For us the winds do blow,
  The earth doth rest, heav'n move, and fountains flow.
  Nothing we see but means our good,
  As our delight, or as our treasure;
  The whole is either our cupboard of food,
  Or cabinet of pleasure.
  George Herbert, 'Man' (2015, p. 87)

- And I have felt
  A presence that disturbs me with the joy
  Of elevated thoughts; a sense sublime
  Of something far more deeply interfused,
  Whose dwelling is the light of setting suns,
  And the round ocean and the living air,
  And the blue sky, and in the mind of man:
  A motion and a spirit, that impels
  All thinking things, all objects of all thought,
  And rolls through all things.
  William Wordsworth,
  'Tintern Abbey' (1996, p. 701)

- Earth's crammed with heaven,
  And every common bush afire with God:
  But only he who sees, takes off his shoes;
  The rest sit round it, and pluck blackberries,
  And daub their natural faces unaware …
  Elizabeth Barrett Browning,
  Aurora Leigh (1866, p. 265)

- An inward spirit feeds earth, heaven, and sea,
  The shining moon, and giant stars;
  a mind Pervades their limbs, and moves the mighty mass.
  Virgil, *Aeneid* (Quoted by Illingworth, 1898, p. 38)

- **St Cyprian**, bishop of Carthage, did not feel at home in the world, indeed, he wrote in *De mortalitate* that he had 'renounced' it, and that he and his fellow Christians were 'sojourning here as foreigners'. Their true home, their 'native land', is paradise, the kingdom of heaven. He look favourably on the prospect of death for it rescues us from 'the snares of the world' (Quoted in Birch, 2021, pp. 87–88).

- Heretically for a Christian, in *A Treatise on Christian Doctrine* (1825) **John Milton** expressed his belief that the universe was not created by God *ex nihilo* (out of nothing) but *ex deo* (out of Himself): 'God did not produce everything out of nothing, but of himself … all things are not only from God, but of God' (p. 183).

To encourage pupils to think more carefully about this cornucopia of extracts, have them place the different writers on a continuum like so:

Pure piffle.   *The resplendent truth.*

> **Concept Check**
>
> John Milton's and Grace Jantzen's views are similar but different. Milton's notion of *creatio ex deo*, which is unusual for a Christian, is a **panentheistic** one. This is the idea that the universe is part, but not the whole, of God. **Pantheism**, on the contrary, is the view that the universe is not part of but *is* God.

Activity 2

Before making their own judgment on the permissibility of planetary destruction, help pupils think more carefully about our moral duties to the natural world by thinking of the ways we can intelligibly speak of wronging an entity. To be completed with a ✓ or ✗, the table below covers various forms of mistreatment.

	Lemur	**Oak tree**	**Mountain**
Hurt			
Harm			
Disrespect			
Wound			
Victimise			
Abuse			
Exploit			
Betray			
Oppress			

Having populated the table, pupils should use their answers to complete the following sentences by substituting the appropriate verbs.

- *It is possible to wrong a lemur by φ-ing it.*
- *It is possible to wrong an oak tree by φ-ing it.*
- *It is possible to wrong a mountain by φ-ing it.*

Activity 3

It's time for pupils to articulate their own views on which of the planets, if any, it would be permissible to destroy. In their answers, pupils should address the question of whether we have a right to destroy the environment. In doing so, they should identify which position most closely aligns with their own: biocentrism, sentiocentrism, anthropocentrism, ecocentrism, deep ecology, ecofeminism, panentheism or pantheism.

Having articulated this, pupils should apply their position to the climate crisis by identifying why exactly the threat to the planet is problematic: is this fundamentally because it threatens human life, or because it threatens other life forms and ecosystems, or because it constitutes a wrong to nature itself?

> **Thought Avenue**
>
> If one is a biocentrist who regards environmental shifts as bad only insofar as they reduce the overall number of living entities on earth, it is not clear that the climate crisis is in fact a crisis. Research has shown, for instance, that warmer soils in subarctic areas have led to an increase in the density of bacteria and fungi. While climate change will lead to the destruction of some living things, it will also lead to the emergence of new species. There is no specific reason to think that climate change will lead to an overall reduction in the number of living entities. So is it something biocentrists ought to worry about?

Activity 4

The final task is to consider what the implications of the pupils' view are for possible state intervention to address the climate crisis. These interventions would inevitably involve a curtailment of our civil liberties. After discussing what these interventions might be, present the following suggestions:

a. Restrictions on leisure air travel.

b. Restrictions on diet: limiting the quantity of meat consumed.

c. Compulsory veganism.

d. Compulsory use of public transport.

e. Cut wages to reduce excess consumption.

f. Restrict the number of children families can have.

Given their response in Activity 4, what lines would have to be crossed to justify implementing these measures? The graph below is almost embarrassingly contrived, and it should be emphasised that the climate crisis will not unfold in this simplistic way (as part of its artificiality, it should also be emphasised that the consequences identified are causally isolated and lead to no further damage). Nevertheless, it is here merely as a tool to help pupils think about when they believe drastic state interference in our lives would be justified. To this end, pupils should add the various measures outlined above to the graph showing at which point they believe the threshold for each has been reached.

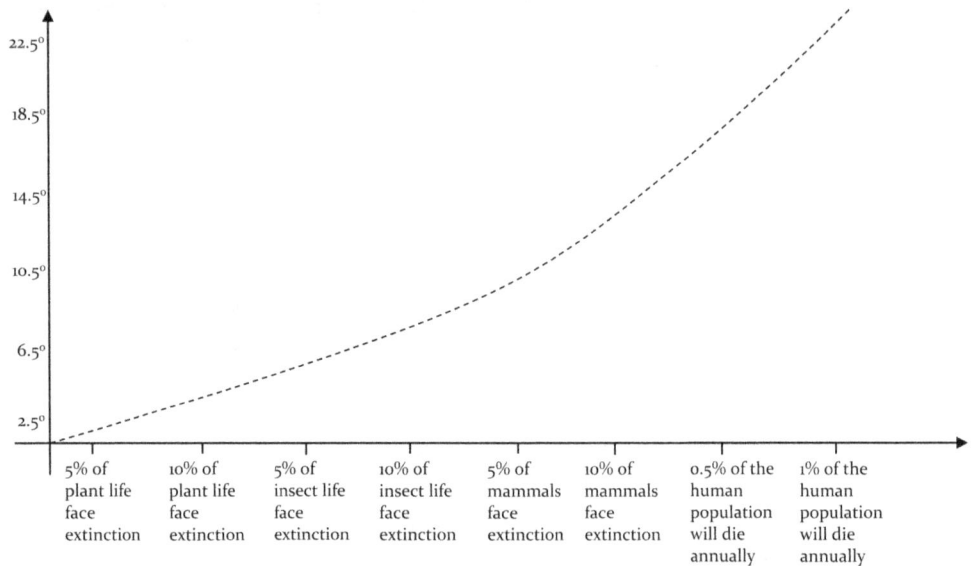

References

Augustine. (2003) [c. 426 CE]. *City of God* (H. Bettenson, Trans.). Penguin Books.
Bentham, J. (1879) [1789]. *An Introduction to the Principles of Morals and Legislation*. Clarendon Press.
Birch, D. (2021). *Pandora's Book: 401 Philosophical Questions to Help You Lose Your Mind (with answers)*. Iff Books.
Browning, E. B. (1866) [1856]. *Aurora Leigh, and Other Poems*. James Miller.
Devall, B., & Sessions, G. (1985). *Deep Ecology: Living as If Nature Mattered*. Peregrine Smith.
Herbert, G. (2015) [1633]. *The Complete Poetry*. Penguin Classics.
Illingworth, J. R. (1898). *Divine Immanence: An Essay on the Spiritual Significance of Matter*. Macmillan & Co.
Jantzen, G. (1984). *God's World, God's Body*. Darton, Longman & Todd.

Kant, I. (1987) [1790]. *Critique of Judgment*, W. S. Pluhar (Trans.). Hackett.

Leopold, A. (1949). *Sand County Almanac and Sketches Here and There*. Oxford University Press.

Milton, J. (1825). *A Treatise on Christian Doctrine: Compiled from the Holy Scriptures Alone* (C. Summer, Trans.). Cambridge University Press.

Naess, A. (1995). Self-realization: An Ecological Approach to Being in the World. In G. Sessions (Ed.), *Deep Ecology for the Twenty-First Century* (pp. 224–240). Shambhala.

Schweitzer, A. (2009). *Out of My Life and Thought (60th Anniversary edition)*. John Hopkins University Press.

Warren, K. (1996). Ecological Feminist Philosophies: An Overview of the Issues. In K. J. Warren (Ed.), *Ecological Feminist Philosophies* (pp. ix–xxvi). Indiana University Press.

Wordsworth, W. (1996) [1798]. Tintern Abbey. *The Norton Anthology of Poetry* (4th ed.). W. W. Norton & Company.

5 War

> **Key Questions**
>
> - Do soldiers have a right to life?
> - By enlisting, do soldiers consent to being killed?
> - When, if ever, is it impermissible for soldiers to kill each other during war?
> - When, if ever, is it permissible to kill the innocent during war?
> - Is knowingly killing innocents morally equivalent to intentionally killing them?
> - Who can we count as truly innocent during war?

As with the previous four chapters, this chapter focuses on the ethics of killing. However, unlike the previous chapters, there is a general presumption in war that killing as such requires no moral justification. We might need to think carefully about exactly who and how one kills, but the fact of killing itself is commonly regarded as an acceptable, albeit regrettable, given. It is, moreover, widely held that the deaths of civilians are morally permissible as collateral damage. But with an estimated 100 million deaths in the 20th century from war, it is important to keep alive the question of the necessary conditions, if indeed there are any, of a just war.

Activity 1

Present the following scenario to the class: two contiguous countries, Redland and Blueland, have discovered there is a vast reserve of a lucrative mineral in the seabed off their coasts. The maritime boundaries of the countries, however, are contested and there is a disagreement over which country the reserve belongs to. After a breakdown in diplomacy, Redland stations a number of battleships to guard the reserve. This sparks a confrontation, which then escalates into a war.

The task is to consider and delineate a set of legal (and moral) conditions to determine what constitutes a war crime by completing the first two columns of the table.

Actions	Morally permissible?	Legally permissible?	Do my views align with IHL? Which statute do they violate/echo?
Killing armed combatants			
Killing armed combatants who were conscripted			
Killing sleeping combatants			
Killing combatants on leave			
Killing combatants who have surrendered			
Killing medics			
Intentionally targeting civilians who have no involvement in the war			
Intentionally targeting civilians who work in munitions factories e.g. destroying a bus of munitions factory employees			
Intentionally targeting militarily significant infrastructure (such as bridges and power stations), which will lead to civilian casualties			
Targeting religious buildings (in the knowledge that no civilians will be harmed)			
The use of laser weapons to blind combatants			
The use of bacteria and viruses to kill combatants			
The use of suffocating gases to kill combatants			

Having filled the first two columns with ✗ and ✓ pupils should now try to extract the general principles governing their thinking. If there are any discrepancies in their answers with respect to the killing of civilians and the killings of combatants, the aim is to identify the reasons for these and thereby determine a set of general rules that could be followed in combat e.g. 'It is legally impermissible to kill any combatant who does not pose a threat', or 'It is legally permissible to kill civilians only if their deaths are a side-effect of trying to achieve a military objective'.

So, to arrive at their *general rules of combat* – rules that can be applied in different contexts – the aim is to complete the following:

- It is legally permissible to attack combatants unless:

- It is legally impermissible to attack civilians unless:

The focus on legality rather than morality is particularly important for those who are pacifists. While they might believe that there is no such thing as a just war, presumably, given the reality of war, they would want laws in place in a bid to mitigate the injustice.

Having completed this, ask pupils to complete the final column of the table by reading through the relevant parts of International Humanitarian Law (IHL) documented below to see the extent of their attitudinal alignment with the law.

> **Concept Check**
>
> **Realism** is a theory that we do not explicitly address in this chapter, but it is useful to keep in mind. Along with pacifism and Just War theory, it is one of three core stances on the morality of war. Both realism and pacifism are united in the belief that there is no such thing as a just war and that it is never morally permissible to kill either civilians or combatants. However, whereas pacifism claims that the reason for this is that war is fundamentally immoral, realism holds that it is because morality does not apply to the actions of states. Unlike the citizens within a state, states themselves do not have moral duties to each other, a view captured by Cicero's adage *inter arma enim silent leges* ('laws are silent when arms are raised'). Given the essential anarchy of international relations, the foreign policy of nations should be governed solely by their own self-interest. Thucydides was the first to articulate realism when he described the 'true causes' of the Peloponnesian War, writing that the Spartans were 'forced into war' by Athens's growth in power. While Athens posed no immediate threat, the Spartans had no choice but to go to war in order to protect Spartan interests by pre-empting a shift in the balance of power.

If there's an ambiguity in the law (the status of sleeping combatants or those on leave, for instance, is not explicitly addressed, though the International Committee of the Red Cross Commentary (ICRC) interprets Article 41 of Protocol I as applicable to 'any unarmed soldier, whether he is surprised in his sleep by the adversary, on leave or in any other similar situation'),[1] the question then becomes how *should* the law be interpreted.

The Convention on Certain Conventional Weapons (CCW)[2]

- It is prohibited to employ laser weapons specifically designed, as their sole combat function or as one of their combat functions, to cause permanent blindness to unenhanced vision, that is, to the naked eye or to the eye with corrective eyesight devices.

Chemical Weapons Convention (CWC)[3]

- **Article 1** – Each State Party to this Convention undertakes never under any circumstances: (a) To develop, produce, otherwise acquire, stockpile or retain chemical weapons, or transfer, directly or indirectly, chemical weapons to anyone; (b) To use chemical weapons; (c) To engage in any military preparations to use chemical weapons; (d) To assist, encourage or induce, in any way, anyone to engage in any activity prohibited to a State Party under this Convention.

> **Fact Check**
>
> International humanitarian law is based on the four Geneva Conventions and its three Additional Protocols. Laws concerning weapons are outlined in separate conventions. While not universally binding, rules on how to behave in war long predate the 1949 Geneva Convention. In the Hindu *Laws of Manu* (500-100 BCE), for instance, proscriptions were issued on the killing of sleeping, naked and unarmed combatants.

Biological Weapons Convention (BWC)[4]

- **Article 1** – Each State Party to this Convention undertakes never in any circumstances to develop, produce, stockpile or otherwise acquire or retain: 1. microbial or other biological agents, or toxins whatever their origin or method of production, of types and in quantities that have no justification for prophylactic, protective or other peaceful purposes; 2. weapons, equipment or means of delivery designed to use such agents or toxins for hostile purposes or in armed conflict.

First Geneva Convention[5]

- **Article 24** – Medical personnel exclusively engaged in the search for, or the collection, transport or treatment of the wounded or sick, or in the prevention of disease, staff exclusively engaged in the administration of medical units and establishments, as well as chaplains attached to the armed forces, shall be respected and protected in all circumstances.

Geneva Conventions Protocol I[6]

- **Article 41** – A person who is recognized or who, in the circumstances, should be recognized to be hors de combat [out of combat] shall not be made the object of attack. A person is hors de combat if: a) he is in the power of an adverse Party; b) he clearly expresses an intention to surrender; or c) he has been rendered unconscious or is otherwise incapacitated by wounds or sickness, and therefore is incapable of defending himself; provided that in any of these cases he abstains from any hostile act and does not attempt to escape.

- **Article 48** – In order to ensure respect for and protection of the civilian population and civilian objects, the Parties to the conflict shall at all times distinguish between the civilian population and combatants and between civilian objects and military objectives and accordingly shall direct their operations only against military objectives.

- **Article 51** – The civilian population as such, as well as individual civilians, shall not be the object of attack. Acts or threats of violence the primary purpose of which is to spread terror among the civilian population are prohibited ... Indiscriminate attacks are prohibited ... Among others, the following types of attacks are to be considered as indiscriminate ... an attack which may be expected to cause incidental loss of civilian life, injury to civilians, damage to civilian objects, or a combination thereof, which would be excessive in relation to the concrete and direct military advantage anticipated.

- **Article 53** – Without prejudice to the provisions of the Hague Convention for the Protection of Cultural Property in the Event of Armed Conflict of 14 May 1954, and of other relevant international instruments, it is prohibited: a) to commit any acts of hostility directed against the historic monuments, works of art or places of worship which constitute the cultural or spiritual heritage of peoples.

Activity 2

IHL draws a distinction between civilians and combatants, with civilians defined by the ICRC as those who are not members of the armed forces. Some philosophers of war, however, find this distinction unhelpful, believing that it would be just to attack, say, engineers working for private companies who are nevertheless developing weapons purchased and used by the armed forces. In a bid for clarity, let's reframe the crucial distinction as not between civilians and combatants, but the 'innocent' and the 'agents of war', with the latter term denoting those who are *responsible* for the war, and thereby *deathworthy*.

Much like God sorting the sheep from the goats, ask the class to determine which of the following are innocent, and which are the agents of war.

Innocent or Agent of War?

a. The Presidents/Prime Ministers/political leaders of the warring nations.

b. Those who voted for the warring leaders.

c. Taxpaying civilians of the warring nations (who indirectly finance the war).

d. Journalists who provide help to sway public opinion in favour of the war.

e. Weapons engineers.

f. Munitions factory workers (those on the assembly line).

g. The steel mill workers who provide steel for the munitions factory.

h. Oil refinery workers who provide fuel for the armed forces.

i. Farmers who provide food for the armed forces.

j. Garment factory workers who manufacture uniforms for the armed forces.

k. Those who design and develop medical equipment purchased by the armed forces.

l. Chaplains who provide spiritual and religious support to service personnel.

The philosopher Michael Walzer (2006) has argued that farmers should not be classified as agents of war. This is because of the crucial difference, as he sees it, between the things a soldier needs to function as a soldier, and the things she needs simply to function as a human being. He has written:

> The relevant distinction is not between those who work for the war effort and those who do not, but between those who make what combatants need to fight and those who make what they need to live, like all the rest of us ... An army, to be sure, has an enormous belly, and it must be fed if it is to fight. But it is not its belly but its arms that make it an army. (p. 145)

Present this passage to the class and firstly ask them to apply Walzer's reasoning to determine who in the list should

Thought Avenue

On case (c) Jeff McMahan (2009) has written the following: 'Most civilians have, on their own, no capacity at all to affect the action of their government. They may pay their taxes, vote or even campaign for particular political candidates ... Military attack exceeds what a person may ordinarily be liable to on the basis of these comparatively trivial sources of responsibility,' (p. 225). There are a number of things one might focus on here; for instance, if McMahan is right with respect to the 'trivial sources of responsibility' of civilians, does this show that we don't live in a true democracy? In the direct democracy of ancient Athens, by contrast, matters of war were decided by an 'ekklesia', which was comprised of every member of the enfranchised public, with each holding an equally weighted vote.

be regarded as innocent and who is an agent of war. Then evaluate his position against these two criteria:

- Is it clear and easily applicable?
- Is it cogent?

If it fails to satisfy the first criterion, this indicates it may well fail the second. On that point, Cécile Fabre (2009) has demurred. She questions whether there is a clear distinction to be drawn between what combatants need to fight and what they need to live. Given that combatants need to live in order to fight, satisfying the former need is seemingly entwined with satisfaction of the latter.

> For although it is true that, strictly speaking, it is the guns as used by combatants which kill, not their specialized rations or wound dressing, it is equally true that combatants are not able to kill if hunger or untreated wounds make it impossible for them to lift their arms and train those guns on the enemy. Generally, meeting combatants' material need for food, shelter, appropriate clothing, and medical care goes a long way toward enabling them to kill in war, even if the resources in question do not in themselves constitute a threat. (pp. 43–44)

Ask pupils to read back through the Walzer passage and identify where exactly Fabre thinks there is a problem (the principal problem is in his first sentence). Then present the following argument tree to the pupils:

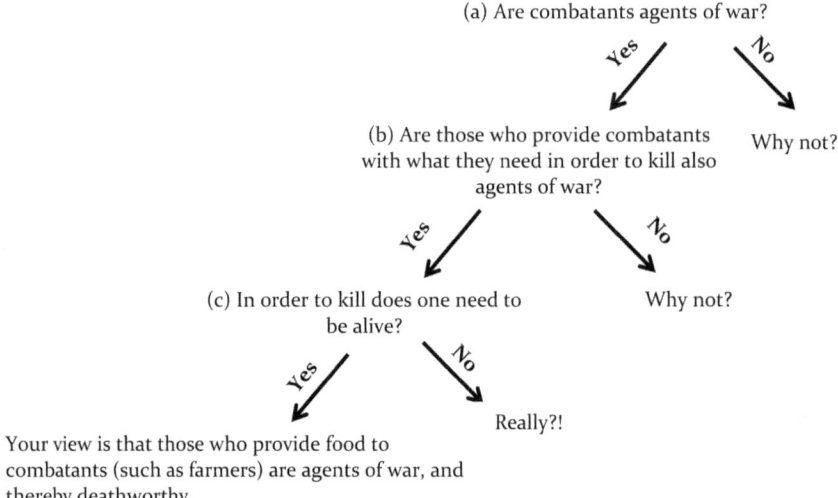

Having worked through the tree, if they end with the bottom view stated as their view and yet don't actually believe it, ask them to determine whether they are being inconsistent (or where the branches don't quite connect as they should).

Present the argument in standard form:

1. *Combatants are agents of war.*

2. *Those who provide combatants with what they need in order to kill are also agents of war.*

3. *In order to kill, one needs to be alive.*

4. *Therefore, those who provide combatants with what they need to live are providing them with what they need to kill.*

5. *Combatants need food to live.*

6. *Therefore, those who provide food to combatants are agents of war and thereby deathworthy.*

The next task is to answer the following:

i. Is the argument valid (does the conclusion logically follow from the premises)?

ii. Are premises 1–3 and 5 true?

iii. For each erroneous premise, explain the error.

iv. If you do accept the argument, explain the reasons that support premises 1 and 2.

Activity 3

For a rather extreme perspective on the permissible scope of killing during war, let's now consider George Orwell's reply to the pacifist Vera Brittain during World War II. In 1944 Brittain published *Seed of Chaos* in which she decried how, owing to the indiscriminate bombings of the RAF, 'thousands of helpless and innocent people in German, Italian and German-occupied cities are being subjected to agonising forms of death and injury comparable to the worst tortures of the Middle Ages' (p. 8). This was Orwell's reply:

> Why is it worse to kill civilians than soldiers? Obviously one must not kill children if it is in any way avoidable, but it is only in propaganda pamphlets that every bomb drops on a school or an orphanage ... Probably a disproportionately large number of bomb

victims will be middle-aged ... On the other hand, "normal" or "legitimate" warfare picks out and slaughters all the healthiest and bravest of the young male population. Every time a German submarine goes to the bottom about fifty young men of fine physique and good nerves are suffocated. Yet people who would hold up their hands at the very words "civilian bombing" will repeat with satisfaction such phrases as "We are winning the Battle of the Atlantic" ... War is not avoidable at this stage of history, and since it has to happen it does not seem to me a bad thing that others should be killed besides young men ... The immunity of the civilian, one of the things that have made war possible, has been shattered. Unlike Miss Brittain, I don't regret that. I can't feel that war is "humanized" by being confined to the slaughter of the young and becomes "barbarous" when the old get killed as well ... War is of its nature barbarous, it is better to admit that.

(Quoted in Branham, 1992, pp. 126–127)

Ask the class to read through the passage to ascertain which of the following sentences most accurately reflects Orwell's views:

a. *There are no innocent people during war; therefore, it is permissible to bomb civilians.*

b. *Everyone is innocent during war. If we permit the killing of one group of innocent people, given their moral equality, we may as well permit the killing of all groups.*

c. *The young (even if they are combatants) are more innocent and deserving of life than the old. Given that war inevitably involves the deaths of those in the first group, the tragedy of war is not significantly increased by the deaths of older civilians.*

d. *Only children are innocent during war; therefore, it is permissible to kill middle-aged civilians.*

Having discussed the comparative accuracy of the statements, ask the class to consider whether any of the statements (irrespective of their proximity to Orwell's own comments) are justifiable, and then to decide whether they are more sympathetic to Orwell or Brittain. It would also be worth dwelling on Orwell's claim that 'one must not kill children'. With his indifference towards middle-aged civilians, what credible justification could he give for his asymmetrical attitude? How could one's age be relevant to one's right to life?

Orwell's views are not aligned with IHL. Article 51 of Protocol I states that 'the civilian population as such, as well as individual civilians, shall not be the object of attack'. Nevertheless, it does permit attacks in which civilians are killed so long as their deaths are 'incidental' and not excessive in relation to the military objective. The historian Howard Zinn (2001), however, believed that this did not go far enough in protecting the innocent, claiming that the deaths of the innocent should not only be unintended, but accidental and unforeseen. He wrote:

> Even if you grant that the intention is not to kill civilians, if they nevertheless become victims, again and again and again, can that be called an accident? If the deaths of civilians are inevitable in bombing, it may not be deliberate, but it is not an accident, and the bombers cannot be considered innocent. They are committing murder as surely as are the terrorists … No killing of innocents, whether deliberate or "accidental," can be justified.

The political scientist Colm McKeogh (2002) has similarly written,

> To be excusable, the deaths of civilians in war must be accidental. The deaths must be, not only unintended but also unforeseen and reasonably unforeseeable (accidental killing is both unintended and unforeseen; collateral killing is foreseen). Where the deaths of civilians is a near certainty or great probability, it is not accidental. For an attack on a military objective to be just, there must be, not only an intention, but also a likelihood of no civilian deaths occurring as a result. (pp. 169–170)

Having read the views of Zinn and McKeogh, lead a discussion on the following:

- Enquiry Question: Is it wrong to knowingly kill the innocent during war?

Activity 4

What's been assumed so far is that combatants are agents of war. But on what grounds is this true? And how attenuated is their right to life compared with that of the innocent? If killing a combatant during war is neither a moral nor criminal offence, presumably combatants have either no or a significantly diminished right to life. According to Thomas Hurka (2007), combatants denude themselves of the right to life by joining the military. Joining the military is effectively consenting to being killed –

> [B]y voluntarily entering military service, soldiers on both sides freely took on the status of soldiers and thereby freely accepted that they may permissibly be killed in the course of war. More specifically, they accepted that they may permissibly be killed by specific people – enemy soldiers who have made a reciprocal surrender of rights – in specific circumstances – those of formally declared hostilities between their and another state. By volunteering, in other words, they freely gave up their right not to be killed in certain circumstances and so made their killing in those circumstances not unjust. (p. 210)

Present the following timeline to the class and ask them to determine at which point, if any, Adam loses the right to life i.e. at which point he may permissibly be killed.

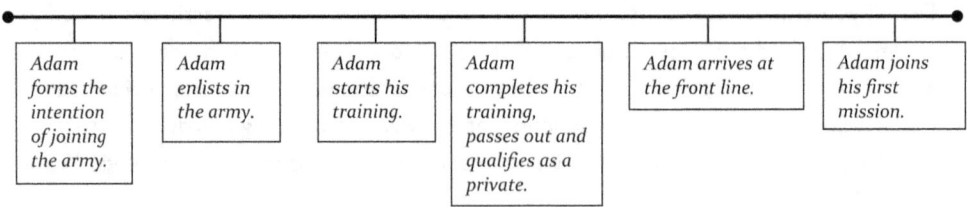

Having identified the point at which he loses the right to life (or it is at least severely diminished), the task now is to explain why that point of transition is so crucial: what personal change in Adam equates to this dramatic moral shift?

You should next consider how attenuated combatants' right to life is when compared with that of the innocent. Consider the following scenario.

> In order to disable a heavily guarded oil refinery, one is faced with a choice: either destroy the refinery with an airstrike, which will (a) kill 40 civilians, or (b) send in troops to take control of it, resulting in 5 civilian deaths but 80 combatant deaths.

Is there a qualitative moral disparity between the lives of civilians and combatants? If we should avoid civilian deaths at the expense of combatants, does this have a limit? When discussing the correct course of action, address both the moral and legal questions: do legal and moral permissibility diverge here?

Concept Check

Much of this lesson is focused on the *jus in bello* conditions of war, that is, the rules that govern the conduct of combatants during war. Another important concept in Just War theory is *jus ad bellum*, which refers to the legitimate grounds for entering into war. Article 51 of the UN Charter, for instance, cites self-defence as a legitimate ground for war. Now, Jeff McMahan's view is that *ad bellum* and *in bello* are not separate matters: if a nation unjustly starts a war, then every act of aggression it perpetrates within that war is unjust.

To further explore the concept of *jus ad bellum* with the class, you could think about whether any of the following constitute just cause:

i. Cicero: 'Only a war waged for revenge or defence can actually be just.'

ii. Humanitarian intervention: would it be just to start a war in order to prevent the genocide of an entire ethnic group consisting of only 15,000 people, if it were expected that doing so, while saving the persecuted group, would lead to the deaths of 20,000 civilians.

iii. Hopelessly attacking an oppressor: would it be just to attack, for the sake of pride alone, a powerful colonising nation when there is no prospect of victory.

(ii) and (iii) respectively probe the following commonly accepted *ad bellum* conditions in Just War theory: that use of violence must be proportional to the wrong being resisted and that war must have a reasonable chance of success.

Activity 5

The current laws of armed conflict hold that combatants do not act illegally simply by fighting in a war, even if they fight on the unjust side. 'Unjust combatants' have the same legal status as 'just combatants'. But consider Robert Fullwinder's (1975) argument for why it is permissible to kill combatants and only combatants –

> Why is any killing at all justified? I claim that a nation may justifiably kill in self-defense. From the point of view of self-defense, only those are justifiably liable to be killed who pose the immediate and direct jeopardy. In the case of war, it is nations' armed forces which are the agents of the jeopardy ... To intentionally kill non-combatants is to kill beyond the scope of self-defense. (p. 94)

The implication is that during a war in which one country has invaded another, combatants of the attacking nation have no justification for killing combatants of the attacked nation. This is at odds with Walzer's view that 'the enemy solider, though his war may well be criminal, is nevertheless as blameless as oneself'.

Jeff McMahan (2006) disagrees with Walzer. If the cause of war is unjust, then every act of aggression within that war is unjust, and the combatants of the unjust nation are acting immorally when they attack enemy combatants. While he doesn't believe that unjust combatants ought to be prosecuted for war crimes, he does believe that their actions are nevertheless wrong. He has written:

> People don't lose moral rights by justifiably defending themselves or other innocent people against an unjust attack ... So, even when unjust combatants confine their attacks to military targets, they kill innocent people ... This means that we must stop reassuring soldiers that they act permissibly when they fight in an unjust war, provided that they conduct themselves honorably on the battlefield by fighting in accordance with the rules of engagement. (p. 379)

To investigate McMahan's views, present to the class a story of two combatants, Daniel and Yousef.

Daniel	Yousef
Daniel was a citizen of the Christian country Polemos. His family had a long history of serving in the armed forces. He was intensely patriotic and fond of saying, 'One does not live *in* Polemos, one lives *for* Polemos'. Wishing to fulfil his duties to the state, Daniel, following in the footsteps of his older brother, enlisted in the armed forces when he turned 16. Four years later, Polemos launched an offensive against its neighbour Eirene with the express aim of conquering and controlling Eirene. Following an address to the country by the President, Daniel was convinced that the war was just. With Eirene's growing military capabilities and its new alliance with another Muslim country in the region, the President claimed that Eirene now posed a direct threat to the security and sovereignty of Polemos. While there was no evidence that Eirene intended to invade Polemos, the President said that its expansionist aims were 'undeniable'. Journalists speculated that the true motive for war was political: the unpopular President wished to trigger a state of emergency in order to suspend elections and extend his stay in power. Following five years of combat, widespread destruction to both countries and the deaths of 40,000 civilians, a peace treaty was signed. Daniel survived the war, though his brother was killed by a mortar bomb launched by Yousef. According to Daniel's own tally, he killed 48 enemy soldiers. At no point did he target civilians or surrendering combatants. He believed in and acted in accordance with the rules of just and honourable combat.	Yousef was a teacher in the Muslim country Eirene, where he was born, raised and lived with his wife. While not pacifists, they both believed that most wars were unjust, and certainly never contemplated joining the armed forces. Nevertheless, after several months following the invasion of Poelmos, with scores of civilians dead and defeat looking a distinct possibility, Yousef and his wife followed thousands of other civilians by voluntarily enlisting. Following an expedited period of basic training, both were sent to the front line. Over the course of the next few years, Yousef, like Daniel, became a prolific killer, causing the bereavement of dozens of families. At no point, again like Daniel, did Yousef target civilians or anyone who was *hors de combat*. Three months before the end of the war, which he survived, Yousef's wife was sniped and instantly killed by Daniel.

Given that Polemos invaded Eirene without any clear just cause, according to McMahan there is a significant moral asymmetry between Daniel and Yousef. Equipped with the above McMahan extract to help guide their thinking, the pupils' task is to determine the extent to which they agree with him. To this end, ask them to imagine that they work at an institution much like the International Criminal Court. Their role is to adjudicate on whether Daniel or Yousef behaved either immorally or criminally. Rather than refer to IHL to make their ruling, they should simply rely on their own views on just combat. In short:

- Case Question: *Should either Daniel or Yousef be punished?*

  Questions to address in their ruling:

  ○ Were their actions morally identical?

  ○ Were both Daniel's brother and Yousef's wife agents of war (and thereby deathworthy) or innocent?

  ○ Was Daniel justified in killing Yousef's wife? Was Yousef justified in killing Daniel's brother?

  ○ By voluntarily enlisting, did all combatants in question renounce their right to life?

  ○ Was Daniel's participation in an unjust invasion excusable?

  ○ Even if an act is excusable, does that make it just?

  ○ Is either Daniel or Yousef a murderer?

  ○ Even if their actions were immoral, should they be deemed illegal?

One way to approach this activity would be to stage a trial for each character, with defence and prosecution lawyers making statements (possibly with statements also made by the defendants) before a team of disinterested judges (whose subsequent task is to determine and explicate their ruling) to summarise the key arguments for whether either Daniel or Yousef ought to be convicted of and punished for murder.

Activity 6

The final task is to collate the views reached in the other activities to effectively draft their own war convention by completing the table.

Action	Answer	Details	Reasons
Is it morally permissible to kill combatants?			
Are all combatants equally deathworthy?			
Should combatants ever be considered hors de combat?			
Besides combatants, are there other deathworthy agents of war?			
During war, is anyone innocent?			
Is it ever permissible to kill the innocent in war?			

Extension Material

Pacifism

The views of Howard Zinn explored above suggest one possible argument for pacifism: if killing civilians is inherently wrong, and war inevitably leads to the deaths of civilians, then war is inherently wrong. However, many pacifists go further than this by arguing that war would be unjust even if civilians weren't killed. The problem is not the killing of civilians but the killing of any person, including combatants. Regardless of its ends, given that the systematic taking of human life is the very means of war, it is an irremediably savage undertaking and can never be just.

Concept Check

Pacifism exists in many forms. **Political pacifism**, for instance, is a principled opposition to war as such. **Personal pacifism**, by contrast, is opposed to killing human beings *tout court*. Both forms of pacifism, therefore, oppose war, but for personal pacifism this is because it is an instance of a more general wrong.

It is worth emphasising that these positions are purely moral and have no necessary psychological implications. The Dalai Lama has said, 'Through inner peace, genuine world peace can

Pupils can use the texts referenced below in tandem with the accompanying summaries to compile a dossier on pacifism. With each passage, they should endeavour to extract the principles, latent or obvious, that support or oppose pacifism. Having done this, they should then undertake an evaluation of these principles, and from there draw the relevant conclusions on the morality, metaphysics and practicality of pacifism.

be achieved ... an atmosphere of peace must first be created within ourselves, then gradually expanded to include our families, our communities, and ultimately the whole planet,' (Quoted in Fox, 2014, p. 189). Irrespective of whether this view is psychologically accurate, a pacifist needn't be philosophically committed to it, nor Plato's belief that within one's soul 'wickedness is discord and virtue harmony'. Indeed, there is no incoherence in a pacifist sympathising with Friedrich Nietzsche's view that 'the price of fruitfulness is to be rich in internal opposition; one remains young only as long as the soul does not stretch itself and desire peace ... One has renounced the great life when one renounces war', (1976, pp. 488–489).

- Robert Graves and George Orwell, both writers and both with direct experience of combat (World War I in the former case and the Spanish Civil War in the latter), expressed a similar resistance to killing unarmed, undressed men. While these are very particular circumstances, it may be possible to draw from them general pacifist principles.
- In the case of Graves, he describes in *Goodbye to All That* (1958) seeing through his sniper scope a German soldier taking a bath. He handed the rifle to the sergeant with him because 'I disliked the idea of shooting a naked man' (p. 116).
- Orwell, also operating a sniper rifle, recounted in *Homage to Catalonia* (1966) spotting a half-dressed enemy soldier dashing along on some business and needing to hold up his trousers with both hands as he ran. Orwell didn't take a shot because, though he had enlisted in order to shoot 'Fascists', 'a man who is holding up his trousers isn't a "Fascist", he is visibly a fellow creature, similar to yourself' (pp. 230–231).
- Graves and Orwell imply that the comportment and uniform of soldiers serve to create a sense of distance and dissociation among rival combatants. According to the philosopher Cheney Ryan, the pacifist cannot help but see beyond these uniforms. In his article 'Self-Defense, Pacifism, and the Possibility of Killing' (1983), he writes that 'the pacifist's problem is that he cannot create, or does not wish to create, the necessary distance between himself and another to make the act of killing possible' (p. 521).
- Writing in *An Encyclopaedia of Pacifism* (1937), Aldous Huxley made an observation which raises doubts about the possibility of an *in bello* just war and therefore the efficacy of IHL. War is, of course, a physical struggle, but according to Huxley 'a physical struggle inevitably arouses hatred, fear,

rage and resentment. In the heat of passion all scruples are thrown to the winds, all the habits of forbearance and humaneness acquired during years of civilized living are forgotten' (p. 79).

- The American pastor Harry Emerson Fosdick alluded to this loss of humanity when he proclaimed his renunciation of war for what it compels us to do to our enemies: 'bombing their mothers and villages, starving their children by blockades, laughing over our coffee cups about every damnable thing we have been able to do to them' (quoted in Leavens, 1929, p. 580). His pacifism was further strengthened by his direct encounters with mutilated soldiers during World War I: 'I have heard the cries of the crazed and the prayers of those who wanted to die and could not' (ibid).

- In his speech 'The American Dream' delivered at Drew University in 1964,[7] Martin Luther King Jr. presented a strategic and pragmatic justification for pacifism. King believed that nonviolent resistance was 'the most potent weapon available to oppressed people in their struggle for freedom and human dignity...' By refusing to engage in a physical struggle one avoids arousing the 'hatred, fear, rage and resentment' that Huxley referred to. Nonviolent resistance instead 'disarms the opponent, it exposes his moral defenses, it weakens his morale and at the same time it works on his conscience, and he just doesn't know how to deal with it'.

> **Thought Avenue**
>
> The Russian novelist and pacifist Leo Tolstoy (1968) wrote that 'no action is more opposed to the will of God than that of killing men. And therefore you cannot obey men if they order you to kill ... [A] Christian cannot be a murderer and therefore cannot be a soldier' (pp. 4–35, 37).
>
> As an exegetical exercise, present the following New Testament verses and ask pupils whether they leave a Christian no choice but to support Tolstoy's claims. Is there any possible interpretation that could exonerate the Christian soldier?
>
> *Blessed are the peacemakers, for they will be called children of God.*
> Matthew 5:9
>
> *Do not resist an evil person. If anyone slaps you on the right cheek, turn to them the other cheek also.*
> Matthew 5:38
>
> *Love your enemies and pray for those who persecute you.*
> Matthew 5:44
>
> *If it is possible, as far as it depends on you, live at peace with everyone ... Do not be overcome by evil, but overcome evil with good.*
> Romans 12:18-21

- One of the criteria for a *jus ad bellum* war is that it is likely to engender an emergent peace. A just war, in other words, must have a reasonable chance of correcting the injustice it was waged to redress. However, King did not believe this condition could be satisfied. He rejected the idea that violence could beget peace because, as he stated in a 1961 address, 'in the long run of history, immoral destructive means cannot bring about moral and constructive ends'. He therefore concluded that 'the end is pre-existent in the means' and so 'the means must be as pure as the end' (1986, p. 45).

- Malcolm X was sceptical about the use of nonviolent resistance to secure racial justice in the US because 'when you're dealing with an enemy who doesn't know what nonviolence is, as far as I'm concerned you're wasting your time' (Clark, 1992, p. 25). What gave King (1986) hope in the efficacy of the method, however, was his conviction that 'the universe is on the side of justice'. King's faith in the future and his faith in the inevitability of the victory of nonviolent resistance were sustained by his belief in the existence of 'a creative force in this universe that works to bring the disconnected aspects of reality into a harmonious whole' (p. 20). This force provides those engaged in a nonviolent struggle for justice with 'cosmic companionship' (ibid).
- In *Guerrilla Warfare* (1998) Che Guevara approvingly quoted Lenin's claim that the exploitative fabric of a society hierarchically organised into distinct classes 'cannot be destroyed without war' (p. 41). Following Lenin's teachings, he believed that violence is the 'midwife of new societies' (ibid).
- In *The Wretched of the Earth* (2004), Frantz Fanon similarly claimed that colonialism, which is 'not a machine capable of thinking' nor 'a body endowed with reason' but 'naked violence', can only be defeated with 'greater violence' (p. 23). Not only is violence a necessary means of decolonisation, for the colonised individual it holds certain medicinal properties; it is a 'cleansing force' that 'rids the colonized of their inferiority complex' and 'restores their self-confidence' (p. 51). Colonial subjugation instils self-hatred at one's compliance and passivity. Violence, Fanon believed, overturns that self-hatred. As Jean-Paul Sartre wrote in the preface, the violence that the colonised visits on the coloniser is 'not a consequence of resentment: it is man reconstructing himself' (p. lv).
- In *Civilization and its Discontents* (1930), the psychoanalyst Sigmund Freud outlined his belief that 'men are not gentle creatures' but 'savage beasts' (pp. 85–86). Aggression is a basic fact of human nature. If we survey the evidence from human history, our own lives, and even our own minds, we find clear support for the Latin proverb *Homo homini lupus* ('Man is to man a wolf'). Freud stressed that our aggression is not simply a mechanism of self-defence but is itself a sort of primitive drive or impulse. While we may say seek to curb and contain the worst excesses of this drive, it remains part of our

Fact Check

Pacifism is often associated with Christianity. This is understandable given the pacifist tendencies of denominations such as the Mennonites, Quakers and Brethren, and of Christian individuals such as Leo Tolstoy and Martin Luther King Jr. With the doctrinal centrality of *ahimsa* (non-violence), it is also 'instinctual endowment' (ibid), and is always in danger of wreaking havoc. At this level of instinct, one human is to another a 'temptation to them to gratify their aggressiveness on him, to exploit his capacity for work without recompense, to use him sexually without his consent, to seize his possessions, to humiliate him, to cause him pain, to torture and to kill him' (ibid). If Freud was right, what hope is there for pacifism?

- In her essay 'War and Murder', the philosopher Elizabeth Anscombe (1981) expressed the concern that the pacifist view that war can never be just risks deregulating warfare. Pacifism 'teaches people to make no distinction between the shedding of innocent blood and the shedding of any human blood', and this failure to distinguish between just and unjust killing effectively licenses the worst atrocities (p. 57). Those who are compelled to engage in warfare but who are persuaded by the pacifist belief that it is absolutely unjust become 'convinced that a number of things are wicked which are not; hence seeing no way of avoiding wickedness, they set no limits to it' (ibid). In short, Anscombe claims that the purity of pacifism is a path that can lead us to the anarchy of realism.

> understandable that Jainism, Hinduism and Buddhism are often similarly associated with pacifism. This is not usually the case, however, with Islam. But it is worth noting that Islam does have a tradition of pacifism. The activism of Abdul Ghaffar Khan is one instance of this. A contemporary and friend of Gandhi, he was from northwest Pakistan and mobilised the 100,000 strong Khudai Khidmatgar, 'Servants of God', in nonviolent resistance against the British Raj. In his pacifism, Khan was directly inspired by the Qur'an and hadiths, and drew particularly from the concept of *sabr* (roughly translated as 'patience'). He told his fellow Pathans: 'I am going to give you such a weapon that the police and army will not be able to stand against it. It is the weapon of the Prophet, but you are not aware of it. That weapon is patience and righteousness. No power on earth can stand against it' (Quoted in Tendulkar, 1967, p. 129). Additionally: 'The Prophet has said that the most pious and God-fearing youth is he who brings comfort to the creatures of God … The mission of the Khudai Khidmatgars is to give comfort to all creatures of God … There is nothing surprising in a Muslim or a Pathan like me subscribing to the creed of nonviolence. It is not a new creed. It was followed fourteen hundred years ago by the Prophet all the time he was in Mecca …' (pp. 128, 94).

Notes

1 https://ihl-databases.icrc.org/en/ihl-treaties/api-1977/article-41/commentary/1987
2 https://www.icrc.org/en/doc/resources/documents/article/other/57jn4y.htm
3 https://ihl-databases.icrc.org/en/ihl-treaties/cwc-1993?activeTab=undefined
4 https://legal.un.org/avl/ha/cpdpsbbtwd/cpdpsbbtwd.html

5 https://ihl-databases.icrc.org/en/ihl-treaties/gci-1949?activeTab=undefined
6 https://ihl-databases.icrc.org/en/ihl-treaties/api-1977?activeTab=undefined
7 https://archive.org/details/the-american-dream-mlk-jr/The+American+Dream_pt.2.mp3

References

Anscombe, G. E. M. (1981). War and Murder. In *Collected Philosophical Papers Vol. III, Ethics, Religion and Politics*. Oxford University Press.
Branham, R. J. (1992). *Debate and Critical Analysis: Harmony in Conflict*. Routledge.
Brittain, V. (1944). *Seeds of Chaos: What Mass Bombing Really Means*. New Vision.
Clark, S. (Ed.) (1992). *February 1965: The Final Speeches: Malcolm X*. Pathfinder.
Fabre, C. (2009). Guns, Food, and Liability to Attack in War. *Ethics*, 120(1), 36–63.
Fanon, F. (2004) [1963]. *The Wretched of the Earth*, R. Philcox (Trans.). Grove Press.
Fox, M. A. (2014). *Understanding Peace: A Comprehensive Introduction*. Routledge.
Freud, S. (1930). *Civilization and Its Discontents*, J. Riviere (Trans.). Hogarth Press.
Fullwinder, R. K. (1975). War and Innocence. *Philosophy & Public Affairs,* 5(1), 90–97.
Graves, R. (1958). *Goodbye to All That* (2nd ed.). Cassell & Company.
Guevara, E. (1998) [1961]. *Guerrilla Warfare*. University of Nebraska Press.
Hurka, T. (2007). Liability and Just Cause. *Ethics & International Affairs,* 21(2), 199–218.
Huxley, A. (1937). *An Encyclopaedia of Pacifism*. Chatto & Windus.
King, M. L. K. (1986). *A Testament of Hope: The Essential Writings and Speeches of Martin Luther King, Jr*, J. M. Washington (Ed.). Harper Collins.
Leavens, M. A. (1929). *Great Companions: Readings on the Meaning and Conduct of Life from Ancient and Modern Sources*. Beacon Press.
McKeogh, C. (2002). *Innocent Civilians: The Morality of Killing in War*. Palgrave.
McMahan, J. (2006). On the Moral Equality of Combatants. *The Journal of Political Philosophy*, 14(4), 377–393.
McMahan, J. (2009). *Killing in War*. Oxford University Press.
Nietzsche, F. (1976) [1889]. Twilight of the Idols. In W. Kaufmann (Ed. and Trans.), *The Portable Nietzsche*. Penguin Books.
Orwell, G. (1966). *Homage to Catalonia*. Harmondsworth.
Ryan, C. (1983). Self-Defense, Pacifism, and the Possibility of Killing. *Ethics*, 93(3), 508–524.
Tendulkar, D. G. (1967). *Abdul Ghaffar Khan: Faith Is a Battle*. Popular Prakashan.
Tolstoy, L. (1968) [1901]. Notes for Soldiers. In *Tolstoy's Writings on Civil Disobedience and Non-Violence*. The New American Library.
Walzer, M. (2006). *Just and Unjust Wars: A Moral Argument with Historical Illustrations* (4th ed.). Basic Books.
Zinn, H. (2001). *A Just Cause, Not a Just War*. The Progressive Magazine. https://progressive.org/magazine/just-cause-just-war-Zinn/

6 Terrorism

> **Key Questions**
>
> - When, if ever, is it permissible to intentionally kill the innocent?
> - Are there circumstances in which it is permissible to do the impermissible?
> - Are we ever required to ignore the call of morality?
> - Is there ever anything admirable or virtuous in the actions of terrorists?

The closest we came in the chapter on war to the view that it is permissible to intentionally target civilians in combat was in George Orwell's reply to Vera Brittain, but even there Orwell qualified his position by stating that it is wrong to kill children. For Orwell there remained a category of people who must never intentionally be killed. This lesson considers whether he was wrong and whether this is a line that, in extreme circumstances, can permissibly be crossed. In other words, is terrorism ever just?

While the precise definition is contested, we shall characterise terrorism in the terms by which it is broadly understood:

1. Intentionally targeting civilian life or property
2. With the intent of spreading terror throughout a population
3. In order to promote a political agenda

Terrorism as defined violates Article 51 of the Geneva Convention Protocol I and is thus illegal under International Humanitarian Law.

Activity 1

Start by presenting the following account of Nat Turner's 1831 slave rebellion.

In August 1831 Nat Turner led a slave rebellion across Southampton County, Virginia. For no more than a day or two, dozens of Black slaves travelled from house to house indiscriminately massacring every White they encountered. Fifty-five people were killed, with at least 18 of the victims aged 10 years old or younger. Many were hacked to death. A decapitated baby was found in the fire place of one house. Though Turner had instructed his followers to kill every White person in their path, it seems he only claimed one victim for himself, whom he bludgeoned to death. Following his capture and arrest, Turner was convicted of 'conspiring to rebel and make insurrection', and sentenced to death. He was hung from a tree on November 11th, 1831.

Turner was born into slavery in 1800. Uncommonly for a slave he was literate, and with his 'uncommon intelligence' he believed that he was destined for 'some great purpose' beyond the life of a slave. In 1828 Turner had a profound religious experience: 'I heard a loud noise in the heavens, and the Spirit instantly appeared to me and said the Serpent was loosened, and Christ had laid down the yoke he had borne for the sins of men, and that I should take it on and fight against the Serpent, for the time was fast approaching when the first should be last and the last should be first [Matthew 20:16] … And by signs in the heavens that it would make known to me when I should commence the great work.'[1] In 1831 that sign appeared to Turner in the form of a solar eclipse. He started to organise the insurrection, which eventually took place on August 21st.

In the dead of night, armed with hatchets, axes and knives, Turner and several co-conspirators approached the house of his owner. Using a ladder to reach a high window, Turner quietly eased himself into the house while the inhabitants slept. He crept downstairs to unlock the door for the others to enter. The four family members were swiftly slaughtered: 'the work of a moment', in Turner's words. With their deaths Turner became a free man for the first time in his life.

Wishing to 'carry terror and devastation wherever we went', the group swept from farm to farm, murdering the proprietors and their families, while encouraging more slaves to join the rebellion. The massacre was only the first stage of the plan. With the acquisition of arms and fighters, it seems the second stage was to form a militia and start gaining territory. It was reported at the time that Turner intended to conquer the country. Following his arrest one interrogator wrote that 'he seems of the opinion that if his time were to go over again, he must necessarily act in the same way'.

Following the rebellion, the state legislature of Virginia contemplated abolishing slavery to ensure the safety of the White population, but the proposal was ultimately rejected. Instead legislation was passed to impose greater restriction on slaves with it becoming illegal, for instance, 'to preach, exhort or conduct, or hold any assembly, or meeting, for religious or other purposes, either in the day time, or at night.'[2]

Ask pupils to circle the statement which best characterises their views on this event –

a. *This wasn't terrorism because no innocent people were killed. All the victims were guilty by virtue of their complicity in the heinous institution of slavery.*

b. *Though innocent people were killed, the slaves did not act immorally. In fact, they ought to be commended for it takes courage to violate the standard norms of morality in order to achieve a greater good.*

c. *While undoubtedly regrettable, the actions of the slaves were not immoral.*

d. *While understandable, the actions of the slaves were nevertheless immoral.*

e. *The actions of the slaves were not 'understandable'. Such was the depravity and immorality of this event that no one should venture to defend, excuse or justify it. It warrants nothing but unmitigated condemnation.*

Ask the class to imagine that Nat Turner sought their counsel on the night of the attack. What would they have told him?

> *I am planning to commit and incite unspeakable atrocities against the guilty and innocent alike. But my soul is troubled. Am I preparing to embark on sin? Are these acts worthy of hell? I fear God's judgment. Tell me, is it wrong? Should I stand down? Should I let them live?*

Activity 2

Michael Walzer (2004) has argued that while 'every act of terrorism is a wrongful act' (p. 52), it can be justified during a 'supreme emergency'. 'A supreme emergency exists', he has written, 'when our deepest values and our collective survival are in imminent danger' (ibid., p. 33). He cites the threat of Nazism to the UK in the early stages of World War II when defeat looked a distinct possibility. As a supreme emergency, the bombing of German cities and targeting of civilians was defensible (the later bombings of cities, most infamously Dresden, when defeat was far less likely, were wholly inexcusable).

Present his overview of the situation to the class:

> The decision to bomb [German] cities was made late in 1940. A directive issued in June of that year had "specifically laid down that targets had to be identified and aimed at. Indiscriminate bombing was forbidden." In November, after the German raid on Coventry, "Bomber Command was instructed simply to aim at the center of a city." What had once been called indiscriminate bombing (and commonly condemned) was now required, and by early 1942, aiming at military or industrial targets was barred: "the aiming points are to be the built-up areas, not, for instance, the dockyards or aircraft factories." The purpose of the raids was explicitly declared to be the destruction of civilian morale. (2006, pp. 255–256)

Using the same range of responses as above, ask pupils to circle the statement which best characterises their views on this event –

a. *This wasn't terrorism because no innocent people were killed. All the victims were guilty by virtue of their complicity in Nazism.*

b. *Though innocent people were killed, the UK did not act immorally. In fact, they ought to be commended for it takes courage to violate the standard norms of morality in order to achieve a greater good.*

c. *While undoubtedly regrettable, the UK's actions were not immoral.*

d. *While understandable, the UK's actions were nevertheless immoral.*

e. *The UK's actions were not 'understandable'. Such was the depravity and immorality of their actions that no one should venture to defend, excuse or justify them. It warrants nothing but unmitigated condemnation.*

Check to see whether there are any discrepancies in pupils' answers between the two cases we've looked at. If there are, those discrepancies should be investigated.

Use a Venn diagram to explore the similarities and differences between the two acts of terrorism, for example –

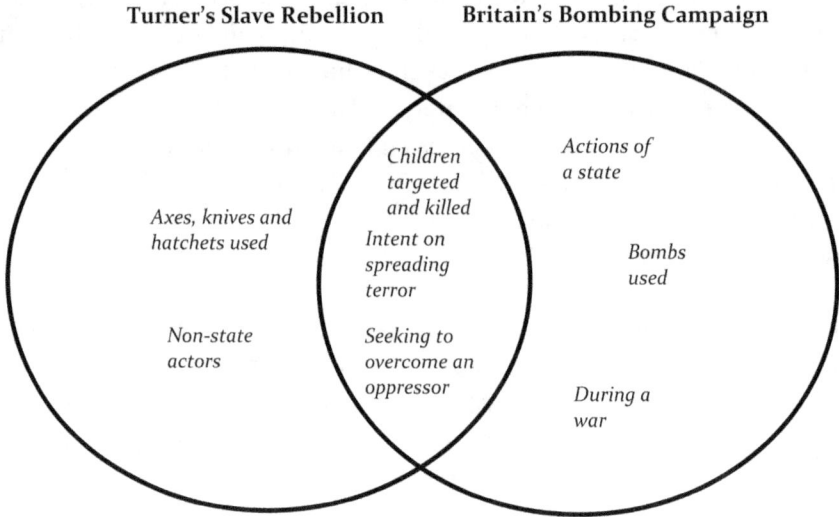

If there are differences in the pupils' moral judgments of the two acts of terrorism, this must of course pertain to one of the facts that doesn't fall in the overlap. The task is then to identify and highlight those pivotal facts and explain why they are morally significant.

Following this, present pupils with Walzer's definition of a 'supreme emergency' and ask them to determine whether it applies to both instances of terrorism. If it doesn't, and yet they view Turner's rebellion as justifiable, this must be because Walzer's condition is not a necessary one. On this point, then, ask pupils to complete the sentence that most aligns with their thinking:

a. *Turner's slave rebellion was a response to a supreme emergency because…*

b. *Turner's slave rebellion was not a response to a supreme emergency because… and was therefore unjustifiable.*

c. *Turner's slave rebellion was not a response to a supreme emergency because… but was nevertheless justifiable because…*

The range of possible responses to the actions of Turner and the British outlined above are certainly not exhaustive. To encourage more nuanced responses, present the two passages below from Walzer (2004), on the left, and Thomas Nagel (1972), on the right. The task is to identify the differences between these two views with respect to committing necessary atrocities (what is sometimes known as the 'problem of dirty hands'). While Walzer refers to such atrocities as immoral but 'morally defensible', Nagel suggests that, despite their necessity, they may be wholly immoral. For Nagel, it is possible that we can be compelled to act in ways for which there is no moral comfort to be found, no way to ameliorate our guilt or excuse our conduct. Walzer seeks to avoid Nagel's simple pessimism by way of paradox and contradiction.

'The intention of the British leaders at that point in the war was to kill and terrorize the civilian population, to attack German morale rather than German military might … In order to display the theoretical issue in all its difficulty, it is enough to say flatly that the intention was wrongful, the bombing criminal; its victims were innocent men, women, and children … But if there was no other way of preventing a Nazi triumph, then the immorality—no less immoral, for what else can the deliberate killing of the innocent be?—was also, simultaneously, morally defensible. That is the provocation and the paradox.' (pp. 34–35)

'In situations of deadly conflict, particularly where a weaker party is threatened with annihilation or enslavement by a stronger one, the argument for resorting to atrocities can be powerful, and the dilemma acute. There may exist principles, not yet codified, which would enable us to resolve such dilemmas. But then again there may not. We must face the pessimistic alternative that … the world can present us with situations in which there is no honorable or moral course for a man to take, no course free of guilt and responsibility for evil.' (pp. 143–144)

Do either of these views help illuminate the actions of the Turner or the British for your pupils? Do either of the following statements align with their views?

a. The actions of the slaves/British were instances of morally defensible immorality.

b. The actions of the slaves/British, though necessary, were wholly immoral and dishonourable.

Activity 3

Pupils should now endeavour to formulate their ultimate views on the morality of terrorism. Drawing on the range of options below, they should outline and justify their position. If they do regard terrorism as sometimes necessary or moral, they should specify under what circumstances that is the case; in other words, they should outline the general criteria for what constitutes a 'supreme emergency'.

a. Terrorism is wholly immoral and should never be considered an option.

b. Terrorism is a sometimes necessary, though wholly immoral, course of action; in times of extreme desperation we are required to ignore the call of morality.

c. *Terrorism, though always immoral, is sometimes necessary and thereby morally defensible.*

d. *There are circumstances under which terrorism is a wholly moral course of action.*

One way to help pupils think about these questions is to consider the moral character of the terrorist who responds to a supreme emergency. To this end, you could offer the following options:

a. *The terrorist is despicable and deserves nothing but condemnation. They are wholly responsible for their depravity.*

b. *The terrorist acts abominably, but we must sympathise with the fact that they were driven to this by the impossible situation they were placed in. Yes, they are dishonourable, but they are not wholly responsible for the moral stain they must now live with.*

c. *Though the terrorist acts immorally and is stained, it is also the case that they act with a kind of valour and fortitude.*

d. *The terrorist is a figure of unqualified goodness. They ought to be commended for their steadfast devotion to the pursuit of justice.*

Activity 4

Having investigated the morality of terrorism, the final activity addresses the question of whether the legal distinction between intentionally killing civilians and killing civilians as an unintended side-effect actually corresponds to a significant moral difference. In other words, is terrorism morally distinct from other legally permissible acts of war?

The relevant piece of legislation is Article 51 of the Geneva Convention Protocol I, as excerpted in the war chapter. From that article, we can extract the following claims:

- It is illegal to intentionally kill civilians in order to gain a military advantage by spreading terror among the civilian population.

- It is legal to kill civilians so long as their deaths are a side-effect of, and in proportion to, the military advantage gained.

Consider the following two scenarios:

i. *In order to erode civilian morale and public support for the war, a civilian hospital is targeted killing 50 patients and doctors. As a consequence, workers at* the local oil refinery, which produces the fuel used in tanks and fighter aircraft, refuse to work, and the refinery is forced to close.

ii. *In order to stop the production of fuel used in tanks and fighter aircraft, an oil refinery is targeted in an air strike killing 50 civilian workers.*

Ask pupils to apply Article 51 to determine which of these actions is illegal. Then discuss:

- Enquiry Question: Is there a significant moral difference between these two scenarios?

    Development Questions:

    o Do the actions in the two scenarios reveal a different attitude towards the value of civilian life?

    o Does Article 51 effectively legalise the murder of civilians?

    o If there is no moral difference, does that mean there should be no legal difference?

    o If there should be no legal difference, is it the case that both or neither act should be legal?

Returning to the views of Howard Zinn (2001) presented in the chapter on war, he would argue that there is no moral difference. Use this extract as an interlude in the discussion:

> Is it really an accident when civilians die under our bombs? Even if you grant that the intention is not to kill civilians, if they nevertheless become victims, again and again and again, can that be called an accident? If the deaths of civilians are inevitable in bombing, it may not be deliberate, but it is not an accident, and the bombers cannot be considered innocent. They are committing murder as surely as are the terrorists.

Ask the class to identify Zinn's reasons for thinking there is no moral difference between the two scenarios. Use his ideas to further propel the discussion by asking the following development question:

- Is there a moral difference between intentionally causing harm and unintentionally causing foreseeable harm?

Notes

1 https://docsouth.unc.edu/neh/turner/turner.html
2 https://www.natturnerproject.org/laws-passed-march-15-1832

References

Nagel, T. (1972). War and Massacre. *Philosophy & Public Affairs*, 1(2), 123–144.

Walzer, M. (2004). *Arguing about War*. Yale University Press.

Walzer, M. (2006). *Just and Unjust Wars: A Moral Argument with Historical Illustrations* (4th ed.). Basic Books.

Zinn, H. (2001). *A Just Cause, Not a Just War*. The Progressive Magazine. https://progressive.org/magazine/just-cause-just-war-Zinn/

Poverty

> **Key Questions**
>
> - Do we have a moral duty to make significant financial sacrifices in order to alleviate extreme poverty?
> - If we ignore the plight of those in extreme poverty, are we moral monsters?
> - Is letting the poor die morally equivalent to killing them?
> - By letting the poor die, are we ourselves killers?
> - By not sharing 'our' wealth, are we morally equivalent to thieves?

Start by outlining the scale of the problem. As of 2023, almost 700 million people were living in extreme poverty. This means that up to 700 million people had inadequate housing, were undernourished, and lacked access to clean water, basic sanitation and essential healthcare.

The millions of annual poverty-related deaths are preventable by ensuring access to such basic goods as antibiotics, mosquito nets, safe water and better nutrition. Adopted by all United Nations members in 2015, the first of the 17 Sustainable Development Goals was ending poverty in all its forms by 2030. It is now projected that this goal will not be met, with almost 600 million people expected to still be living in extreme poverty.

One in six of the world's children live in poverty. As a result of this material vulnerability, many of these children are coerced into child labour, prostitution and joining militias. This is how the United Nations has explained the degradation of poverty:

> Poverty is about more than a lack of income. It has a range of different socioeconomic dimensions, including: the ability to access services and social protection measures and to express opinions and choice; the power to negotiate; and social status, decent work

and opportunities. Poverty is also the root cause of many human rights and labour rights violations. For example, child labour, forced labour and human trafficking are each deeply connected to poverty.[1]

The economist Marc Fleurbaey (2007) shares the view that poverty is not simply a lack of income or having fewer resources than others. The difference between the impoverished and the rest is not merely quantitative. Poverty is not a matter of being at a lower point on a continuum of wealth but of having an entirely distinct form of life, a distinct way of being in the world. He writes:

> [P]overty is not experienced only in terms of "less": less consumption, less leisure, reduced opportunities, etc. It is experienced in qualitatively different terms: fear of the future, shame, absence of control over one's destiny, submission to the arbitrary power of the boss or the civil servant, etc. (p. 143)

Further, an implication of Arjun Sengupta's (2007) description of poverty is that its existence seemingly contravenes the Universal Declaration of Human Rights, which states in Article 1 that 'All human beings are born free and equal in dignity…' A world that does not actively seek to eradicate poverty is one that does not take seriously the dignity and self-respect of all people. He writes:

> Poverty has always been considered a degradation of human dignity, extreme poverty a form of extreme degradation: Poor people cannot lead a life commensurate with the standards of civilized existence. They are afflicted with hunger, malnutrition, ill health, unsanitary housing and living conditions, and often lack education … They lose their self-respect and ability to participate in any kind of fulfilling social life. (p. 324)

Activity 1

Does the problem of extreme global poverty impose any duties on the relatively rich? Peter Singer (1972), who has said he donates 40% of his income to charity, believes it does. He famously used the analogy of saving a child drowning in a pond to illustrate this. Present his analogy to the class:

> [I]f I am walking past a shallow pond and see a child drowning in it, I ought to wade in and pull the child out. This will mean getting my clothes muddy, but this is insignificant, while the death of the child would presumably be a very bad thing. (p. 231)

Ask pupils to try to extract the implied moral principle – one that we can apply to any issue, not just drowning children – at work here using this structure:

Implied Moral Principle: If a person is x, then another person, who y, is under an obligation to z.

The aim here is to identify what conditions two people must satisfy in order to give rise to a duty between them e.g. *If a person is suffering, then another person, who is able to alleviate their suffering, is under an obligation to do just that.*

- Enquiry Question: Is this moral principle correct?

    Development Question:

    ○ If the *y*-condition seems too demanding, to what extent should it be loosened to render the principle acceptable?

Activity 2

Having discussed this, present the principle as Singer formulates it:

> If it is in our power to prevent something bad from happening, without thereby sacrificing anything of comparable moral importance, we ought, morally, to do it. By "without sacrificing anything of comparable moral importance" I mean without causing anything else comparably bad to happen, or doing something that is wrong in itself, or failing to promote some moral good, comparable in significance to the bad thing that we can prevent. (p. 231)

Ask pupils to apply Singer's principle to the cases in the table, determining both the prescribed course of action and their own views:

	According to Singer's principle, do you have a duty to give?	'I believe you have a duty to give.'	'I believe if you don't give you are responsible for that person's suffering.'	'I believe you don't have a duty to give, but it would be morally praiseworthy if you were you to.'	'It would be foolish to give, not praiseworthy.'
An emergency blood transfusion is required in order to save the life of a person who has been bitten by a shark. As you lie on the sand watching, the paramedic calls out imploring you to donate your blood.					

A teenager is being pursued by a number of gang members who are intent on causing him physical harm. He asks whether he can take your bike in order to escape.					
On safari, a woman unknown to you is being stalked by a lioness. The only way to save the woman's life is to attack the lion yourself, leading to your probable death.					
You have just bought a pair of trainers, your third, and are carrying them home. A homeless person without shoes notices the bag and asks you to gift them to him.					
Your budget allows for £150 leisure spending every month. You're about to purchase opera tickets when an ad pops up from a humanitarian organisation asking for a one-off donation of £150 which will help save the lives of 10 people suffering in a famine in a distant part of the world.					

A stranger who is unable to get the kidney he needs to survive has resorted to the desperate measure of putting letters through people's doors asking for one of theirs. If you were to act as a donor, this would slightly shorten your life, but it would save his.						

Having worked through this, present Singer's own words on the morality of shopping, specifically, buying clothes in order to look 'well-dressed' rather than keep ourselves warm:

> We would not be sacrificing anything significant if we were to continue to wear our old clothes, and give the money to famine relief ... [Therefore] we ought to give money away, rather than spend it on clothes which we do not need ... To do so is not charitable, or generous. Nor is it the kind of act which philosophers and theologians have called "supererogatory" ... If you are living comfortably while others are hungry or dying from easily preventable diseases, and you are doing nothing about it, there is something wrong with your behaviour. (p. 235)

The table should give pupils a clear picture of whether they agree with Singer's principle. At this stage, there are three possible positions:

1. *I agree with both Singer's conclusion (that we have a duty to donate money instead of buying things we don't need) and his principle.*

Concept Check

A **supererogatory** act is one that is good but not obligatory. It is an act that goes beyond the call of duty, often heroically so. The Memorial to Heroic Self-Sacrifice in Postman's Park, London, honours those who performed supererogatory acts by dying to save the lives of others. While we praise those who perform such acts, we don't condemn those who don't. Libertarians are liable to claim that any positive act of assistance is supererogatory. This is because they believe that, in the absence of contracts or promises, there are no **positive duties**. These are duties that require us to actively help others. They believe that we only have **negative duties**, which are the duties to refrain from interfering with or harming others. As such, the libertarian would claim that we have no duty to rescue the drowning child.

2. *I agree with Singer's conclusion but I don't agree with his principle.*

3. *I neither agree with Singer's conclusions nor his principle.*

For 2 and 3, pupils should provide reasons for their divergence from Singer. With 2, they should endeavour to modify the principle in order to make it palatable and align with their answers in the table. Returning to the Implied Moral Principle may help with this.

Activity 3

If many pupils are clustering around 2, it may be that Singer's principle is a distraction. So let's put it to one side and treat the argument as an argument from analogy. The question, then, becomes: if you have a duty to sacrifice your clean, dry clothes to rescue the drowning child, do you similarly have a duty to sacrifice buying inessential goods to donate money to charities that alleviate extreme poverty? To answer this question, have pupils complete the following argument schematic, selecting operators ~ (morally similar to) or ≁ (not morally similar to), then → (entails that) or ↛ (does not entail that).

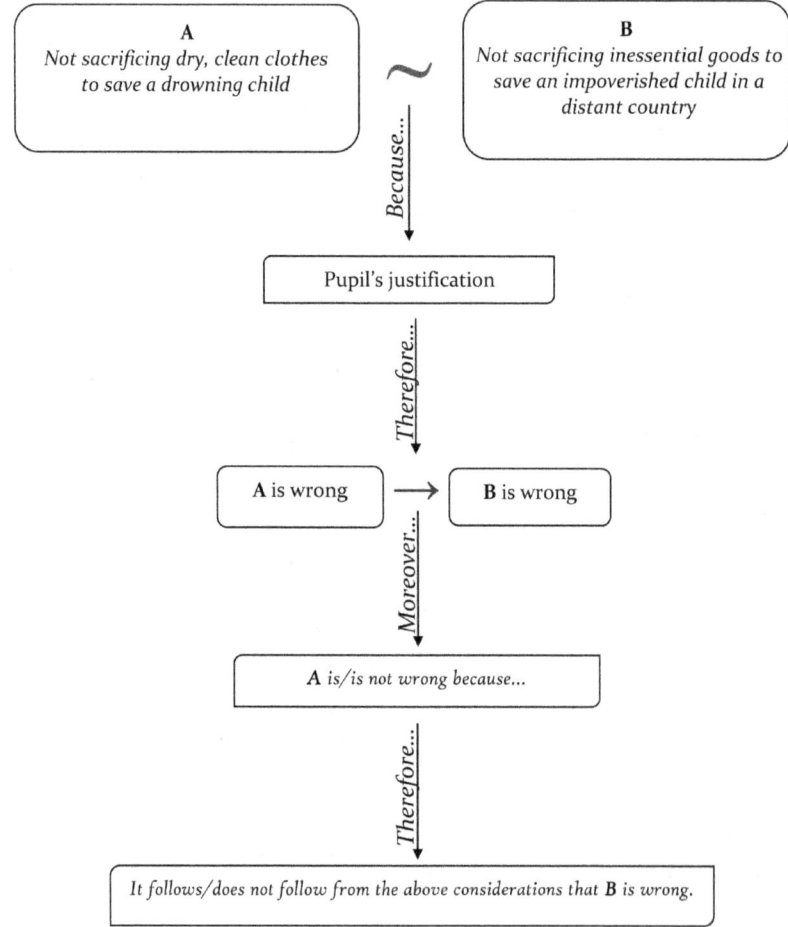

Activity 4

As a final way to illustrate Singer's moral conception of the duties we face, you might present this scenario:

Imagine a world where keys are our unit of currency. We are paid in keys. We purchase goods with keys. When we receive our wages, the number of keys sufficient to cover our basic living costs – energy bills, travel expenses, food, etc. – are coloured blue. The additional keys which we use to spend on inessential items are coloured red.

There is a distant country where people are suffering because they don't have sufficient access to food, medicine, and other vital provisions such as mosquito nets. These basic goods do actually exist in this country, but they are in locked boxes. The boxes can only be opened using red keys, but the people in this country have an inadequate supply.

You are considering purchasing a video game which will cost several red keys. You, of course, know that these keys could be sent to the impoverished country where they would be used to unlock a number of boxes containing vital provisions for the suffering people there.

- Enquiry Question: Would it be wrong to purchase a video game?

Development Question:

○ Is this a good analogy for the moral situation we actually face in relation to global poverty?

Have pupils then complete the following schematic, selecting operators ~ (morally similar to) or ≁ (not morally similar to), then → (entails that) or ↛ (does not entail that).

> **Thought Avenue**
>
> When discussing the pond scenario Singer commented: 'It makes no moral difference whether the person I can help is a neighbor's child ten yards from me or a Bengali whose name I shall never know, ten thousand miles away ... The fact that a person is physically near to us ... does not show that we ought to help him rather than another who happens to be further away' (pp. 231–232). While this doesn't imply that we ought not help the Bengali, David Miller (2007) has argued that our moral duties to our compatriots are greater than our duties to those in other countries: 'we owe more to our fellow-nationals than we owe to human beings in general merely by virtue of the fact that we share with them the various cultural and other features that make up a national identity ... our responsibilities to the world's poor are [not] in principle exactly the same as our responsibilities to our fellow citizens' (pp. 30, 231). To explore this alleged asymmetry, ask pupils to imagine there are two people drowning. They, the pupils, are only able to save one. Would they be morally justified in saving one person over the other because that person was their (a) brother, (b) friend, (c) neighbour, (d) compatriot, (e) religion, (f) ethnicity? Relatedly, would it be wrong *not* to so prioritise any of these people?

118 Navigating the Moral Maze

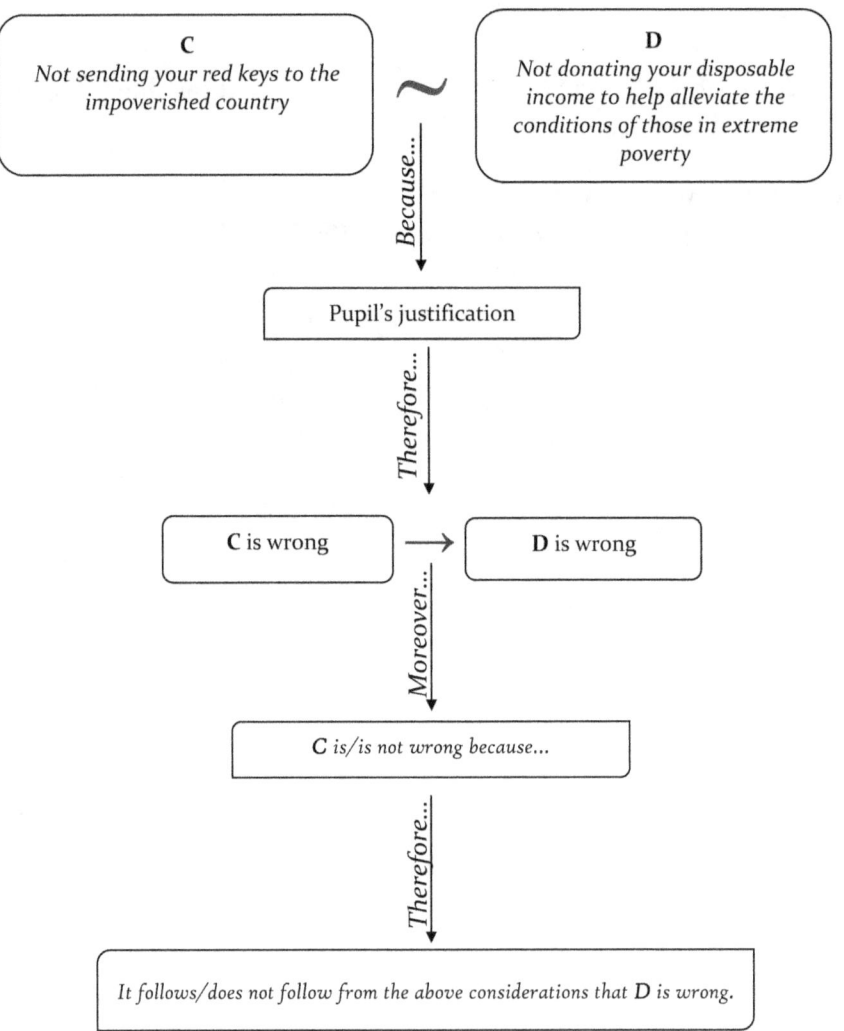

Activity 5

Singer argues that we ought to help those in extreme poverty, but how wrong is it if we don't? James Rachels (1979) argues that letting the poor die makes us 'moral monsters'. It is, he states, morally equivalent to killing them: 'Although we do not know exactly how many people die each year of malnutrition or related health problems, the number is very high, in millions. By giving money to support famine relief efforts, each of us could save at least some of them. By not giving, we let them die … [And] letting die is just as bad as killing …' (p. 159). Given that the reason why you shouldn't kill is the same as the reason why you shouldn't let someone die, Rachels argues that the actions are morally equivalent.

Let's start by looking at his first claim that not giving to charity makes us morally monstrous. He reaches this conclusion by arguing from analogy on the basis of a hypothetical case in which there is a room with a starving child. Also in the room is a man, whom Rachels calls Jack Palance, with a sandwich on the table beside him. The man is completely indifferent to the suffering of the child and lets her die of starvation. Rachels claims that Jack Palance is clearly a 'moral monster'. But, if he is a moral monster, then what does that say about us?

> [W]e feel intuitively that we are not so monstrous, even though we also let starving children die when we could feed them almost as easily. If this intuition is correct, there must be some important difference between him and us. But when we examine the most obvious differences between his conduct and ours – the location of the dying, the differences in numbers – we find no real basis for judging ourselves less harshly than we judge him. (p. 160)

Rachels therefore concludes that, if Jack Palance is a moral monster, then we, the indifferent rich, are monsters too. This scenario is equivalent to Singer's pond story, but what Rachels is doing differently is articulating the precise moral judgment that is appropriate to Palance and, by extension, the miserly rich. Having already established whether the acts of not saving a child in your vicinity and not saving a distant child are morally similar, pupils should refer back to their earlier schematic to complete the following:

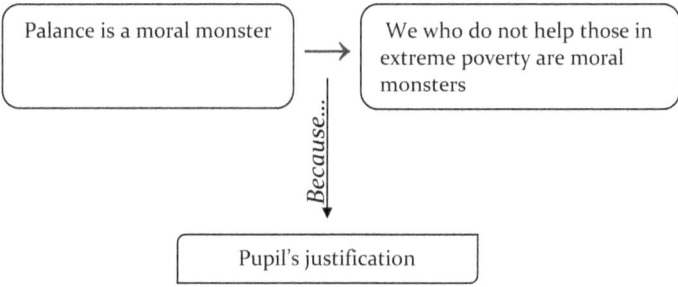

Rachels offers an interesting explanation of why we might recoil from thinking of ourselves as moral monsters. He writes:

> How guilty we feel about something depends, to some extent, on how we compare with those around us. If we were surrounded by people who regularly sacrificed to feed the starving, and we did not, we would probably feel ashamed. But because our neighbours do not do any better than we, we are not so ashamed. (p. 162)

Is it the case that we do not think we are moral monsters because we feel no guilt? And do we feel no guilt because we live in a world where most people will not judge us for our inaction?

Rachels goes on to draw an equivalence (familiar from his arguments against the distinction between passive and active euthanasia) between letting die and killing.

> The primary reason why killing is wrong is that something very bad is done to the victim himself: he ends up dead; he no longer has a good – his life – which he possessed before. But notice that exactly the same can be said about letting someone die. The primary reason why it is morally objectionable to let someone die, when we could save him, is that he ends up dead; he no longer has a good – his life – which he possessed before. Thus, the explanation of why killing is bad mentions features of killing that are also features of letting die, and vice versa. (p. 165)

Rachels doesn't think there is a difference that can be identified to show that killing is worse than letting die, and therefore concludes that they are morally equivalent.

Let's blend the Palance and key scenarios to see whether our intuitions align with Rachels' analysis.

A starving child was detained in a room. A guard who knew that a starving child was due to be detained, and knew that the child would die if it was deprived of food, nevertheless was feeling peckish and ate the sandwich that had been left for the chid. The child thus slowly and inevitably died as a result. By knowingly depriving the child of what it needed to survive, he thus killed the child.	*You and a starving child are both being detained in a room in which there is a box containing a sandwich. You have a red key in your pocket that could open the box. You know that the child will die if you don't open it. Nevertheless, you want to use your red key to go to the cinema when you're released, so you choose not to open the box. You close your eyes to spare yourself the sight of the child's agonising death.*

- Enquiry Question: Are your actions morally equivalent to the guard's?

    Development Questions:

    ○ Are both you and the guard equally despicable?

    ○ Would the explanations for the wrongness in each case be identical?

    ○ If two actions are wrong for the same reasons, are they wrong to the same extent?

Following the discussion, have pupils complete the following, using either ≡ (morally equivalent) or ≢ (not morally equivalent), and → (entails that) or ↛ (does not entail that).

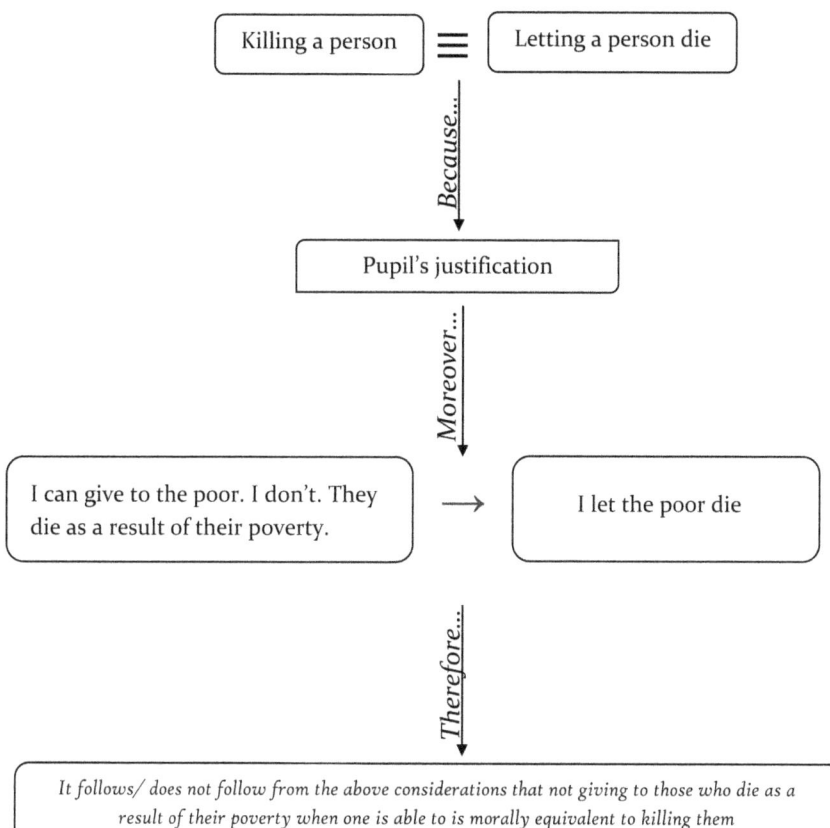

Activity 6

We shall now consider a different approach, one which addresses the injustice of poverty, inspired by the 4th century Church Father St Basil of Caesarea (1948) who wrote:

Is he not called a thief who strips a man of his clothes? And he who will not clothe the naked when he can — is he deserving of a different appellation? The bread that you keep in your possession belongs to the hungry; the cloak in your closet, to the naked; the shoes that you allow to rot, to the barefooted, and your hoarded silver, to the indigent. Hence you have done injustice to as many as you have failed to help. (p. 61)

Thought Avenue

Many philosophers have argued that there is a human right to subsistence. If the right to subsistence is entailed by our right to minimally flourishing life, would it also follow that we have a right to love and friendship, since these are also necessary for a minimally flourishing life (according to The Samaritans

This is a fascinating passage but with certain gaps in its reasoning. As an act of intellectual charity, ask pupils to suppose that Basil is correct in what he writes. Their task, then, is to kindly fill the philosophical lacunae on his behalf. To that end, ask them to complete the following:

> 'Loneliness is a serious public health issue. There is an association between suicide and loneliness')? If the poor have a right to our property, does it follow that the lonely have a right to our love?

- *The bread in your pantry belongs to the poor because...*
- *Keeping hold of an object which belongs to another is the same as theft because...*

Below is an attempt to provide an argument in support of Basil's claims. This is too complex to be presented as an argument tree, so work through it with the pupils.

1. Everyone is entitled to a minimally flourishing life.
2. Extreme poverty prevents a minimally flourishing life.
3. Therefore, everyone is entitled not to live in extreme poverty.
4. If everyone is entitled not to live in extreme poverty, then the poor are entitled to financial aid.
5. If the poor are entitled to financial aid, that means there is money in the world that they have a rightful claim to.
6. The poor have a rightful claim to the financial resources of anyone who is able to help them.
7. You have the financial resources to help them.
8. Therefore, the poor have a rightful claim to your money.
9. If they have a rightful claim to your money, one that supersedes your own claim, then the money in your possession is theirs (what is owed to them is owned by them).
10. To possess the property of another person against their wishes is (*morally equivalent to*) theft.

> **Thought Avenue**
>
> Does poverty bestow any moral benefit? This is an odd and somewhat glib question. But in the context of Jesus's pronouncement that 'Blessed are you who are poor for yours is the kingdom of God' (Luke 6:20), for some it is very much a live one. Francis of Assisi strongly believed in the value of poverty. On the rare occasions that he ate cooked food he made sure to subdue the flavours by seasoning it with ash. When he witnessed extreme poverty his reaction was not one of compassion but envy. For Francis

11. Therefore, if you do not give to those in extreme poverty, you *are* (*morally equivalent to*) a thief.

In premise 10 and the conclusion, I've added the parenthetical qualifications to enable the argument to take two forms: one which reaches a metaphysical conclusion about the nature of our actions (that they constitute theft), and one which reaches a moral conclusion about the morality of our actions (that they are morally equivalent to theft). It's possible for one to accept the latter argument while rejecting the former.

> being 'rich in poverty' was an entirely coherent state of affairs. He even spoke of his relationship to poverty in marital terms: 'Lady Poverty', queen of virtues, a source of great beauty and wisdom, was his bride. Crucially, however, for Francis the truly admirable state was not being in poverty, but choosing to be in poverty.

This argument can be used to support a claim propounded by the Second Vatican Council:

Feed the man dying of hunger, for if you have not fed him you have killed him.[2]

This is a striking claim, one that goes further than Rachels. Instead of saying there is a moral equivalence between letting die and killing, it claims that letting die *is* killing. Again, no justification is offered for this view, so ask pupils to repeat their prior act of intellectual charity by trying to find a credible way of completing the following statement:

- *By letting the poor die we are killing them because…*

To marry the version of Basil's argument above and the Second Vatican Council, we might argue:

1. If I steal what A needs to survive, and A subsequently dies, I have killed A.

2. By not giving financial aid to those in extreme poverty, we are stealing from them.

3. Therefore, if those in extreme poverty die for lack of financial aid, we have killed them.

Watering the metaphysical claim down slightly, discuss the extent to which the class would subscribe to this position:

The more easily I can prevent a bad thing from happening, the more I am responsible for its happening if I do nothing. We can easily prevent some of those in extreme poverty from dying, therefore, if we do nothing, we are significantly responsible for their deaths.

Activity 7

It's time to take stock. Have pupils complete the following.

	Agree	Disagree
Singer's principle: *'If it is in our power to prevent something bad from happening, without thereby sacrificing anything of comparable moral importance, we ought, morally, to do it.'*		
A is a morally impermissible.		
A's wrongness entails **B**'s wrongness.		
C is morally impermissible.		
C's wrongness entails **D**'s wrongness.		
Letting someone die is morally equivalent to killing them.		
Not giving to the poor is morally equivalent to theft.		
Letting someone die *is* killing them.		
Letting someone die when we might easily save them makes us significantly responsible for their death.		

With everything laid out, have pupils complete the concluding statements:

I believe that we have a moral duty to make a significant/some/minimal/no financial sacrifice in order to help those in extreme poverty. The moral principle which has led me to this conclusion is the following…

I, moreover, agree/disagree with Rachels that by not making financial sacrifices we are moral monsters. And I believe he is correct/incorrect to say that we are thereby morally equivalent to killers because…

Additionally, I accept/reject Basil of Caesarea's claim that by not giving to the poor we are thieves because… I also think the Second Vatican Council is right/wrong to say that not giving to the poor is killing them because…

I believe that individuals who are able to help those who die in extreme poverty and do nothing are entirely/significantly/minimally/not at all responsible for their deaths because…

In summary, I believe that giving to those in extreme poverty is a moral option/moral necessity and a person who makes no such financial sacrifice is…

Notes

1 https://unglobalcompact.org/what-is-gc/our-work/social/poverty
2 https://www.vatican.va/archive/hist_councils/ii_vatican_council/documents/vat-ii_const_19651207_gaudium-et-spes_en.html

References

Basil. (1948) [4th C CE]. The Rich Fool. In W. Shewring (Trans.), *Rich and Poor in Christian Tradition*. Burns Oates & Washbourne.

Fleurbaey, M. (2007). Poverty as a Form of Oppression. In T. Pogge (Ed.), *Freedom from Poverty as a Human Right: Who Owes What to the Very Poor?* (pp. 133–155). Oxford University Press.

Miller, D. (2007). *National Responsibility and Global Justice*. Oxford University Press.

Rachels, J. (1979). Killing and Starving to Death. *Philosophy*, 54(208), 159–171.

Sengupta, A. (2007). Poverty Eradication and Human Rights. In T. Pogge (Ed.), *Freedom from Poverty As a Human Right: Who Owes What to the Very Poor?* (pp. 323–345). Oxford University Press.

Singer, P. (1972). Famine, Affluence, and Morality. *Philosophy & Public Affairs,* 1(3), 229–243.

8 Wealth

> **Key Questions**
>
> - Is it wrong to tax the rich to help the poor?
> - Do the rich deserve their wealth?
> - Is taxation theft?
> - Is taxation slavery?
> - Is property a natural or legal right?
> - Does your right to property supersede my right to a minimally flourishing life?

In the preceding chapter, we considered whether the rich have a duty to help the poor. This chapter now turns to the question of whether it is acceptable to coercively take from the rich in order to help the poor. We shall do this by first exploring the notion of private property and then analysing the political theory of libertarianism.

Though libertarianism is something of a fringe view within political philosophy, engaging with it prompts pupils to think about a host of other key questions, such as whether we are essentially individual or interconnected beings. I have found that evaluating libertarianism often provokes pupils to be at their most brilliant and insightful.

PART I: PRIVATE PROPERTY

In the 17th and 18th centuries, there was a dispute among philosophers regarding the nature of property. Some philosophers, such as John Locke, thought that property was established by natural right, which means that it still exists within a state of nature, independent of political structures. Locke argued that if you were to find an apple tree on an uninhabited island and proceeded to pluck off one of its apples, you would thereby own that apple. By virtue of plucking the fruit, it has become 'mixed' with your body and your labour and is consequently yours.

> **Concept Check**
>
> The **state of nature** is a hypothetical state in which humans lived prior to establishing a government or organised political system; in the state of nature, there are no laws or contracts. The 17th-century philosopher **Thomas Hobbes** famously wrote that in the state of nature, life would be 'solitary, poor, nasty brutish, and short'.

Other philosophers, such as David Hume (1978), believed property was merely a matter of convention and legal right: 'Our property is nothing but those goods, whose constant possession is establish'd by the laws of society,' he wrote in *Treatise of Human Nature* (p. 491).

Activity 1

Invite a volunteer (*x*) to perform a version of Locke's thought experiment, miming while you narrate:

> *Our story starts with x lying face down on the sandy beach of a deserted island. She has been lying there unconscious for several hours. Suddenly, she starts to stir. Her right leg twitches. Then she coughs. Slowly, wearily, she rises to her knees, and then her feet. Squinting, she looks around. Behind her is the endless sea, before her the forest of an unknown land. How did she get here? Was she shipwrecked? Kidnapped? She tries to remember, but she can't. She can't even recall her own name. She's forgotten who she is. Her confusion is swiftly cast aside by a sharp pain that pierces her stomach causing her to wince. The pain strikes again. It's hunger. Desperately, she stumbles up the beach to the forest hoping to find some food. Turning from naked bough to naked bough her hopes start to fade. Then, like a miracle, she sees a scarlet red apple hanging high overhead. Frantically, like a squirrel, she scales the tree, reaches out, grabs the apple and jumps to the ground. She looks at it mesmerised, as though it were a rare jewel. Then, with the spell quickly broken by her returning hunger, she spits on it and rubs it clean.*

- Enquiry Question (a): Is the apple now *x*'s property?

Development Questions:

○ If yes, at which point did it become *x*'s property?

○ If yes, would it be a squirrel's property if a squirrel had plucked it? Do animals have property?

○ If not, whose property is it? The tree's?

○ Is the fact that she's forgotten her identity relevant to the question?

While facilitating the discussion, use the board to note down the pupils' ideas in a table divided into the 'Yes' answers and the 'No' answers. This will help with their written work.

● Enquiry Question (b): Would it be x's property if she ate it?

For this question, target those pupils who answered no to (a). Doing so should yield some further and novel ideas about what constitutes property. (If a pupil says that it's not her property because it no longer exists, reply by referring specifically to the indigestible seeds of the apple.)

You will now need another volunteer (y) to perform the next part of the story:

Feeling invigorated, x continued to explore the island. Certainly, she felt some fear, for she had no notion of what other creatures might inhabit this strange land. Treading carefully, biting her nails, her aquiline eyes took note of even the slightest movement. All the while thoughts of undiscovered beasts ran through her mind: three-headed rats, flying snakes, carnivorous trees. Suddenly, something struck her on the head. She froze, petrified. Silence. Stillness. No sign of monsters. Slowly, fearfully, she looked up. Her eyes widened, her heart raced, her jaw dropped – fear was replaced with glee. She had walked into a grove of orange trees. Hanging overhead, like a garden of tiny suns, were hundreds of oranges. Joyfully, she danced from tree to tree grabbing as many oranges as she could handle. With a bale of them in her arms, she trundled over to a nearby patch of shade, dropped the oranges to the ground, and then dropped herself. Exhausted, she closed her eyes and started to snore.

Once her arms had flopped down by her sides and her breathing had deepened, y emerged from behind a bush. x was not alone. The island was not empty. On another beach, y had similarly woken without any recollection of who he was, and had been similarly pained by hunger. But y, unfortunately, had suffered some sort of injury to his leg and was only able to hobble along. Though he had tried, he was unable to climb the trees to reach the oranges. And so, desperate for food, he slowly approached the sleeping x. Carefully, he picked up a few of the oranges from the pile and stuffed them in his pocket. He limped back to his bush and started to peel them.

● Enquiry Question (c): Are these oranges now y's property?

Development Questions:

○ Has y done something wrong?

○ Has y worked for the oranges?

- Does *y* deserve the oranges?
- Would *x* be justified in harming *y* to reclaim the oranges?

Activity 2

The aim now is for pupils to apply the ideas gathered from the previous activity in order to formulate their thoughts on the nature of property. Before starting on this, however, spend a few minutes outlining the differences between **natural rights** and **legal rights**.

- **Natural right:** a right that is guaranteed by nature. Within a state of nature where there are no governments, natural rights still exist.
- **Legal right:** a right that is guaranteed by law. Within a state of nature where there are no governments, legal rights do not exist.

This distinction invites much thought. To explore it, you could ask whether the pupils believe the right to life is a natural or merely legal right. You should also highlight that answering 'yes' to question (a) is seemingly in support of property as a natural right because this implies that property can exist within a state of nature.

Ask the pupils to complete the following:

I believe that for an object to be your personal property it has to be the case that… This is because… As such, I believe that property is a natural/merely legal right. This being so, my view of theft within the state of nature is that it is morally permissible/impermissible. This is because… Within a society where theft is illegal, I believe that it is morally permissible/impermissible because…

Once this has been completed, ask neighbours to swap books with each other. They are to read through their neighbour's answer and beneath it complete the following:

If everyone held these beliefs, then the world be like this: … But if everyone held the opposite of these beliefs, then the world be like this: … I would rather live in the former/latter world because… This shows that I regard your views as convincing/unconvincing. Indeed/Nevertheless, I think you need to explain your point that … in more detail. Overall, I think your most interesting point is …

Extension paragraph:

A consequence of my theory of property is that animals can/cannot own property. This is because… As such, one can/cannot steal from animals. The implications of this for dairy farming in which the produce (eggs or milk) of animals is taken is that it is morally permissible/impermissible. I fully/somewhat/struggle to accept these implications of my theory.

Activity 3

The following extract is from John Locke's (1988) *Two Treatises of Government:*

> Though the earth, and all inferior creatures, be common to all men, yet every man has a property in his own person: this no body has any right to but himself. The labour of his body, and the work of his hands, we may say, are properly his. Whatsoever then he removes out of the state that nature hath provided, and left it in, he hath mixed his labour with, and joined to it something that is his own, and thereby makes it his property. It being by him removed from the common state nature hath placed it in, it hath by this labour something annexed to it, that excludes the common right of other men: for this labour being the unquestionable property of the labourer, no man but he can have a right to what that is once joined to, at least where there is enough, and as good, left in common for others.
>
> He that is nourished by the acorns he picked up under an oak, or the apples he gathered from the trees in the wood, has certainly appropriated them to himself. I ask then, when did they begin to be his? when he digested? or when he eat? or when he boiled? or when he brought them home? or when he picked them up? and it is plain, if the first gathering made them not his, nothing else could. That labour put a distinction between them and common: that added something to them more than nature, the common mother of all, had done; and so they became his private right. (pp. 287–288)

> **Thought Avenue**
>
> The Theft Act 1968 states the following:
>
> *A person who picks mushrooms growing wild on any land, or who picks flowers, fruit or foliage from a plant growing wild on any land, does not (although not in possession of the land) steal what he picks, unless he does it for reward or for sale or other commercial purpose.*
>
> Given that the law merely states and doesn't justify, ask the pupils to devise a justification for the legality of foraging. This will then serve as a prelude to a discussion on whether they agree with this law.

Read through the passage with the class clarifying any terms or phrases they're uncertain of. Ask pupils to underline the moments in the passage that explain Locke's reasons for thinking that property is a natural right and then complete the following:

John Locke believed that property was a natural right because… However, what he didn't fully explain is… My view is that Locke's theory of property is right/broadly right/wrong. This is shown by my previous answer where I wrote that…

Finally, ask the pupils to draw a timeline like the one below, writing both their initials and Locke's initials to show the respective points at which they believe the apple became the person's property.

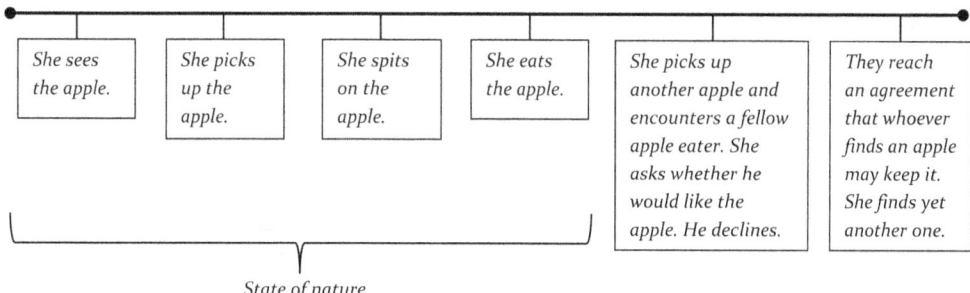

PART II: LIBERTARIANISM

Libertarians are strongly committed to the right to individual liberty and the concomitant institution of private property. They think that the role of the state is simply to uphold and protect these rights. As such, they are opposed to redistributive taxation. While the rich may *choose* to help the poor by donating a portion of their earnings, it is wrong of the state to force the rich to help the poor via redistributive taxation.

As a prelude to exploring libertarianism, it'd be worth explaining what redistributive taxation is and how it can be used to redress income inequality (in the US, for instance, it is estimated that the richest 10% of households own 70% of all the wealth), with the rich being taxed to support public services that they may rarely, if ever, use. Is this fair? Use the following as a question to bridge this lesson to the last:

- Enquiry Question (a): If property is a natural right, is it wrong to take from the rich to help the poor?

An effective way of encouraging pupils to understand and engage with these ideas is by watching a segment of a lecture by the Harvard philosopher Michael Sandel. His 'Justice' series of lectures don't merely explain different philosophical theories; they feature Sandel facilitating discussions among the students. Pupils find it immensely stimulating to watch other young people in the education system (albeit higher education) absorbed by and immersed in the live process of thinking through theories and experimenting with new concepts.

The relevant lecture is episode 3 on Harvard University's YouTube channel. Give the pupils a worksheet to complete while they watch. Starting with Sandel's outline of libertarianism, these are the key concepts and ideas to grasp (the final two belong to the libertarian philosopher Robert Nozick):

- **The right that libertarians regard as the most important:** The right to liberty.

- **Paternalist legislation, which is opposed by libertarianism:** Coercive laws designed to protect us from ourselves.

- **Morals legislation, which is opposed by libertarianism:** Coercive laws designed to protect our moral integrity.

- **Justice in acquisition:** our wealth is justly ours if the means by which we made it were fair e.g. the dairy farmer didn't steal his cows.

- **Justice in transfer:** our wealth is justly ours if the product we sell is purchased freely and without coercion.

To help pupils understand the difference between paternalist and morals legislation, use a simple sorting exercise in which they try to categorise the following class of laws (of course, depending on the age and maturity of your class, you may wish to avoid some of these):

○ **Drug laws**

○ **Pornography laws:** *In England and Wales, the Coroners and Justice Act 2009 prohibits the possession of cartoons depicting child pornography.*

○ **Bigamy laws:** *The Offences against the Person Act 1861 prohibits bigamy.*

○ **Organ trade laws:** *In England and Wales, the Human Tissue Act 2004 prohibits commercial dealings in human material for transplantation.*

○ **Suicide:** *This was illegal in England and Wales till the Suicide Act of 1961.*

○ **Homosexuality:** *In England, there were still prosecutions for homosexual acts as late as 1998 (with the case of the 'Boston Seven').*

In order to probe the 'Justice in Acquisition' condition, present the following scenarios and ask whether the individual's wealth in each case is just

> **Thought Avenue**
>
> In the New Testament, Jesus categorically denounces wealth:
>
> "It is easier for a camel to go through the eye of a needle than for a rich person to enter the kingdom of God."
> Mark 10:25
>
> "You cannot serve both God and money."
> Matthew 6:24

or unjust. If the wealth is unjust but neither of Nozick's principles violated, what additional principles are required?

i. *He is a Wyoming dairy farmer. He didn't steal the cows that produce the milk he sells. Nevertheless, the land on which the animals graze was violently acquired by his great-great-grandfather, who participated in the massacre of the tribe of Native Americans who had inhabited the region for hundreds of years.*

ii. *She is a bestselling author. Before she became successful, she was unemployed, wrote every day, and financially supported herself with money she'd inherited from her mother. This money had been passed down through the family for several generations. It originated with her great-great-great-great grandfather, who had amassed the fortune through his sugar company, the vast profitability of which was enabled by its use of slave labour.*

> "If you want to be perfect, go, sell your possessions."
> Matthew 19:21
>
> "Do not store up for yourselves treasures on earth, where moths and vermin destroy, and where thieves break in and steal ... For where your treasure is, there your heart will be also."
> Matthew 6:19-21
>
> Jesus believed that wealth distances us from the ultimate good of life. An implication of this view is that by taking from the rich and reducing their wealth we are helping them; indeed, the early Christian theologian St Cyprian wrote, 'We must avoid all property, as we should avoid an enemy' (Quoted in Chroust & Affeldt, 1951, p. 164). Discuss with the class whether there is any truth to these views (do they contain any truth for non-Christians?) and whether there is such a thing as excessive wealth.

iii. *He owns a successful graphic design company. While he has never stolen the computers and software that are essential to his work, they are produced by a company that uses child labour.*

iv. *She is a KC who earns close to £1 million a year. In addition to years of hard work, she was also given a golden start to life with an expensive education at an elite boarding school. Later, family connections enabled her to secure invaluable internships.*

v. *She, a multimillionaire, owns a highly successful clothing company with factories deliberately placed in poor countries with weak labour protections. Her employees, while not forced to work for the company, are paid extremely low wages (they live in shacks and have no access to healthcare), work extremely long days and do not receive paid leave.*

Though your pupils should also try to sketch out Nozick's argument that taxation is slavery, don't worry about them capturing this precisely; they'll analyse the argument in detail in the activities below. The most enjoyable and stimulating aspect of watching the lecture is engaging with the student contributions. To facilitate this, give pupils a table of names for the various speakers (Julia, John, Raul etc.) with columns for the following: whether they are for or against libertarianism, what their key point is, and a simple emoji evaluation (a tick for smile, frown or not sure).

PART III: EVALUATING LIBERTARIANISM

As a starter, present the following statements and ask your pupils to choose and justify the one they think is true (allow them to suggest an alternative if their view isn't articulated here):

a. *The rich do not deserve their wealth.*

b. *The rich do deserve their wealth, and they ought to share it, but they should be free to choose not to.*

c. *The rich do deserve their wealth, and they should be forced to share it.*

d. *The rich do deserve their wealth and they are under no obligation to share it.*

To evaluate the libertarian claim that taxation is theft, start by presenting the following argument tree (these are effective and more accessible primers for evaluating the argument in standard form). If they fall out of the tree with a 'no', they need to explain why this is. If they climb the entire way to the final fruit, they need to outline whether it does reflect their views, and if not, to find the fault with the tree.

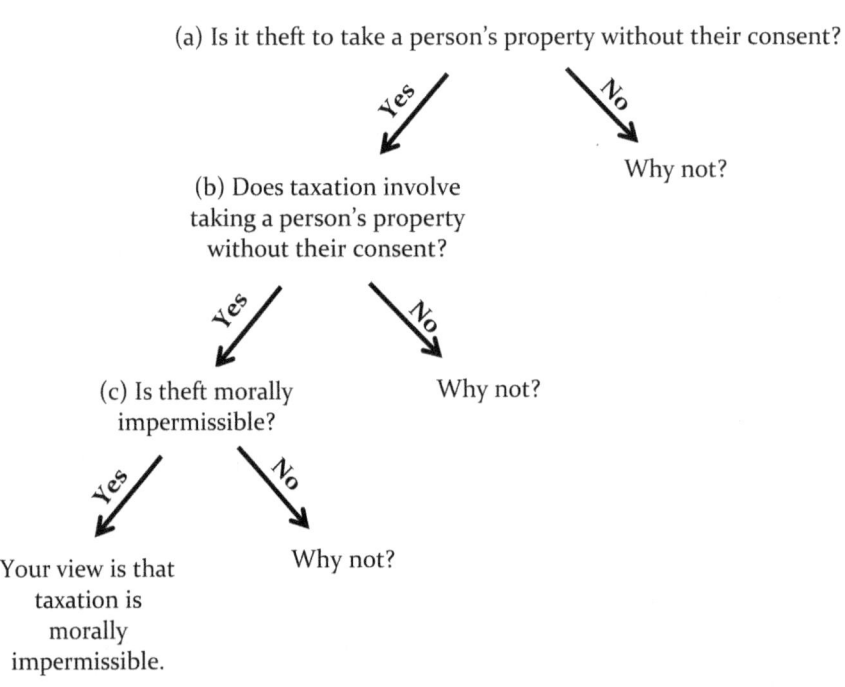

Having worked through the tree, present the class with the argument stated in standard form:

1. *To take a person's property without their consent is theft.*
2. *Taxation involves taking a person's property without (in some instances) their consent.*
3. *Therefore, taxation is theft.*
4. *Theft is morally impermissible.*
5. *Therefore, taxation is morally impermissible.*
6. *Therefore, we shouldn't tax the rich to help the poor.*

The next task is to answer the following:

i. Is the argument valid (does the conclusion logically follow from the premises)?
ii. Are premises 1, 2 and 4 true?
iii. For each erroneous premise, explain the error.
iv. If you do accept the argument, explain the reasons that support premises 1, 2 and 4.

To examine premise 1 in more detail and help with task (ii), present the following options, asking your pupils to identify and justify the claim they agree with. Welcome the possibility that there are alternative positions not articulated here.

a. *No one's money is their property because they don't own themselves and therefore do not own the fruits of 'their' labour. Therefore, taxation is not theft.*

b. *No one's money is their property because it is never justly acquired. Therefore, taxation is not theft.*

c. *In most cases, a person's money is their property. Therefore, non-consensual taxation is theft, but it is morally permissible theft.*

d. *In most cases, a person's money is their property. Therefore, non-consensual taxation is theft, and as such is morally impermissible.*

To examine premise 2 introduce the distinction between tacit, express and hypothetical consent:

a. **Tacit:** when we implicitly accept a situation by not avoiding or leaving it.

b. **Express:** when we explicitly accept a situation e.g. verbally or in writing.

c. **Hypothetical:** when we would explicitly accept a situation were we asked or able to.

Two questions that need to be asked:

- Can any of these forms of consent be applied to taxation? For instance, could it be argued that we tacitly consent to being taxed by not leaving the country?

- Should this notion of consent be accepted as genuine consent? Is it at all problematic?

We will now turn to Nozick's more radical claim that taxation is tantamount to slavery. In his book, *Anarchy, State and Utopia* (1974), he wrote:

> Taxation of earnings from labor is on a par with forced labor. Some persons find this claim obviously true: taking the earnings of n hours of labor is like taking n hours from the person; it is like forcing the person to work n hours for another's purpose. (p. 169)

> **Thought Avenue**
>
> In the New Testament (Acts 4: 32–35) early Christian communities are described as communist:
>
> > "All the believers were one in heart and mind. No one claimed that any of their possessions was their own, but they shared everything they had … there were no needy persons among them. For from time to time those who owned land or houses sold them, brought the money from the sales and put it at the apostles' feet, and it was distributed to anyone who had need."
>
> By abolishing private property, the apostles were able to eradicate poverty among themselves. The ancient Greek philosopher Plato also believed that the ruling class of society should not have private property because it leads us to regard ourselves as autonomous individuals rather than as parts of the state. Discuss with the class whether we should be inspired by these views. Would the world be better if we abolished private property?

To analyse these ideas, start by asking your pupils to work through the following arguments tree. As above, if they fall out of the tree with a 'no', they need to explain why this is. If they climb the entire way to the final fruit, they need to outline whether it does reflect their views, and if not, to find the fault with the tree.

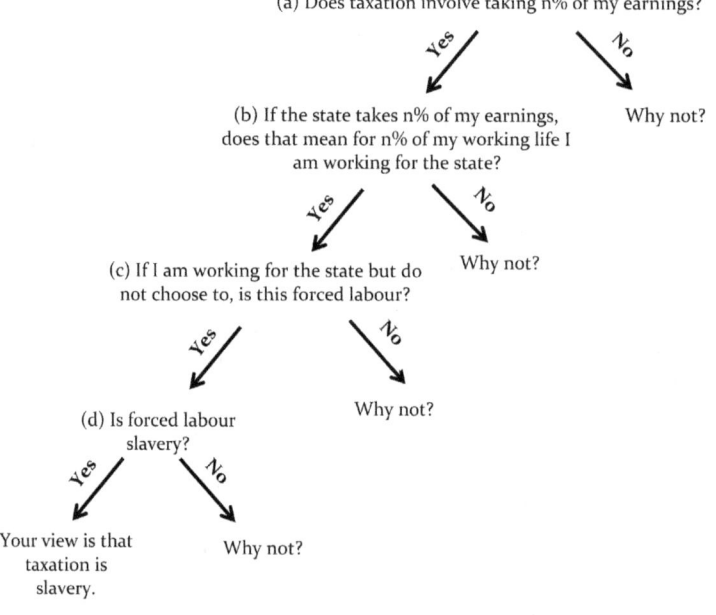

Now, analyse the argument in standard form:

1. *Taxation involves the state taking n% of my earnings.*
2. *If n% of my earnings are taken, then n% of my working life I am working for the state.*
3. *I do not choose to work for the state.*
4. *Therefore, I am being forced to work for the state.*
5. *Forced labour is slavery.*
6. *Therefore, taxation is slavery.*

i. Is the argument valid (does the conclusion logically follow from the premises)?

ii. Are premises 1–3 and 5 true?

iii. For each erroneous premise, explain the error.

iv. If you do accept the argument, explain the reasons that support premises 1, 2, 3 and 5.

With the arguments now in place, pupils should be sufficiently equipped to embark on an extended piece of writing which addresses arguments and counterarguments on the question below and incorporates the bullet-pointed concepts.

- **Extended writing:** Is it wrong to tax the rich to help the poor?

  ○ Libertarianism (Nozick)

  ○ Natural right and legal right (Locke)

  ○ Justice in acquisition

  ○ Justice in transfer

  ○ Consent

There's a lot to juggle here, so as a guide, present a few of the available positions so pupils can work out where they stand.

a. *Redistributive taxation is wrong because property is a natural right and should therefore be an absolute legal right, meaning taxation of justly acquired wealth is theft/slavery.*

b. *Redistributive taxation is wrong because, whilst not a natural right, property should still be an absolute legal right, meaning taxation of justly acquired wealth is theft/slavery.*

c. *Redistributive taxation is not wrong because property is not a natural right and it shouldn't be an absolute legal right. Therefore, taxation is not theft/slavery.*

d. *Redistributive taxation is not wrong because, though property is a natural right and ought to be an absolute legal right, vast wealth is not a person's property because it is never justly acquired.*

References

Chroust, H. & Affeldt, R. J. (1951). The Problem of Private Property, According to St Thomas Aquinas. *Marquette Law Review*, 34(3), 151–182.

Hume, D. (1978) [1739]. *A Treatise of Human Nature*. Clarendon Press.

Locke, J. (1988) [1689]. *Two Treatises of Government*, P. Laslett (Ed.). Cambridge University Press.

Nozick, R. (1974). *Anarchy, State, and Utopia*. Blackwell.

Borders

Key Questions

- Is there a human right to immigrate?
- Do states have the right to exclude?
- Do states have the right to exclude on racial grounds?
- Does the right of states to self-determination supersede the right to immigrate?
- Is the right to immigrate necessitated by the freedom rights enshrined in the Universal Declaration of Human Rights?
- Does equality of opportunity necessitate the right to immigrate?

Activity 1

Ask pupils to imagine that they have control over the UK's borders. They are presented with a list of people who have arrived in the UK and are seeking permission to remain here. Their task is to determine which applications to approve.

Welcome or not?

a. *A Hong Kong businessman with a net worth of £35 million.*

b. *An unemployed Brazilian with no qualifications who wants to live with a Brit she has been in an online relationship with for several years.*

c. *A non-English-speaking low-skilled Pakistani with a criminal record whose family has been living in the UK for several years.*

> d. *A gay man who faces persecution in his native country for his sexual orientation.*
>
> e. *A Russian journalist who wants to live in a country with greater press freedom.*
>
> f. *A virulent Canadian republican who is on a mission to persuade the British to abolish the monarchy.*
>
> g. *A middle-aged man with kidney disease whose native country, Somalia, lacks a healthcare system capable of giving him the treatment he needs. He wishes to reside in the UK in order to access the NHS.*
>
> h. *An exceptionally gifted mathematics student who wishes to study at a UK university but fully intends to leave once her degree is completed.*
>
> i. *An Ethiopian family fleeing drought and famine.*

Following this, ask the class to determine which of the applicants it would *be morally impermissible* to deny entry to. They should then complete the following claims:

- *The UK ought not to admit the following people... This is because...*
- *It would be morally impermissible to exclude the following people... This is because...*

> **Fact Check**
>
> The UK is a signatory to the 1951 Refugee Convention and is thus legally obliged to ensure the safety of those who are unable or unwilling to return to their country of origin owing to a well-founded fear of being persecuted for reasons of race, religion, nationality, membership of a particular social group, or political opinion. As such the UK would likely have legal obligations to case d). Those fleeing natural disasters do not satisfy the refugee criteria outlined in the 1951 convention, which is centred on the threat of persecution. Case h) would therefore not be entitled to the legal protections of a refugee.

Activity 2

Ask pupils to imagine a series of countries exercising their self-determination and sovereignty by permanently forbidding entry or access to certain areas within their territories to citizens of other countries. In any of these cases, do pupils think the country in question should be under international legal obligations to allow access to their territories?

   a. *Italy permanently preventing access to Venice.*

   b. *Saudi Arabia permanently preventing access to Mecca.*

   c. *Egypt permanently preventing access to the pyramids.*

   d. *The US permanently preventing access to the Grand Canyon.*

Drawing on the cases in activities 1 and 2, pupils should endeavour to make the case for both perspectives before determining which is the more convincing:

- *States should have the absolute right to control and regulate entry to their territories by those who are not citizens because…*

- *States should not have the absolute right to control and regulate entry to their territories by those who are not citizens because…*

An additional way to approach the second statement would be to question whether the right to exclude would weaken with profound population decline. If, for instance, a deadly pandemic struck the US leaving the entire land mass with a population of, say, 2,000, or even just 2, surviving Americans, would the remaining few still have the right to exclude?

Activity 3

Let's test the limits of national self-determination, specifically the right to exclude, by looking at the White Australia policy. Present the following details:

- On January 1st, 1901, the British parliament passed legislation allowing the six colonies of Australia to federate into a self-governing nation.

- In March 1901, an editorial in the *Sydney Morning Herald* outlined what it viewed as a legislative priority for the new nation: 'The experience of all countries shows the danger of unrestricted coloured immigration and if we are to have "a white Australia", the Federal Parliament must devote its attention to the matter at an early stage.'[1]

- While debating an immigration bill, the Labor member for South Melbourne expressed similar sentiments: 'Let us keep before us the noble ideal of a white Australia, a snow-white Australia if you will. Let us be pure and spotless' (Quoted in Evans, 2001, p. 46).

- The eventual Commonwealth Immigration Restriction Act became law in December that year. The aim of this legislation was to limit non-British immigration to Australia and create a racially homogenous population.

- Immigrants could be required to take a dictation test. This involved writing down 50 words in a European language of the immigration officer's choosing. The test was designed to ensure that non-whites, or otherwise undesirable applicants, could be easily made to fail (in order to exclude the polyglot communist Egon Kisch, the immigration officer asked him to write in Gaelic).

- On its own terms, the White Australia policy was a success. The Asian population, which was only 1.25% of the population in 1901, had dwindled to 0.21% in the late 1940s. By 1947, the non-white population was just 1.3% (the 2021 non-white population in England and Wales was 18.3%).

In defence of the White Australia policy, an Australian minister of immigration said:

> We seek to create a homogeneous nation. Can anyone reasonably object to that? Is not this the elementary right of every government, to decide the composition of the nation? It is just the same prerogative as the head of a family exercises as to who is to live in his own house. (Quoted in Carens, 1988, p. 45)

- Enquiry Question: Should countries have the right to racial exclusion?

Present the following argument from Christopher Wellman (2014):

> [A]s much as I abhor racism, I believe that racist individuals cannot permissibly be forced to marry someone (or adopt a child) outside of their race. And if the importance of freedom of association entitles racist individuals to marry exclusively within their race, why does it not similarly entitle racist citizens to exclude immigrants based upon race? At the very least, one must explain why the immigration case is dissimilar to the marital one. (p. 206)

Wellman ends the passage by issuing a challenge to determine whether there is a crucial dissimilarity between an individual's right to freedom of association and a nation's right to exclude. To meet this challenge, have pupils complete the schematic below, choosing between one of these two operators, ~ (similar to) or ≁ (not similar to):

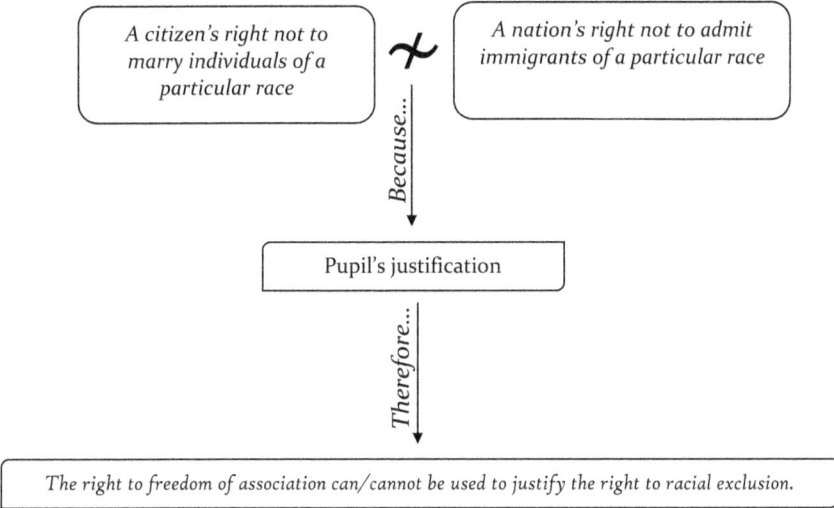

Wellman uses the same analogy to support the right to exclude *tout court:*

And just as an individual's freedom of association entitles one to remain single, a legitimate state's freedom of association entitles it to exclude all foreigners from its political community. (p. 187)

Have pupils repeat the previous task to see whether these different points make the analogy any more or less successful:

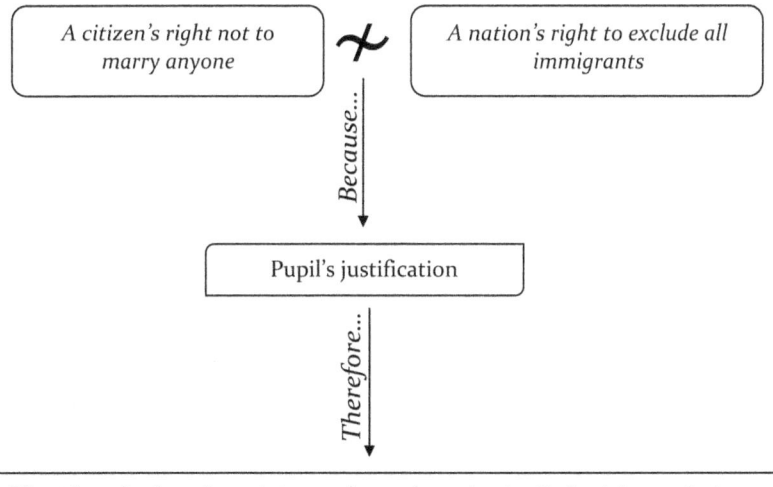

Michael Walzer (1983) has offered this justification for the right to exclude:

> The distinctiveness of cultures and groups depends upon closure and, without it, cannot be conceived as a stable feature of human life ... Admission and exclusion are at the core of communal independence. They suggest the deepest meaning of self-determination. Without them, there could not be communities of character, historically stable, ongoing associations of men and women with some special commitment to one another and some special sense of their common life. (pp. 39, 62)

Walzer suggests that free movement would threaten the existence of cultural particularity. It would also undo and undermine the special bonds that obtain between people within a community. Let's try to present his views in standard form. Ask the pupils to identify which of the premises (3) are not explicitly stated by Walzer in the extract.

1. *Communities of character are valuable because they foster special commitments between people.*
2. *Communities of character require the right to exclude.*
3. *The good of sustaining communities of character supersedes the good of individuals' right to free movement.*
4. *Therefore, communities (or states) should have the right to exclude.*

1. *The existence of a variety of distinct cultures is valuable.*
2. *Distinct cultures require the right to exclude.*
3. *The good of sustaining distinct cultures supersedes the good of individuals' right to free movement.*
4. *Therefore, states should have the right to exclude (in order to protect their distinct cultures).*

- Enquiry Question: Do the facts outlined below regarding movement within a state prove that the 2nd premises in Walzer's arguments are wrong?

People have an absolute right to freedom of movement within the UK: a Mancunian can move to London, if they wish, or a Londoner to Glasgow, or a Glaswegian to Liverpool, or a Liverpudlian to Swansea. This, however, hasn't resulted in any of these cities losing their particular cultures or character (*most residents of these cities would regard them as having distinct and unique identities*).

> **Fact Check**
>
> Article 12 of the Covenant on Civil and Political Rights, which the UK ratified in 1976, ensures that 'Everyone lawfully within the territory of a State shall, within that territory, have the right to liberty of movement and freedom to choose his residence.'

Activity 4

In Activity 1, did any pupil opine that it would be impermissible to exclude any of the applicants? Both Kieran Oberman and Joseph Carens effectively hold this view. They believe that there exists a human right to immigrate. The first argument we'll explore in support of this view comes from Carens (2013). He writes:

> Every reason why one might want to move within a state may also be a reason for moving between states. One might want a job; one might fall in love with someone from another country; one might want to belong to a religion that has few adherents in one's native state and many in another; one might want to pursue cultural opportunities that are only available in another land. The radical disjuncture that treats freedom of movement within the state as a human right while granting states discretionary control over freedom of movement across state borders makes no moral sense. (p. 239)

We'll distil this argument like so:

1. *If there is a legal right to move within states, then there ought to be a legal right to move between states.*
2. *There is a legal right to move within states.*
3. *Therefore, there ought to be a legal right to move within states.*

Have pupils assess the merits of this argument by completing the following schematic, using either of these logical connectives: → or ↛ to show the relationship between the two rights, where → shows that one right does entail the other, and ↛ shows the contrary.

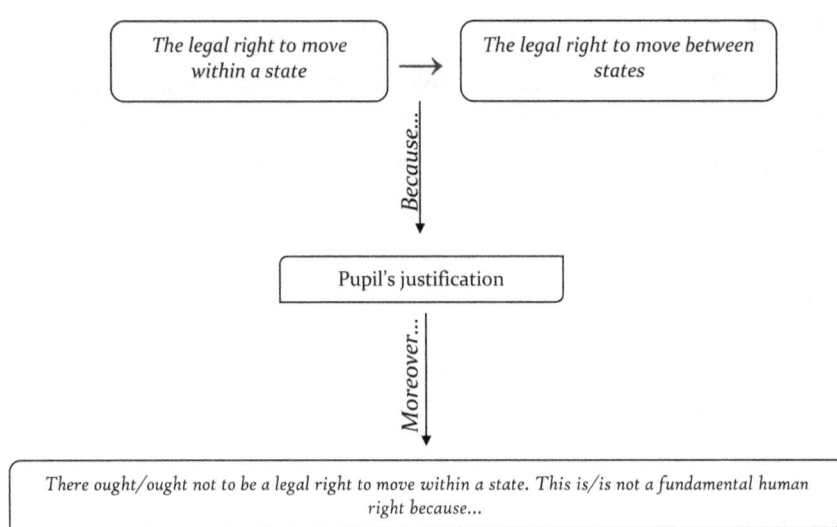

Activity 5

Kieran Oberman (2016) believes that the human right to immigrate is necessitated by our other human freedom rights, such as the right to association, religion, occupational choice and marry. He writes:

> Immigration restrictions place a bar between citizens and excluded foreigners. They interfere with the freedom of both to decide for themselves with whom they communicate, associate, worship, work, study, or marry. They cut people off from careers they may wish to pursue, religions they may wish to practice, ideas they may wish to explore, and people with whom they may wish to pursue relationships ... Our set of human freedom rights is thus incomplete without the human right to immigrate. (pp. 38)

Present the following Articles from the Universal Declaration of Human Rights to the class and ask pupils to think about how each might require a British individual the right to immigrate. They should think of specific examples with specific destinations.

- **Article 16**: Men and women of full age, without any limitation due to race, nationality or religion, have the right to marry and to found a family.
- **Article 18**: Everyone has the right to freedom of thought, conscience and religion; this right includes freedom to change his religion or belief, and freedom,

either alone or in community with others and in public or private, to manifest his religion or belief in teaching, practice, worship and observance.

- **Article 19**: Everyone has the right to freedom of opinion and expression.
- **Article 20:** Everyone has the right to freedom of peaceful assembly and association.
- **Article 23**: Everyone has the right to work, to free choice of employment.
- **Article 26**: Everyone has the right to education.

David Miller (2020) disagrees with Oberman that 'Our set of human freedom rights is thus incomplete without the human right to immigrate'. He writes:

> [A] person may have a specific aim that can only be realized by migrating, such as joining a particular religious cult, or studying a rare species of butterfly, but aims such as this are always liable to being thwarted by material costs, rules of property, or the unwillingness of other people to collaborate. There is no human right to carry out your ideal plan of life … [Human rights] are meant to protect basic human interests, or, in another formulation, provide the conditions for a minimally decent life. (pp. 400–401)

Let's isolate his two key claims here:

- *'There is no human right to carry out your ideal plan of life.'*
- *'[Human rights] are meant to protect basic human interests, or, in another formulation, provide the conditions for a minimally decent life.'*

Remind pupils that these are questions of justice and what human beings are fundamentally entitled to *qua* human beings. In the language of the Universal Declaration of Human Rights, our rights ought to recognise our 'inherent dignity' and honour our status as beings 'endowed with reason'. As such, we can say that we have a right to *x* if the denial of this right would compromise our dignity and fail to acknowledge our status as rational beings.

With that in mind, have pupils respond to Miller on Oberman's behalf. Of course, they might be sympathetic to Miller's points, but as an act of intellectual charity, ask them to momentarily suspend their own views and imagine how Oberman would or could reply to Miller. Having done that, they should determine which position they are more convinced by.

Thought Avenue

One possible argument for the right to immigrate would be grounded in the cosmopolitan claim that the earth fundamentally belongs to humankind as a whole. Jean-Jacques Rousseau (1998) expressed such a view when he wrote: *'The first man who, having*

> enclosed a piece of ground, bethought himself of saying "This is mine," and found people simple enough to believe him, was the real founder of civil society. Humanity would have been spared infinite crimes, wars, homicides, murders, if only someone had ripped up the fences or filled in the ditches and said, "Do not listen to this pretender! You are eternally lost if you do not remember that the fruits of the earth are everyone's property and that the land is no-one's property!"' (p. 27)
>
> The Roman emperor Marcus Aurelius also rejected the significance of borders: 'If mind is common to us, so also is reason, in virtue of which we are rational. If that is so, the reason which prescribes what is and is not to be done is also common. If that is so, law also is common; if that is so, we are citizens; if that is so, we partake in a kind of political system; if that is so, the universe is as it were a city' (Quoted in Schofield, 1991, p. 68). Since we share reason, we are subject to the same laws of reason (reason is universal), and being subject to the same laws means we are all citizens of the same polity.

Activity 6

Jospeh Carens (2015) has also argued for the right to immigrate from the principle of equality of opportunity and global justice. One's nationality, like one's ethnicity, is an arbitrary feature of one's identity and should not determine the limits of what one can hope to do and become. He writes:

> Freedom of movement is essential for equality of opportunity… This ideal of equal opportunity is intimately linked to the view that all human beings are of equal moral worth, that there are no natural hierarchies of birth that entitle people to advantageous social positions. But you have to be able to move to where the opportunities are in order to take advantage of them … The exclusion of so many poor and desperate people seems hard to justify from a perspective that takes seriously the claims of all individuals as free and equal moral persons.

Having looked at the passage, present Carens' position in the form of an argument tree. If pupils fall out of the tree with at any point, they need to explain why this is. If they reach the final fruit, they need to outline whether it reflects their views, and if not, to find the fault with the tree.

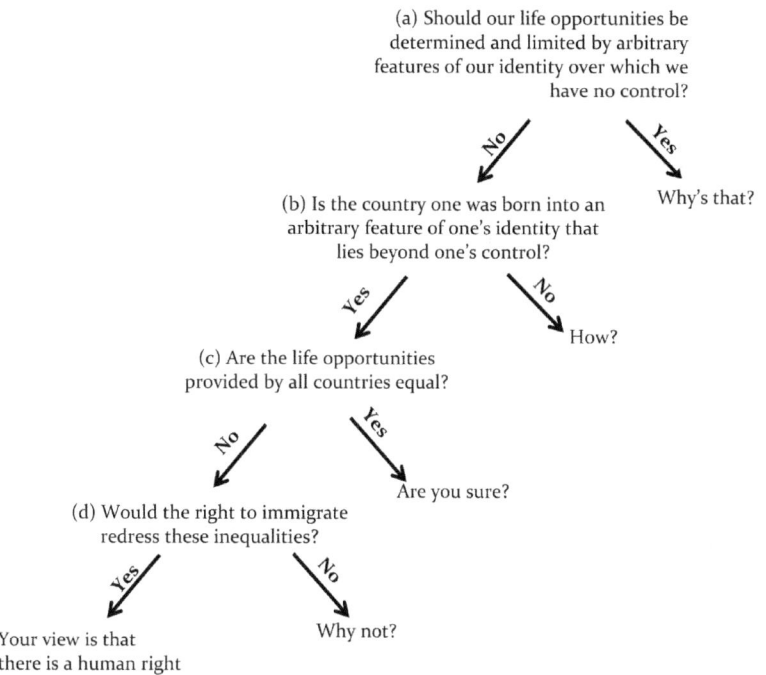

Having worked through this, pupils should be well placed to complete the following schematic using → or ↛ to show whether equality of opportunity does entail the right to immigrate.

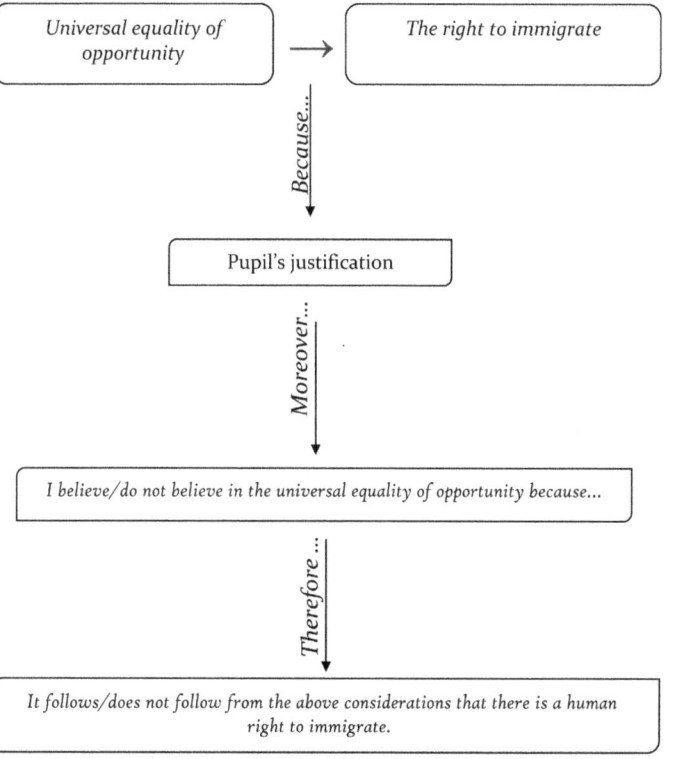

Activity 7

Pupils should now return to Activity 1 to see whether they wish to revise their answers to the first task. Finally, they should synthesise all of the above to offer their concluding view on whether there is a right to immigrate. In doing this, they should cite and dismiss, or cite and embrace, the arguments of Walzer, Wellman, Oberman, Miller and Carens.

Note

1 https://www.newspapers.com/article/the-sydney-morning-herald/24980288/

References

Carens, J. (1988). Nationalism and the Exclusion of Immigrants: Lessons from Australian Immigration Policy. In M. Gibney (Ed.), *Open Borders? Closed Societies? The Ethical and Political Issues* (pp. 41–61). Greenwood Press.

Carens, J. (2013). *The Ethics of Immigration.* Oxford University Press.

Carens, J. (2015). *The Case for Open Borders.* Open Democracy. https://www.opendemocracy.net/en/beyond-trafficking-and-slavery/case-for-open-borders/

Evans, R. (2001). The White Australia Policy. In J. Jupp (Ed.), *The Australian People: An Encyclopedia of the Nation, Its People and Their Origins* (pp. 44–49) (2nd ed.). Cambridge University Press.

Miller, D. (2020). Immigration. In T. Brooks (Ed.), *The Oxford Handbook of Global Justice* (pp. 395–411). Oxford University Press.

Oberman, K. (2016). Immigration as a Human Right. In S. Fine & L. Ypi (Eds.), *Migration in Political Theory: The Ethics of Movement and Membership* (pp. 32–57). Oxford University Press.

Rousseau, J.-J. (1998) [1755]. *Discourse on Inequality* (G. D. H. Cole Trans.). Kesinger Reprints.

Schofield, M. (1991). *The Stoic Idea of a City.* Cambridge University Press.

Walzer, M. (1983). *Spheres of Justice.* Basic Books.

Wellman, C. H. (2014). *Liberal Rights and Responsibilities: Essays on Citizenship and Sovereignty.* Oxford University Press.

10 Punishment

> **Key Questions**
>
> - What makes it permissible to harm those who have harmed?
> - Does anyone truly deserve to be harmed?
> - Does anyone truly deserve to die?
> - What is the justification for punishing acts that are *mala prohibita*?
> - Does the state have a right to take the lives of those who break the law?
> - Is capital punishment morally equivalent to torture?
> - Should we abolish prisons? (*Extension*)

PART I: PUNISHMENT

Most of us share the view that it is morally impermissible to intentionally harm another person. Strangely, however, our disapprobation disappears when the victim of our harm is someone who has broken the law or caused harm to another. Through a strange sort of alchemy, an act which would otherwise be seen as abhorrent – incarceration – is regarded as just. Is this transmutation of the bad into the good via the name of 'punishment' an intelligible or viable one? Is there any justification for this? This is the problem of punishment.

Most pupils do not recognise punishment as a problem. While they might appreciate that there are competing reasons for why we punish, the fact that we do punish is regarded as a given. The first aim is to try to alert them to and delineate the problem of punishment.

Activity 1

> This is the story of Alice Wood. In 2022 she was abducted and taken captive. Naturally, she wanted to escape but her captors showed no interest in her wishes or fears. In fact, it seems they wanted, and want, to see her suffer. She remains in captivity, utterly powerless, completely helpless. In all likelihood this victim of a profound wrong is going to be held captive for many, many years. Prior to her kidnapping this young woman was a philosophy student at the University of Manchester and had been offered a scholarship to undertake a master's degree at the University of Cambridge. That is no longer a possibility. Deprived of her liberty, confined to a cage, her life has effectively been taken from her. She will not be able to pursue an education, start a family, see the world, have a career, or even enjoy the everyday pleasures of going to the cinema, the theatre, seeing live music, going to restaurants, going for walks, being spontaneous. Obsessed with order and obedience, her captors control and regulate every second of her day. She is treated like a child and is told when to sleep, when to eat, when to wash. She has been stripped of her autonomy and free will, of the ability to live and move as she chooses, and lives at the mercy of her kidnappers, who often demean her.
>
> With the Universal Declaration of Human Rights in hand, it is clear that she is not being treated with the dignity a human being deserves: she is subject to 'degrading treatment' (Article 5), has no 'freedom of movement' (Article 13), cannot 'found a family' (Article 16), does not have the 'freedom of peaceful assembly and association', cannot take part in the government of her own country (Article 21), does not have 'the free choice of employment' (Article 23), and cannot 'participate in the cultural life of the community' (Article 27).
>
> Why did she become the victim of this profound wrong? Why has she been subject to these human rights abuses? Why has her humanity been so utterly disregarded?
>
> Because, on May 26th 2022, following her abduction (by the police, working at the state's behest), she was charged with the murder of her fiancé Ryan Watson after she ran him down in a car following an argument. In 2024 she was ultimately convicted of murder and sentenced to 18 years in prison (she admitted to running him down, even asking a neighbour to call an ambulance immediately after it had happened, but claimed she intended to scare him; the judge, however, concluded that her intent was to kill).

Ask pupils to read through the passage and highlight every characterisation of Alice Wood's situation that they disagree with. For each underlined phrase or sentence, pupils should complete the following sentence: '*This is a mischaracterisation because...*'

As a group discuss whether they agree with any of these statements:

1. *Her life has effectively been taken from her*
2. *She is subject to 'degrading treatment'*
3. *She is not being treated with the dignity a human being deserves*
4. *She is subject to human rights abuses*

- Enquiry Question: Is Alice Wood the victim of a profound wrong?

Development Questions:

- Is it morally permissible to deprive Wood of the rights identified?

- Is she being intentionally made to suffer?

- If she is not a victim of a profound wrong, what treatment of her would constitute a profound wrong and why?

- Would it be morally permissible *not* to punish her?

Development Thoughts:

In their book *Not Just Deserts: A Republican Theory of Criminal Justice* (2002) John Braithwaite and Philip Pettit question the penal value of incarcerating murderers. They highlight that the reason murder is not susceptible to deterrence is that these offences are often 'one-off crimes of passion' (p. 175). They cite a generic example of a 'woman who murders her husband in a moment of provoked anger', which sounds rather like Alice Wood, and write that such a woman 'who understands the enormity of what she has done, who is already punishing herself terribly with guilt and remorse, who is never likely to reoffend, it may be better to leave her in the hands of the informal social control of her family …' (pp. 175–176).

Gather these answers to arrive at a collective and multifarious completion of the following claim:

- *It is morally permissible to incarcerate Alice Wood because…*

Activity 2

After pupils have written down their own particular justification of her treatment, present this range of theories:

- **Retributivism:** punishment is morally permissible because the offender deserves to be punished. The severity of this punishment ought to be congruent with the severity of the offence.

    - One particular version of retributivism adheres to the principle of *lex talionis*, which says that the punishment ought not only be proportionate to the offence but equivalent to it. This has alarming implications for acts such as rape and torture.

- **Reductivism:** punishment is morally permissible if and only if the punishment helps to reduce the incidence of crime.

    - According to the **deterrence** approach, punishment ought to reduce the incidence of crime by providing a disincentive to commit crime.

- Punishment is justified insofar as it **incapacitates** the offender, thereby preventing them from reoffending.

- Punishment ought to reduce the incidence of crime by **reforming** the character of the offender.

● **Denunciation:** society ought to be able to express its abhorrence and denunciation of an offence, and this is achieved through punishment. The justification of punishment, then, is that it enables society to express its condemnation of certain acts and thereby reassert and champion its values. The difficulty of this approach is explaining why acts of denunciation necessitate the suffering of the offender. Why not, say, burn effigies of the offender instead? Why not sacrifice a lamb in the offender's stead? Why not stage collective days of rage where we gather and scream at the firmament?

● **Restorative justice:** punishment is morally permissible if and only if it repairs the effects of the offence and restores the relationship between the offender and those who have been harmed by the offence. To start with, the offender must acknowledge their guilt by taking responsibility for the crime and its consequences. Then they must seek to repair the damage caused. This might be achieved by compensating those harmed by the offence or performing some compensatory service for the affected community. Part of the aim is to create the conditions whereby the affected community will allow the offenders readmission into society. Often the process involves a dialogue (with the aid of mediators) between the offender and those affected by the offence.

● **Transformative justice:** Like restorative justice, transformative justice requires the offender to accept accountability and work to repair the damage done. Transformative justice, however, objects to the simplistic notion that the offender is wholly responsible and the victim wholly innocent. It believes that violence and abuse are influenced, perpetuated and reinforced by social conditions, which must be identified and changed. Transformative justice places the individual offender in a larger social context and aims to redress the social conditions (e.g. inequality, militarism, imperialism, classism, heteronormativity, patriarchy, misogyny, racism, ableism) that led them to offend. It believes in collective as well as individual responsibility, and it holds that the response to crime should not only be interpersonal but political.

Ask pupils to identify which approach to criminal justice each of the following summaries and extracts aligns with:

● 'But if any harm follows, then you must take life for life, eye for eye, tooth for tooth, hand for hand, foot for foot, burning for burning, wound for wound, and bruise for bruise.'

Exodus 21:23–25

- 'General prevention ought to be the chief end of punishment, as it is its real justification. If we could consider an offence which has been committed as an isolated fact, the like of which would never recur, punishment would be useless. It would be only adding one evil to another. But when we consider that an unpunished crime leaves the path of crime open not only to the same delinquent, but also to all those who may have the same motives and opportunities for entering upon it, we perceive that the punishment inflicted on the individual becomes a source of security to all. That punishment, which, considered in itself, appeared base and repugnant to all generous sentiments, is elevated to the first rank of benefits, when it is regarded not as an act of wrath or of vengeance against a guilty or unfortunate individual who has given way to mischievous inclinations, but as an indispensable sacrifice to the common safety.'
  Jeremy Bentham (1838, p. 396)

- **Bertrand Russell** (1961) believed we ought to approach the issue of punishment in a 'purely scientific spirit'. In the case of murder, for instance, 'We should ask simply: What is the best method of preventing murder?' (p. 31) He went on to observe that prisons are far less effective in 'curing criminal tendencies' than hospitals are in curing disease. To redress this asymmetry, he believed we ought to treat a criminal as we treat those suffering from plague. While both are a danger to the public and both require a curtailment of their liberty till they are no longer a danger, we regard both classes of people very differently: 'the man suffering from plague is an object of sympathy and commiseration, whereas the criminal is an object of execration' (ibid.). This attitudinal difference is 'quite irrational' and the reason prisons are much less successful than hospitals.

- 'If a builder build a house for someone, and does not construct it properly, and the house which he built fall in and kill its owner, then that builder shall be put to death. If it kill the son of the owner, the son of that builder shall be put to death.'
  Code of Hammurabi, a record of Babylonian laws dating 1792–1750 BCE (1904, p. 81)

- The criminologist **John Braithwaite** (1999) believes that justice ought to be a process by which those who have been affected by an offence come together to agree on how to repair the harm caused. The aim of justice should be to remedy the wounds of crime, not cause greater hurt. Punishment usually 'adds to the amount of hurt in the world, but justice has more meaning if it is about healing rather than hurting' (p. 1743). Essentially for Braithwaite, crime hurts and justice heals. And so the paradigm shift he wishes to see in criminal justice 'involves rejection of a justice that balances the hurt of the crime with proportionately hurtful punishment' (ibid.).

- The Danish philosopher **Søren Kierkegaard** (1998) believed that we have a duty to love, where love is a distinctively Christian concept (agape, caritas) that encompasses our neighbours, our enemies, the whole human race. Jesus, whom Kierkegaard believed Christians ought to live in imitation of, practiced this love when he refused to renounce Peter, who had betrayed and disavowed him. Through his love, he sought to help Peter become another person. In imitation of Jesus, and fulfilling our duty to love, Kierkegaard believed that we should 'never unlovingly give up on any human being or give up hope for that person, since it is possible that even the most prodigal son could still be saved, that even the most embittered enemy – alas, he who was your friend – it is still possible that he could again become your friend' (p. 254). To love, then, is to 'hope all things' and 'not despair, even at the last moment' because 'It is possible that the one who sank the deepest – alas, because he stood so high – it is still possible that he could again be raised up' (ibid.).

- 'The punishment for grave crimes should adequately reflect the revulsion felt by the great majority of citizens for them ... from this point of view there are some murders which, in the present state of public opinion, demand the most emphatic denunciation of all, namely the death penalty.'

  Lord Denning, *The Report of the Royal Commission on Capital Punishment, 1949–1953* (1953, para. 53)

- **Ernest van den Haag** was a prominent advocate of the death penalty. Echoing Thomas Aquinas's view that by acting contrary to reason sinners lose their human dignity and are therefore demoted to the moral status of animals, Haag (1986) wrote that 'the murderer has so dehumanised himself that he cannot remain among the living'. Execution, then, is 'the social recognition of his self-degradation' (p. 1669).

Having studied the different accounts of justice, ask pupils to return to their answer to the question on Alice Wood and ask them to identify which account of criminal justice their views are closest to.

Activity 3

To help pupils think through the implications of these different theories, present the following scenarios.

- **Scenario 1**
  A 1990 UK government White Paper reported the following:

  It was once believed that prison, properly used, could encourage a high proportion of offenders to start an honest life on their release. Nobody now regards imprisonment, in itself, as an effective means of reform for most prisoners ... The prospects of reforming offenders are usually much better if they stay in the community, provided the public is properly protected ... [M]uch crime is committed on impulse, given the opportunity presented by an open window or unlocked door, and it is committed by offenders who live from moment to moment; their crimes are as impulsive as the rest of their feckless, sad or pathetic lives. It is unrealistic to construct sentencing arrangements on the assumption that most offenders will weigh up the possibilities in advance and base their conduct on rational calculation. Often they do not. (Home Office, 1990, p. 6)

Firstly, ask pupils which theories of criminal justice would regard this description, if accurate, as rendering the prison system in England and Wales unjust.

Ask pupils to imagine that following this White paper that the government opted to abolish punishment. Having determined that the level of crime would be the same – the addition of opportunism and vigilantism cancelled out by the criminogenic effects of prison (which is described in the White Paper as 'an expensive way of making bad people worse') – and a vast amount of money would be saved. Of course, the law would still exist, and the police would seek to prevent crime. But those who committed offences would face no punishment. Would this situation be more just than the one we currently have?

- **Scenario 2**

    In the future a drug called Euphoria has been developed which rids those who take it of their malevolent impulses. While preserving the core features of a person's personality and in no way erasing their individuality, it manages to induce a general and lasting sense of well-being and gratitude. Those who have undergone a course of treatment are far less likely to act violently or deviously than individuals of a similar profile. With its wondrous properties the government has found that giving Euphoria to prisoners has a profoundly positive effect on recidivism rates. Following release, those who undergo a course of treatment become more motivated, hopeful and ambitious in pursuing their life goals.

    It's become apparent that the drug is more effective if the treatment occurs in a calm and supportive environment. As such, in order to unlock the full power of the drug, offenders (murderers, rapists and war criminals among them) are not sent to prison but are taken to a remote and exotic destination, which has come to be known as Euphoria Island, where they stay in luxury accommodation for a period of time. Rather than dwell on the immorality of their past actions, there they are taught not to think about their criminal offences (focusing on negative or violent experiences limits the effectiveness of the drug).

    Of course, were this 'punishment' to become public knowledge, others may deliberately seek to be convicted of an offence (besides the social damage this would do, resources are stretched and the government would struggle to deal with an explosion in 'prisoner' numbers) in the hope of a trip to the island, so the government maintains the pretence that offenders are incarcerated in prison. In fact, to deliver a more powerful deterrent, the government has enacted and done much to publicise a law which permits the torture of non-compliant prisoners (of course, this isn't actually practiced). After their treatment on Euphoria Island, convicts are happy to assist the government in maintaining this noble lie.

Before expressing their personal views on the justice of this system, pupils should determine which theories of criminal justice would support and which oppose this system.

- **Scenario 3**

    a. *After a night of partying and heavy drinking, James, despite the protestations of his friends, decided to drive home. He subsequently swerved off the road and killed a pedestrian.*

    b. *After a night of partying and heavy drinking, Jack, despite the protestations of his friends, decided to drive home. Despite swerving off the road at one point, there were no pedestrians on the pavement, so he made it home without causing any harm.*

Ask pupils to decide whether, having acted in exactly the same way, James and Jack deserve equally severe punishments. If not, why might this be a problem for retributivism? Which theories of punishment could respect the widely held intuition that James should face more severe consequences?

- **Scenario 4**

    A drug has been invented which has the ability to systematically rewire one's brain. Taking it erases one's memories and profoundly alters one's personality. Those who take it no longer know who they are or the lives they've led.

    Imagine there were a grotesquely sadistic person who had an overwhelming desire to kill, a desire that he ultimately satisfied. With the aim of avoiding prosecution by rendering himself unfit to plead (see the case of Lord Janner for reference), he acquired and took the brain-changing drug. Later when he was arrested and charged, he had no understanding of why this was happening and was horrified to hear of what he'd done.

Should the post-drug person be punished for the actions committed by the pre-drug sadist? Which theories of punishment could justify his facing some kind of penalty?

Activity 4

Below are diagrammatic summaries of the problems facing reductivism and retributivism. Though I've completed some, I'd suggest leaving pupils to complete the boxes with dashed lines. Once completed, they should draw on this to offer their evaluation of each approach, citing the most significant problem with it, if there are any, or an explanation of why, if they support the theory, the problems can be avoided e.g.

- *I think that the reductivist appeal to deterrence fails as a justification of punishment because…*

- *I think that retributivism (though not in the form of lex talionis) succeeds as a justification of punishment. Despite the putative problem that… I believe there is a credible reply to this which is that…*

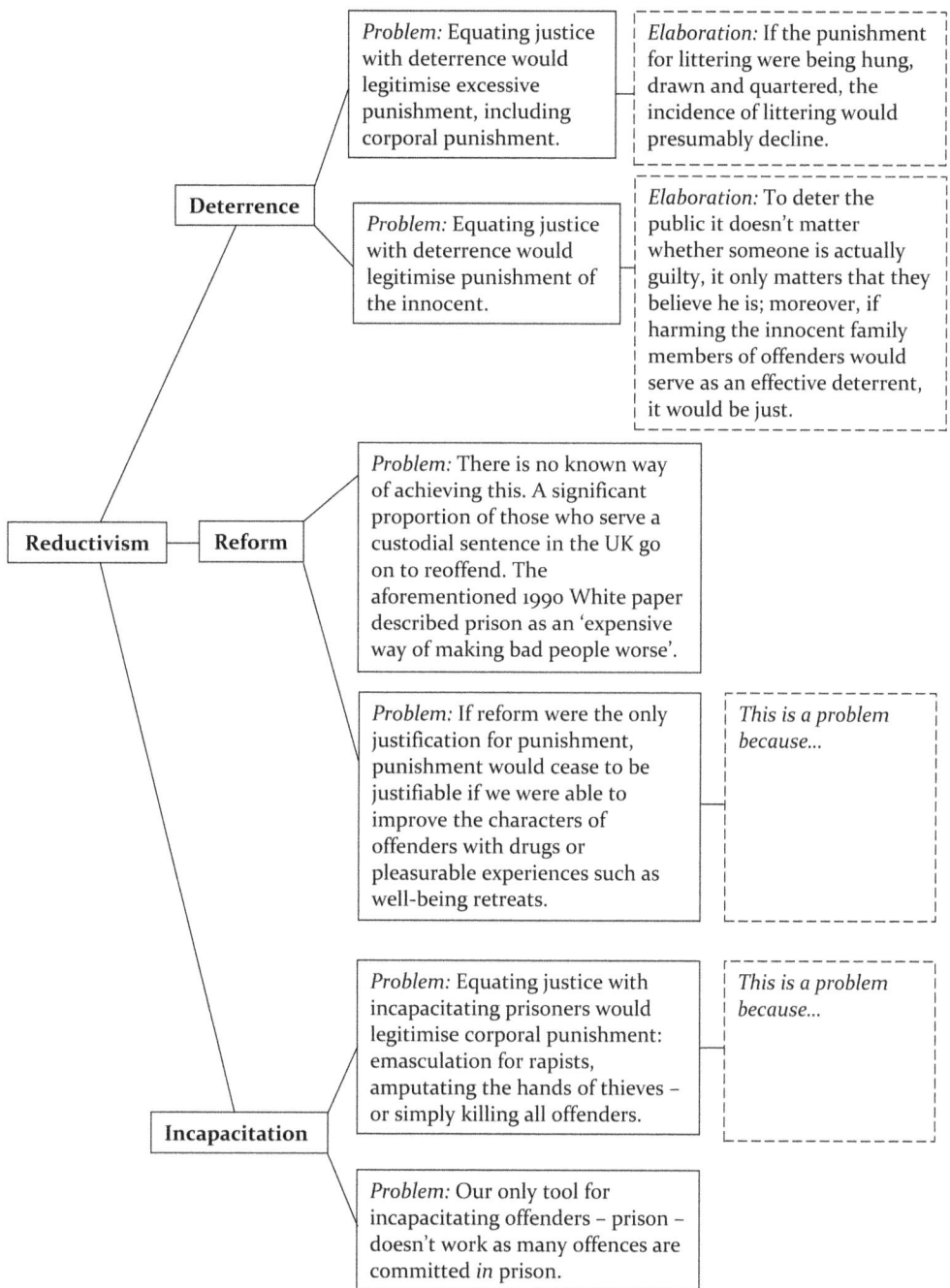

Retributivism

Problem: It cannot justify the punishment of *mala prohibita* crimes (crimes that do not correspond to moral wrongs) e.g. according to the Licensing Act 2003, which deems it an offence to knowingly serve a drunk person alcohol, it would be illegal for the landlord of a pub to serve a whiskey to his merrily drunk friend whom he was reminiscing with at the bar, yet it certainly wouldn't be immoral.

Problem: Retributivism conflates the act with the agent. An act may be morally abhorrent and deserving of censure, but it doesn't thereby follow that we should punish the person who performed the act, unless we are willing to define that person purely in terms of that offence. Condemning an act and punishing a person are two fundamentally different things, but retributivism treats them as one and the same.

Problem: It fails to honour the intuition that identical acts can sometimes warrant different punishments (such as Jack and James).

Problem: Some crimes are so unspeakably heinous that there is no proportionate punishment e.g. the crimes of Fred and Rose West.

Problem: As depicted in the film *Minority Report*, it is logically possible that determinism is true and we have no free will, it's also logically possible for clairvoyant beings to exist who can 'see' the future. If these things were true, while we may be justified in preventing crimes, we would not be justified in punishing those pre-offenders for their pre-crimes.

Problem: The logic behind retribution is unclear. If I deserve pain because I caused pain, why do I not deserve pleasure if I cause pleasure? If retributivism is correct, is it not an injustice that there are no institutions ensuring that the pleasure-givers are duly rewarded? If I help replace a stranger's flat tire, is it an injustice that the state doesn't allocate me an equivalent good?

Problem: If it is morally permissible to inflict harm on an offender because they deserve it, then it would not be wrong for a member of the public to inflict the necessary harm e.g. by keeping them captive in their house. According to retributivism that wouldn't be immoral.

Problem: If there were a pill that 'rewired' one's brain, erasing one's memories and completely altering one's personality, the retributivist approach to punishment could not justify punishing a person who committed an offence and then took the pill (because *they* didn't commit the offence).

Activity 5

As a final activity to help pupils develop a clearer and more concrete sense of their views on the justification for punishment, have them complete the table, only disclosing the actual punishments once finished.

Crime	Punishment in accordance with lex talionis	Appropriate punishment	Justification	Actual punishment
Between June 2015 and June 2016, Lucy Letby used a variety of methods to secretly attack a total of 13 babies on the neonatal ward she worked on as a nurse. Seven babies died as a result. In addition to being convicted of their murders, Letby was also found guilty of seven counts of attempted murder relating to six other babies.				[Whole life order.]
In 2011, Jacob Dunne got into an altercation in Nottingham on a night out. Following a single unprovoked punch to the jaw by Dunne, the victim fell to the ground. The fall resulted in a brain haemorrhage and he became comatose, dying nine days later. Dunne, who is now an advocate of restorative justice (he has given a TEDx talk, which can be found online, on the positive effect it has had on his life), was convicted of manslaughter.				[30 months in prison.]

In 1967, Robert Lipman and Claudie Delbarre took LSD together. Lipman had a bad trip and experienced the illusion of descending to the centre of the earth, where he fought off attacking snakes. Delbarre was later found dead. She had suffered two blows on the head causing haemorrhage of the brain but had died of asphyxia as a result of some eight inches of sheet having been crammed into her mouth. Lipman said he had no knowledge of what he was doing and no intention to harm her; in court it was not disputed that he had killed the victim in the course of this experience. He was charged with manslaughter.				[6 years in prison.]
On October 30th, 2016, during the 'killer clown craze', Michael March, a 17-year-old from Gateshead, tried to scare a woman by hitting the ground with an axe while wearing a clown mask as she walked by him. The woman was so terrified that she threw a brick at him in self-defence. The judge said, 'Carrying a real axe and threatening innocent people goes beyond anything that is acceptable at Halloween. Wearing a clown mask is not an offence but you had armed yourself with an axe, not a fake axe, a real one. The fact you were wearing a clown mask in an aggravating factor.' March was convicted of possession of a bladed article.				[6 months in a youth offender institution.]

In 2014, Samuel Lees drove through a large puddle splashing two children and their mother. The attending officer reported the following: 'The vehicle was driven through the puddle at a relatively fast speed making no attempt to slow down or avoid it. As a consequence, a large wave of water absolutely soaked the children and their parents. We could hear the screams from the children as they got drenched in the cold dirty rain water. His actions caused distress to the young children.' Lees, who said 'I did not mean to splash the family … It was one lapse of concentration and nothing more than that. People drive through puddles and people do get splashed – it's unavoidable unfortunately', was convicted of driving without due care and attention.				[£500 fine and six points removed his driving licence (as a new driver, this meant that he lost his licence).]

Activity 6

Having looked at a range of theories of punishment, pupils should now be in a position to complete something like the following:

I stand by/have changed my views on the moral permissibility of incarcerating Alice Wood. I believe that the fundamental justification for punishment is… This is because… The most problematic and misguided approach to punishment is… because… As such, I believe that the appropriate consequence for Alice Wood's actions is…

> **Thought Avenue**
>
> In 1974, Robert Blaue stabbed Jacolyn Woodhead after she had refused his advances. With a blood transfusion, it is believed that she would have lived. However, she was a Jehovah's Witness and rejected the transfusion on religious grounds. She subsequently died, and Blaue was charged with manslaughter. He later appealed on the basis that he did not cause her death because her refusal to accept a blood transfusion broke the causal chain between the stabbing and her death. The appeal was rejected.
>
> This isn't so much a normative question of how Blaue should have been punished but the metaphysical one of what offence he was guilty of in the first place. I include it as tangential point of interest, with the question being: Was his conviction accurate? Did Blaue kill Woodhead?

PART II: CAPITAL PUNISHMENT

Activity 1

The first thing to clarify is which theories of punishment the death penalty violates: reform, restorative justice and transformative justice. Following this, have pupils think of rebuttals to the counterarguments on the following pages, creating argument streams for each point which end with their verdict of whether the argument succeeds or fails, like so:

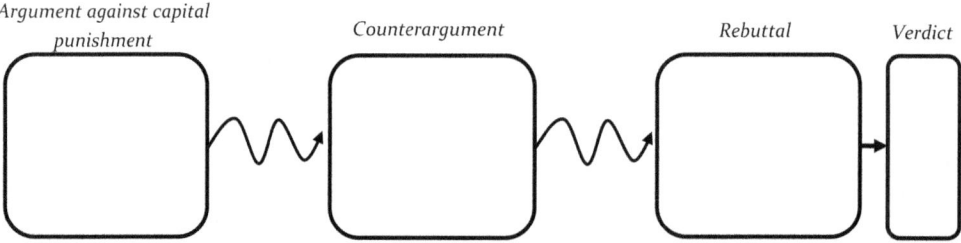

Humans are fallible (between 1989–2020 the use of DNA testing has established 375 wrongful convictions in the US with 69% of these cases involving eyewitness misidentification – innocenceproject.org). Inevitably, innocent people will be executed (between 1973–2023, 196 people in the US were sentenced to death and later exonerated – deathpenaltyinfo.org). Unlike a prison sentence, capital punishment cannot be overturned or compensated for if it transpires there has been a wrongful conviction.	According to Ernest van den Haag (1986), 'for those who think the death penalty just, miscarriages of justice are offset by the moral benefits and the usefulness of doing justice' (p. 1665). Analogously, driving is legal despite the fact that well over 1,000 people die in the UK every year in road collisions. Here, as in capital punishment, the advantages, whether moral or material, outweigh the unintended costs.
The financial cost to the state of capital punishment far exceeds the costs of lifetime incarceration.	The value of achieving justice is infinitely greater than the economic gain of not doing so.
Capital punishment violates Article 3 of the Universal Declaration of Human Rights: the right to life.	Rights are conditional and can be forfeited. A prison sentence similarly deprives a person of their liberty, but is not a violation of the right to liberty because the criminal forfeits that right.
The right to life is unique. Unlike other rights, which can be forfeited, the right to life is absolute.	If the right to life were absolute, this would render killing people in self-defence or in war morally impermissible.
A great deal of evidence indicates that capital punishment doesn't work as a deterrent. The relative murder rates in the US states where capital punishment is used to those where it is not are not comparable.	Its effectiveness as a deterrent is irrelevant. The value of the death penalty lies in its retributive and denunciatory functions. As was said by the Supreme Court in 1976, 'The decision that capital punishment may be the appropriate sanction in extreme cases is an expression of the community's belief that certain crimes are themselves so grievous an affront to humanity that the only adequate response may be the penalty of death.'

All human life is sacred.	Two replies: i. If this claim cannot be justified without reference to a deity, it is irrelevant to the UK, where the fastest-growing religious affiliation is 'no religion'. ii. While all human life might be sacred, the murderer has so dehumanised himself that he can no longer be considered a person. As Thomas Aquinas said, killing the wicked is no worse than killing an animal.
Capital punishment violates Article 5 of the Universal Declaration of Human Rights, which states that no one shall be subject to 'cruel, inhuman or degrading' punishment.	Capital punishment is more humane than life imprisonment. It is better not to exist than to live a monotonous life, which, in J. S. Mill's words, is 'debarred from all pleasant sights and sounds, and cut off from all earthly hope'. Mill (1868) argues that '[i]t is not human life only, not human life as such, that ought to be sacred to us, but human feelings. The human capacity of suffering is what we should cause to be respected, not the mere capacity of existing'.
Capital punishment fails as a form of retributive justice for the punishment is, in most cases, disproportionate to the offence. As Albert Camus (2020) wrote, '[W]hat is capital punishment but the most premeditated of murders, to which no criminal's deed, however calculated it may be, can be compared? For there to be equivalence, the death penalty would have to punish a criminal who had warned his victim of the date at which he would inflict a horrible death on him and who, from that moment onward, had confined him at his mercy for months' (p. 35).	Though it may fail as a proportionate punishment, this is not because it is too severe. The offender dies with the comforting knowledge that their death serves the noble end of upholding justice. It would be more just if the offender were executed without notice or forewarning.
My existence must fall beyond state control because my existence is not a privilege of my citizenship but a condition of it. The state, in other words, is not responsible for my existence, no one is. The act of bestowing or annihilating existence requires a metaphysical, not a political, justification. Just as suicide is not illegal because my existence is not a possession of the state, neither should capital punishment.	There is no distinction between the metaphysical and the political since, as St Paul explained, 'the authorities that exist have been established by God' (Romans 13:1). If the state is acting at God's behest, then capital punishment is effectively ordained by one's creator. He is responsible for your existence.

Activity 2

Does capital punishment violate Article 5 of the Universal Declaration of Human Rights, which asserts that 'No one shall be subjected to torture or to cruel, inhuman or degrading treatment or punishment'? Jeffrey Reiman (1985) argues that execution is morally similar to torture and as a practice it is an impediment to 'the taming of the human species that we call civilization'. Even if an offender deserves to die, it does not necessarily follow, he argues, that we ought to kill them (similarly, it would be wrong to rape the rapist or beat the assaulter, even if this is what they deserve). The implication of his position is that there are more important things than justice, and our status as civilised beings is one of those. He writes:

> I believe we view torture as especially awful because of two of its features, which also characterize execution: intense pain and the spectacle of one human being completely subject to the power of another ... By placing execution alongside torture in the category of things we will never do to our fellow human beings even when they deserve them, we broadcast the message that totally subjugating a person to the power of others and confronting him with the advent of his own humanly administered demise is too horrible to be done by civilized human beings to their fellows even when they have earned it: too horrible to do, and too horrible to be capable of doing. (pp. 134, 142)

Having discussed the passage, pupils should complete the following argument schematic:

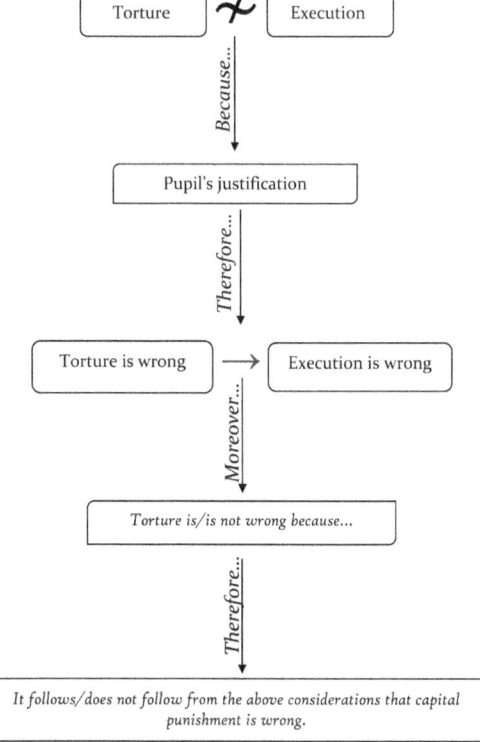

Present Jacques Louis David's painting 'The Death of Socrates', explaining that it depicts the moment just prior to Socrates's self-administered execution following an earlier conviction by the Athenian court. Ask whether this – the stolid and dignified acceptance of his punishment – might present a problem for Reiman's argument. Is there a crucial difference between execution and torture that while someone of a sufficiently phlegmatic disposition can face death with calm acceptance, even with a belief in the justice of it, the same is not true of torture? Indeed, where is the barbarity in David's painting? Are we faced with an affront to our values as civilised beings?

To accompany the painting, here is Plato's (1942) description from the *Phaedo* of his final moments:

Crito made a sign to the servant, who was standing by; and he went out, and having been absent for some time, returned with the jailer carrying the cup of poison. Socrates said: You, my good friend, who are experienced in these matters, shall give me directions how I am to proceed. The man answered: You have only to walk about until your legs are heavy, and then to lie down, and the poison will act. At the same time he handed the cup to Socrates, who in the easiest and gentlest manner, without the least fear or change of colour or feature, looking at the man with all his eyes, Echecrates, as his manner was, took the cup and said: What do you say about making a libation out of this cup to any god? May I, or not? The man answered: We only prepare, Socrates, just so much as we deem enough. I understand, he said: but I may and must ask the gods to prosper my journey from this to the other world—even so—and so be it according to my prayer. Then raising the cup to his lips, quite readily and cheerfully he drank off the poison. And hitherto most of us had been able to control our sorrow; but now when we saw him drinking, and saw too that he had finished the draught, we could no longer forbear, and in spite of myself my own tears were flowing fast; so that I covered my face and wept, not for him, but at the thought of my own calamity in having to part from such a friend. Nor was I the first; for Crito, when he found himself unable to restrain his tears, had got up, and I followed; and at that moment, Apollodorus, who had been weeping all the time, broke out in a loud and passionate cry which made cowards of us all. Socrates alone retained his calmness: What is this strange outcry? he said. I sent away the women mainly in order that they might not misbehave in this way, for I have been told that a man should die in peace. (p. 152)

> **Thought Avenue**
>
> In Iran, under the *qisas* (retribution in kind) principle, the next of kin of a murder victim must decide the murderer's fate: execution, or forgiveness in exchange for 'blood money', known as *diya* (the latter option still leads to a prison sentence of up to 10 years at the judge's discretion). Families can request any amount of money they please. Those who choose capital punishment for the offender must be present at the execution and are encouraged to participate. In 2021, the execution of Maryam Karimi was carried out by her own daughter. Is there any sense or wisdom in this system of justice?

Extension Material

Prison Abolition

Following the murder of George Floyd in 2020 by a police officer and the Black Lives Matter movement it catalysed, prison abolitionism has received a considerable degree of mainstream media and political attention. Many activists within BLM advocate abolition and believe that the murder of citizens, particularly Black citizens such as Floyd, is an inevitable outcome of seeking carceral and punitive solutions to crime. Though abolitionism has gained prominence in recent years, it is a project that has been growing, particularly in the US, for several decades. The points below address some of the key ideas and antecedents.

- As indicated by the following passage from the New Testament, Jesus was arguably in favour of prison abolition.

  > He went to Nazareth, where he had been brought up, and on the Sabbath day he went into the synagogue, as was his custom. He stood up to read, and the scroll of the prophet Isaiah was handed to him. Unrolling it, he found the place where it is written:

  > "The Spirit of the Lord is on me,
  > because he has anointed me
  > to proclaim good news to the poor.
  > He has sent me to proclaim freedom for the prisoners
  > and recovery of sight for the blind,
  > to set the oppressed free,
  > to proclaim the year of the Lord's favour."
  >
  > Luke 4:16–19

- Charles Dickens (1882) wrote of his visit to an American prison in 1842, where he witnessed prisoners living in solitary confinement, a state he described as tantamount to being buried alive. He wrote:

  > 'I believe it, in its effects, to be cruel and wrong. In its intention, I am well convinced that it is kind, humane, and meant for reformation; but I am persuaded that those who devised this system of Prison Discipline, and those benevolent gentlemen who carry it into execution, do not know what it is that they are doing. I believe that very few men are capable of estimating the immense amount of torture and agony which this dreadful punishment, prolonged for years, inflicts upon the sufferers ... I am only the more convinced that there is a depth of terrible endurance in it which none but the sufferers themselves can fathom, and which no man has a right to inflict upon his fellow-creature. I hold this slow and daily tampering with the mysteries of the brain, to be immeasurably worse than any torture of the body.' (p. 107)

- Addressing the inmates at the Cook County Jail in Chicago in 1902, the renowned American lawyer Clarence Darrow (2012) expressed his view that 'there ought to be no jails' (p. 4). He believed that the best approach to crime reduction was one that focused on achieving equality: 'Nobody would steal if he could get something of his own some easier way. Nobody will commit burglary when he has a house full' (p. 14). Jails are 'a blot upon any civilization' for they testify to the deficiencies of charity of the societies they exist within (p. 15).
- Article 5 of the Universal Declaration of Human Rights prohibits and states, 'No one shall be subjected to torture or to cruel, inhuman or degrading treatment or punishment.' As the prison abolitionist Angela Davis (2003) highlights, prisoners are 'denied access to their families, their communities, to educational opportunities, to productive and creative work, to physical and mental recreation' (p. 38). Does this meet the threshold of 'cruel, inhuman and degrading' treatment?
- The Old Testament outlines the following principles of justice:
   - 'The child will not share the guilt of the parent, nor will the parent share the guilt of the child,' Ezekiel 18:20.
   - 'Parents are not to be put to death for their children, nor children put to death for their parents; each will die for their own sin,' Deuteronomy 24:16.

   By depriving children of their parents for extended periods, prison arguably violates these principles of justice by imposing a penalty on the child.
- In *Abolitionism. Feminism. Now.* (2022) co-authors Angela Davis, Gina Dent and Erica Meiners frame abolitionism as an approach to criminal justice that seeks to place crime in a systemic and holistic context. They express the central abolitionist question like so: 'What would we have to change in our existing societies in order to render them less dependent on the putative security associated with carceral approaches to justice?' (p. 58)
- The '8 to Abolition' organisers Leila Raven, Mon Mohpatrra and Rachel Kuo (2020) claim that the resources used to fund the police and carceral system should instead be used on housing and health in order to redress systemic inequality and deprivation and ensure all people have access to economic opportunities. Our approach to criminal justice should not be one of 'retribution, revenge and penance', but seeking to make violence less likely to occur. This involves a paradigm shift that 'moves us away from questions like "Who is to blame?" and "Who will be punished?" toward questions [like] "What is needed to make things right? What changes can be made to prevent this harm from happening again?"'
- Abolitionists are often confronted with the challenge that prison abolition would leave us vulnerable to acts of extreme violence. In *We Do This Til' We Free Us: Abolitionist Organizing and Transforming Justice*, abolition activist Mariame Kaba (2021) has addressed this point by first highlighting

that the current system is not effective in ensuring our safety, particularly in relation to sexual violence, where 'most rapists never see the inside of a courtroom. Two-thirds of people who experience sexual violence never report it to anyone. Those who file police reports are often dissatisfied with the response. Additionally, police officers themselves commit sexual assault alarmingly often' (p. 52).

She explains that abolishing punishment doesn't mean tolerating violence or injustice. Instead of punishment, there will be 'consequences' where these 'might include restricted access to specific groups or spaces, or ineligibility for positions of leadership. Consequences might also include being required to make a public apology' (p. 199). Crucially, these consequences will be agreed upon by those directly affected by the harm that has been caused.

References

Bentham, J. (1838). The Principles of Penal Law. In J. Bowring (Ed.), *The Works of Jeremy Bentham*. Simpkin, Marshall, & Co.

Braithwaite, J. (1999). A Future Where Punishment Is Marginalized: Realistic or Utopian? *UCLA Law Review*, 46(6), 1727–1750.

Braithwaite, J. & Pettit, P. (2002). *Not Just Deserts: A Republican Theory of Criminal Justice*. Oxford University Press.

Camus, A. (2020). *Reflections on the Guillotine* (J. O'Brien, Trans.). Penguin Books.

Code of Hammurabi. (1904). Trans. By R. H. Francis. The University of Chicago Press.

Darrow, C. (2012). *Attorney for the Damned: Clarence Darrow in the Courtroom*, A. Weinberg (Ed.). University of Chicago Press.

Davis, A. (2003). *Are Prisons Obsolete?* Seven Stories Press.

Davis, A., Dent, G., Meiners, E. & Richie, B. (2022). *Abolition. Feminism. Now*. Penguin Books.

Dickens, C. (1882). *American Notes and Pictures from Italy*. Chapman and Hall.

Haag, E. (1986). The Ultimate Punishment: A Defense. *Harvard Law Review*, 99(7), 1662–1669.

Home Office. (1990). *Crime, Justice, and Protecting the Public*. Cm. 965. HMSO.

Kaba, M. (2021). *We Do This Til' We Free Us: Abolitionist Organizing and Transforming Justice*, T. Nopper (Ed.). Haymarket Books.

Kierkegaard, S. (1998). *Works of Love*, H. V. Hong & E. H. Hong (Eds. & Trans.). Princeton University Press.

Mill, J. S. (1868). *Parliamentary Debate on Capital Punishment within Prisons Bill*. Hansard. https://hansard.parliament.uk/Commons/1868-04-21/debates/a89d84e2-fc94-487d-a7e2-4274cdbe9e12/CapitalPunishmentWithinPrisonsBill%E2%80%94Bill36

Plato. (1942) [c. 380 BCE]. Phaedo. In L. R. Loomis (Ed.) & B. Jowett (Trans.), *Five Great Dialogues* (pp. 81–155). D. Van Nostrand Company.

Raven, L., Mohpatrra, M. & Kuo, R. (2020). *8 to Abolition Is Advocating to Abolish Police to Keep Us All Safe*. Teen Vogue. https://www.teenvogue.com/story/8-to-abolition-abolish-police-keep-us-safe-op-ed

Reiman, J. H. (1985). Justice, Civilization, and the Death Penalty: Answering van den Haag. *Philosophy & Public Affairs*, 14(2), 115–148.

Royal Commission on Capital Punishment 1949–1953. (1953). Cmd.8932. HMSO.

Russell, B. (1961). What I Believe. In R. Egner & L. Denonn (Eds.), *The Basic Writings of Bertrand Russell 1903–1959* (pp. 367–391). Simon and Schuster.

# The State

> **Key Questions**
>
> - Whom, if anyone, or what, if anything, should we obey?
> - Do we have a moral duty to obey the law?
> - Do we *owe* the state our obedience?
> - Have we consented to obeying the law?
> - Do we have a moral duty *not* to comply with state authority?
> - Do we have a right to civil disobedience? (*Extension*)
> - Do we have a right to uncivil disobedience? (*Extension*)

Start by explaining what we mean by the state and outlining its various powers, including: the power to take our income (via taxation), the power to evict us from our homes (via Compulsory Purchase Orders), the power to detain us in a hospital and forcibly administer medication (via the Mental Health Act 1983), the power to take children from their parents (via the Children Act 1989), the power to incarcerate us, and the power to enact conscription laws that force us to risk our lives in wars that serve its interests.

The question of political obligation is the question of whether we have a moral duty to obey the state by following the law.

Activity 1

Start with a couple of quick enquiry questions to introduce the topic.

- Enquiry Question (a): In the Ten Commandments issued by God, there is no rule stating that we must follow the Ten Commandments. Does this mean that Christians and Jews are free not to follow them?

- Enquiry Question (b): In the UK, there is no law stating that we must follow the law. Does that mean we are free not to follow them?

One analogous response to both questions is that a self-referential law or commandment ('You must obey all commandments/laws including this one') is not required because it's morally axiomatic that we must obey the law and God. In other words, the requirement to follow the law is itself not a legal duty but a moral one.

To probe this a little further, ask whether the following is a reasonable claim to make, and if so, what it is about God's nature that means his commands are binding:

> It goes without saying that a Jew or Christian ought to do what God commands.

Now, can we make the following analogous claim? If so, in what ways and to what extent does the state resemble God? And if not, why not? In what ways and to what extent is the state different to God?

> It goes without saying that a citizen ought to do what the state commands.

Activity 2

Brainstorm with the class the range of authorities that they are expected to obey. Nudge them towards the following: God (for the sake of this exercise assume His existence), teachers, parents, the law, their own conscience. Having done this, the next task is to convert their answers into a triangular hierarchy with the source of greatest authority (not the authority that has the most power over them, but the one that most deserves their obedience) at the top of the triangle, for example:

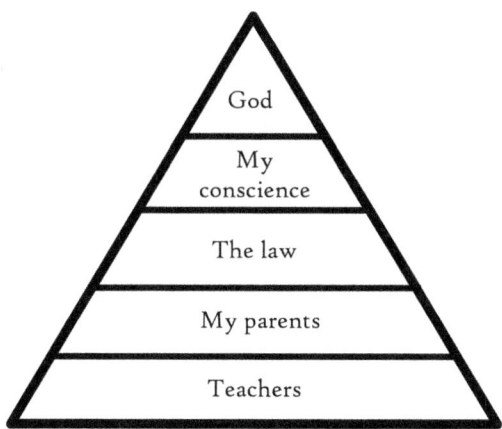

One way to think about this is to imagine each of these authorities issuing conflicting demands. Which should you follow?

Below the triangle, ask pupils to write the same order of authorities, but now in a row, using the size of their writing to illustrate the relative magnitude of authority, for instance:

God   My conscience   The law   My parents   Teachers

In 1963, Martin Luther King Jr. published an open letter from a jail in Birmingham, Alabama, where he was being held for violating a court injunction against civil rights marches. There he defended his illegal acts by citing St Augustine's claim that an unjust law is no law at all. He explained that any law that 'degrades human personality is unjust', and any person who breaks such pseudo-laws while willingly accepting imprisonment 'in order to arouse the conscience of the community over its injustice is in reality expressing the highest respect for law' (1986, pp. 293–294).

On the basis of this information, have pupils determine which source of authority they believe would stand at the summit of King's own triangle. Then repeat with each of the extracts presented below.

> I remember an answer which when quite young I was prompted to make to a valued adviser, who was wont to importune me with the dear old doctrines of the church. On my saying, What have I to do with the sacredness of traditions, if I live wholly from within? my friend suggested, — "But these impulses may be from below, not from above." I replied, "They do not seem to me to be such; but if I am the Devil's child, I will live then from the Devil." No law can be sacred to me but that of my nature. Good and bad are but names very readily transferable to that or this; the only right is what is after my constitution, the only wrong what is against it. A man is to carry himself in the presence of all opposition, as if every thing were titular and ephemeral but he. I am ashamed to think how easily we capitulate to badges and names, to large societies and dead institutions.
>
> Ralph Waldo Emerson (1985, pp. 178–179)

> True law is right reason conformable to nature, universal, unchangeable, eternal ... This law cannot be contradicted by any other law, and is not liable either to derogation or abrogation. Neither the senate nor the people can give us any dispensation for not obeying this universal law of justice. It needs no other expositor and interpreter than our own conscience. It is not one thing at Rome, and another at Athens; one thing today, and another tomorrow; but in all times and nations this universal law must forever reign, eternal and imperishable. It is the sovereign master and emperor of all beings. God himself is its author, its promulgator, its enforcer. And he who does not obey it flies from himself, and does violence to the very nature of man.
>
> Cicero (1894, pp. 437–438)

> Someone came and said, "Behold, the men whom you put in prison are in the temple, standing and teaching the people." Then the captain went with the officers, and brought

the apostles ... When they had brought them, they set them before the council. The high priest questioned them, saying, "Didn't we strictly command you not to teach in this name? Behold, you have filled Jerusalem with your teaching, and intend to bring this man's blood on us." But Peter and the apostles answered, "We must obey God rather than human beings!"

Acts 5:25–29

Let everyone be in subjection to the governing authorities, for there is no authority except from God, and those authorities who exist are established by God. So that he who sets himself in opposition to the authority rebels against what God has instituted; and they who thus resist shall bring the sentence of guilt on themselves.

Romans 13:1–2

Must the citizen ever for a moment, or in the least degree, resign his conscience to the legislator? Why has every man a conscience, then? I think that we should be men first, and subjects afterward. It is not desirable to cultivate a respect for the law, so much as for the right. The only obligation which I have a right to assume is to do at any time what I think right.

Henry David Thoreau (1995, p. 5)

These extracts may well have shaped and invigorated pupils' own views on this topic, and they should now be in a stronger position to complete the next task, which is to annotate their hierarchies of authority with explications:

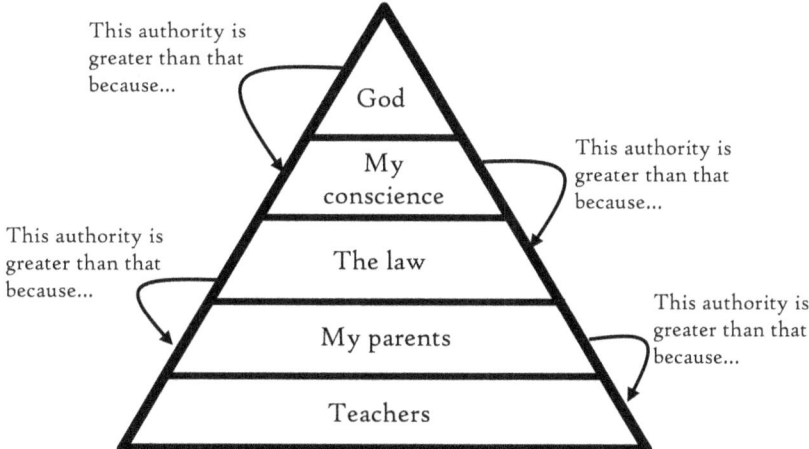

Activity 3

The above extracts address the question of which authority we ought to obey in the event of conflicting demands. Political obligation, however, isn't a question of whether we ought to obey the law above all else, but whether we ought to obey the law at all. Do we have *any* moral obligation to obey the law? Would it be morally permissible to violate the law simply because I wanted to?

This question of political obligation was a matter of life and death for Socrates:

> In 399 BCE, Socrates, at 70 years of age, was charged with impiety and corrupting the young. Socrates' friends begged him to flee Athens, but his inner voice, a personal spirit that had guided him throughout this life, was silent on the matter, indicating that there was no good reason to avoid the trial. And so before a jury of 501 Athenians Socrates defended himself.
>
> 'It is foolish to call me impious,' he argued, 'when I consider myself the god's gift to you. By encouraging you to think about goodness and how we ought to live, I have done this city the greatest possible service. If anything, I do not deserve punishment but gratitude.
>
> 'With respect to the charge of corrupting the young, how is this possible when I have never taught them a single thing? How am I capable of polluting their minds when I do not even know what I think?'
>
> His arguments failed to persuade the jury who, by a margin of 30 votes, sentenced him to death. While in jail awaiting execution Socrates was visited by his friend Crito who had come to help Socrates escape. Socrates said he would only leave with Crito on the condition that he could be persuaded that violating the law would be just. Crito failed in this and Socrates duly downed a cup of hemlock.

Before looking at Socrates' reasons (as presented by Plato) for not escaping, discuss the following:

- Enquiry Question: Would it have been wrong for Socrates to escape with Crito?

Following that, present the following extract from Plato's (1892) *Crito*:

> "In the first place did we [the state] not bring you into existence? Your father married your mother by our aid and begat you. Say whether you have any objection to urge against those of us who regulate marriage?" None, I should reply. "Or against those of us who regulate the system of nurture and education of children in which you were trained? ... [S]ince you were brought into the world and nurtured and educated by us, can you deny in the first place that you are our child and slave, as your fathers were before you? And if this is true you are not on equal terms with us; nor can you think that you have a right to do to us what we are doing to you. Would you have any right to strike or revile or do any other evil to a father or to your master, if you had one, when you have been struck or reviled by him, or received some other evil at his hands? – you would not say this? And because we think right to destroy you, do you think that you have any right to destroy us in return, and your country as far as in you lies? ... And when we are punished by her [the state], whether with imprisonment or stripes, the punishment is to be endured in silence; and if she [the state] leads us to wounds or death in battle, thither we follow as is right; neither may anyone yield or retreat or leave his rank, but whether in battle or in a court of law, or in any other place, he must do what his city and his country order him; or he must change their view of what is just: and if he may do no violence to his father or mother, much less may he do violence to his country ...

[A]fter having brought you into the world, and nurtured and educated you, and given you and every other citizen a share in every good that we had to give, we further proclaim and give the right to every Athenian, that if he does not like us when he has come of age and has seen the ways of the city, and made our acquaintance, he may go where he pleases and take his goods with him; and none of us laws will forbid him or interfere with him. Any of you who does not like us and the city, and who wants to go to a colony or to any other city, may go where he likes, and take his goods with him. But he who has experience of the manner in which we order justice and administer the State, and still remains, has entered into an implied contract that he will do as we command him. And he who disobeys us is, as we maintain, thrice wrong: first, because in disobeying us he is disobeying his parents; secondly, because we are the authors of his education; thirdly, because he has made an agreement with us that he will duly obey our commands ... (pp. 152–153)

To aid with comprehension, have pupils determine the following:

- *First paragraph:*

    1. What does Socrates compare the state to?

    2. In what ways do these two things resemble each other?

    3. As such, what is disobeying the state morally equivalent to?

- *Second paragraph:*

    1. What are citizens who dislike the state free to do?

    2. Those citizens who do not do this are thereby agreeing to what?

    3. As such, what is disobeying the state morally equivalent to?

Activity 4

Before analysing the claims made in the first paragraph, discuss the benefits that the state has arguably bestowed on us. This might include:

- Providing the medical services that ensure our safe birth and continued health.

- Providing education to ensure our intellectual and cultural development.

- Ensuring our safety and well-being, both domestically (via the police) and internationally (via the armed forces).

- Providing a justice system to protect us from unfair treatment.

- Providing housing.

- Overseeing and ensuring the continued operations of the infrastructure that makes society possible e.g. energy, water, transport.

178 Navigating the Moral Maze

Present the following summary of the first paragraph and ask pupils to complete the basic task of converting it into standard form.

The relationship between the state and its citizens is like the relationship between a parent and its children. Children have a moral duty to obey their parents, therefore citizens have a moral duty to obey the state.

In standard form:

1. *The relationship between the state and its citizens is like the relationship between a parent and its children.*
2. *Children have a moral duty to obey their parents.*
3. *Therefore, citizens have a moral duty to obey the state.*

Socrates' argument here approximates what is known as the association model of political obligation. Associative duties are those believed to exist simply by virtue of one's occupying a role in a special type of relationship, for instance, with friends, siblings, parents, neighbours. On this model of political obligation, citizenship is akin to friendship, with both entailing a set of associative duties. And just as children are born into a relationship with a parent, they are also born into a relationship with the state.

Socrates' way of convincing us that we have associative duties to the state is by highlighting the resemblance between the relationships between us and the state, on the one hand, and us and our parents, on the other. With arguments from analogy, the first task is to investigate the extent of the resemblance. Venn diagrams are helpful here, so have pupils complete the following:

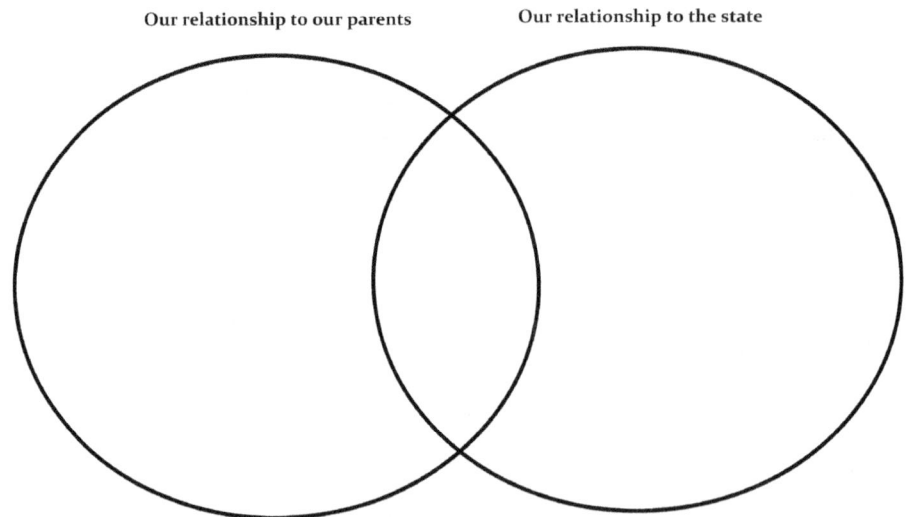

As a potential catalyst, present this comment made by Albert Einstein and consider what reasons he might have had for holding this view:

> The state to which I belong as citizen does not play the least role in my spiritual life; I regard allegiance to a government as a business matter, somewhat like the relationship with a life insurance company. (Quoted in Snyder, 1976, p. ix)

With the Venn complete, the task is to identify whether any of the qualities that don't feature in the overlap are significant enough to undermine the claim that there is a significant resemblance.

The next task is to evaluate premise 2. To this end, ask pupils to sort the following, sometimes conflicting, statements into logically consistent piles (one statement can go into more than pile, and there may need to be more than two piles). Of course, as ambivalent beings, this range of conflicting attitudes can exist within us, nevertheless, the aim is to establish precisely which attitudes are conflicting:

a. *I respect my parents.*

b. *I do not respect my parents.*

c. *I love my parents.*

d. *I hate my parents.*

e. *I feel gratitude to my parents.*

f. *I feel no gratitude to my parents.*

g. *I believe that my parents have authority over me.*

h. *My parents have no authority over me.*

i. *I always obey my parents.*

j. *I do not always obey my parents.*

k. *I believe that I do not owe my parents anything.*

l. *I believe that I am indebted to my parents.*

Since it may be believed that we ought to have certain attitudes towards our (good enough) parents, the aim of this exercise is to establish whether one can consistently disobey one's parents while holding these attitudes. Is it logically consistent to love, respect and feel gratitude towards one's parents while disobeying them? If so, then it seems obedience is not entailed by our associative attitudes.

Activity 5

Present the following summary of the argument in the second paragraph and have pupils convert it into standard form:

> *Those who live within a state are obliged to obey its laws. By not leaving the state, as we are free to do, we have consented to this obligation, and have thus entered into a contract with state (one that says we will obey the law). Since we have a moral duty to honour our contacts, we have a moral duty to obey the state.*

In standard form:

1. *Living within a state involves an obligation to obey its laws.*
2. *By not leaving the state, we have consented to this obligation.*
3. *By consenting to this obligation, we have thus entered into a contract with the state (one that says we will obey the law).*
4. *We have a moral duty to honour our contracts.*
5. *Therefore, we have a moral duty to obey the state.*

Socrates's argument here approximates the consent theory of political obligation. The form of consent that Socrates appeals to is tacit consent. As stated in premise 2, by virtue of not leaving the state, we have agreed to obey its laws. To think about this suggestion, ask pupils to consider an analogous case: the school rules.

- Enquiry Question: Have you consented to the school rules?

  Development Questions:

  ○ By not leaving the school, are you thereby consenting to its rules?

  ○ By not leaving a particular teacher's lesson, are you thereby consenting to that teacher's rules?

  ○ By breaking the school rules, are you violating your contract with the school?

  ○ Do any of your answers here also apply to the laws of the state?

Pupils may object that they do not choose to go to school, that their freedom to move schools is limited, and that even if they could move, all schools have similar rules. Addressing the last development question, ask whether analogous complaints can be made by the citizens of the UK? On this point, explore the extent to which they agree with David Hume's (1966) thoughts on this matter:

> *Can we seriously say that a poor peasant or artisan has a free choice to leave his country, when he knows no foreign language or manners, and lives, from day to day, by the small wages which he acquires? We may as well assert that a man, by remaining in a*

vessel, freely consents to the dominion of the master; though he was carried on board while asleep, and must leap into the ocean and perish, the moment he leaves her. (p. 462)

When the anarchist Emma Goldman was on trial in 1893 for inciting a riot, this exchange took place during the trial:

> Is there any government on earth whose laws you approve?
> No, sir, for they are all against the people.
> Why don't you leave this country if you don't like its laws?
> Where shall I go? Everywhere on earth the laws are against the poor, and they tell me I cannot go to heaven, nor do I want to go there.
>
> (Quoted in Birch, 2021, p. 143)

Present the two passages and ask pupils to determine whether Hume and Goldman are making the same or different points.

Activity 6

Before arriving at an overall synthesis of this topic's core ideas, we're going to turn to Robert Wolff's argument against political obligation from his book *In Defense of Anarchism*. His argument is not merely that we have no moral duty to obey the state, but that we have a moral duty *not* to obey the state. This doesn't mean that we should endeavour to break every law. It means we should never comply with the law, even if our actions do often coincide with it.

Start by presenting this passage from Wolff (1998) and task pupils with trying to explicate Wolff's reasoning. Given the centrality of the concept of autonomy, to enable greater understanding outline its etymology (*auto*. self and *nomos*. laws). This should help clarify the fact that the first sentence is effectively true by definition. The second claim is the pivotal one for which the passage provides no justification. This is where the substantive philosophical work needs to be done.

Concept Check

Anarchism is the view that the abolition of the state is both possible and desirable. The state's abolition is desirable because all forms of domination and coercion are impermissible. While **philosophical anarchism**, the theory associated with Robert Wolff, shares the belief that all authority is illegitimate, it is not committed to the political project of abolishing the state. Philosophical anarchism holds that autonomy and obedience are fundamentally incompatible, and given that we have an inviolable duty to act autonomously, we thereby have a duty to never obey the state, or any other authority. This theory is consistent with state's existence and is not in principle committed to achieving a stateless society.

> For the autonomous man, there is no such thing, strictly speaking, as a *command* ... The primary obligation of man is autonomy, the refusal to be ruled ... Insofar as a man fulfills

his obligation to make himself the author of his decisions, he will resist the state's claim to have authority over him. That is to say, he will deny that he has a duty to obey the laws of the state *simply because they are the laws*. (pp. 12, 18–19)

Use the following exegetical schematic to help pupils work through the extract.

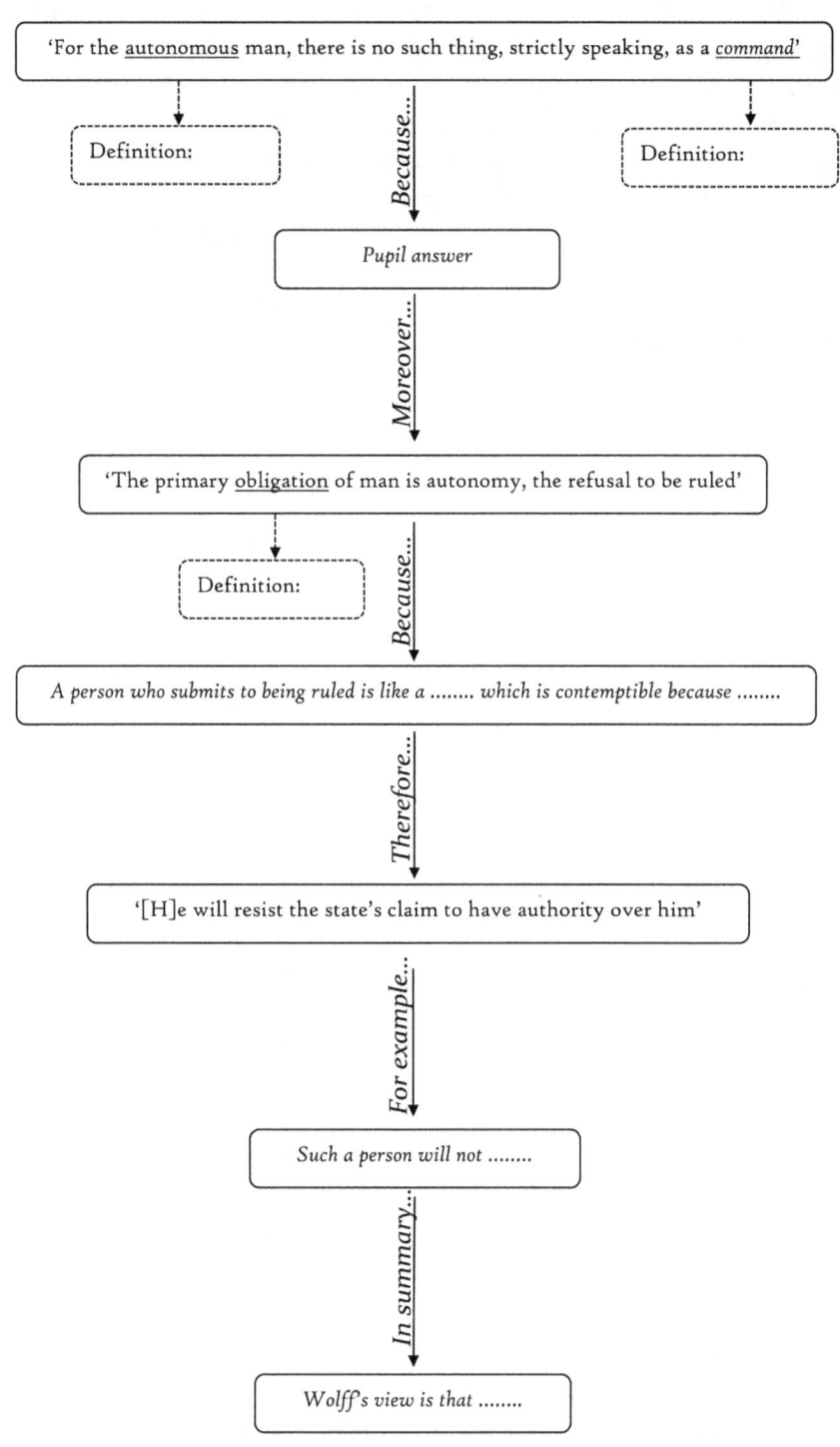

The schematic guides pupils to crack the second claim by way of analogy. The following thought experiment follows this approach by drawing an analogy between the compliant person and an android. This, of course, is just one possible way of making sense of Wolff's views. So, to further guide pupils' thinking, present the following scenario:

In Future School most pupils are human, but there are two new androids who recently joined the school. One of the androids, Goodroid, is programmed to follow orders from authority figures and perform helpful actions. If a teacher tells Goodroid to stop talking, it stops talking. If it sees a peer drop their books, it helps pick them up. Contrariwise, Badroid is programmed to disobey orders and perform unhelpful acts. If Badroid is told to stop talking, it talks even louder. If it sees a peer drop their books, it kicks and scatters them.

In Future School there is an annual ceremony where the most morally impressive pupil is rewarded and the most morally deficient person shamed. In most years Lola wins the former (she is an invariably kind and thoughtful person) and Honey receives the latter (she is an invariably boorish and self-centred person). However, this year Goodroid is rewarded and Badroid is shamed. Lola feels aggrieved by this, while Honey, of course, is relieved.

- Enquiry Question: Should Lola and Honey have respectively received the prize and the punishment?

Development Questions:

○ Is it possible to be good if one is not a free and self-conscious being?

○ Are the androids responsible for their actions?

Use this thought experiment to think about the necessary requirements for moral actions, then apply these to determine the soundness of the following argument:

1. *There is no such thing as a morally good android.*
2. *To act obediently is to act like an android.*
3. *Therefore, there are no morally good obedient acts.*
4. *We should always act morally.*
5. *Therefore, we should never act obediently.*
6. *Complying with the law is acting obediently.*
7. *Therefore, we should never comply with the law.*

Activity 7

Having investigated Socrates's two arguments for political obligation, pupils should have a good sense of whether they think the arguments are successful. As a final synthesising task, have them adopt the role of Crito and, utilising the ideas explored throughout this lesson, write a response to Socrates identifying the potential weaknesses in his arguments. Of course, if they are ultimately sympathetic to either of his arguments, they will also need to rebut these objections.

Extension Material

Civil Disobedience

- Even if we do have a moral duty to obey the law, is it ever permissible to violate that duty in the form of civil disobedience? Indeed, in the pursuit of justice, can one say that we ever have a moral duty to *break* the law?
- Civil disobedience is a non-violent and principled breach of the law. It is a public act meant to draw attention to an injustice in a bid to effect a change in the government's policies or laws. There is no attempt to evade punishment; receiving punishment is an integral part of the communicative act. In the words of John Rawls (1971), 'Civil disobedience is giving voice to conscientious and deeply held convictions; while it may warn and admonish, it is not itself a threat' (p. 366).
- Is it accurate to say, then, that civil disobedience doesn't violate political obligation since it still maintains a respect for the law and the authority of the state? And if those who engage in civil disobedience have a fundamental respect for the law, should they be punished? Should there exist a right to civil disobedience?
- Henry David Thoreau's refusal to pay the state poll tax in protest against slavery, the war on Mexico, and the treatment of Native Americans is a famous example of civil disobedience. He spent a night in jail and was released the next day after his aunt paid the tax.
- Greta Thunberg (2019) has said, '[E]veryone out there: it is now time for civil disobedience. It is time to rebel' (p. 11). If civil disobedience proves ineffectual, is there a point at which climate protest should become uncivil?
- Uncivil disobedience is also a principled breach of the law in the advancement of a cause. However, it transgresses the bounds of civility through acts that are offensive, covert or violent. One objection to uncivil disobedience is that it is not so much communicative (it might be argued that violence cannot be communicative) as threatening. As such, it is coercive and a violation of the principles of democratic participation.
- An example of uncivil disobedience is what Avia Pasternak (2018) calls 'political rioting', which she defines as 'spontaneous, disorganized, public collective violence in order to protest against and to defy their political order,' citing as an example the riot that followed the death-in-custody of Freddie Gray in 2015 (p. 385). Though rioting involves damage to public

and private property, as well as attacks on police officers, she believes that it is permissible. She writes:

> [T]he political riot is a communicative episode – its participants intending to deliver a message to the police, the government, and to fellow citizens … [P]olitical rioters communicate various messages to these audiences: anger and condemnation of the injustice, a demand for a change of public policy, and a message of defiance of the legal order … Taking part in an act of collective defiance can also give participants and their community a sense of empowerment and self-respect, as they assert themselves as agents who are not cowed by oppression. (pp. 391, 397)

- Examples of organisations, movements and events you might consider when exploring the permissibility and limits of both civil and uncivil disobedience include the Femen protests, Pussy Riot, Just Stop Oil, Extinction Rebellion, the Occupy Movement, the Gilets Jaunes protests, the Ferguson unrest, and the toppling of the statue of Edward Colston.

Anarchism

- The anarchist Pierre-Joseph Proudhon (1923) denounced the state in no uncertain terms:

> To be governed is to be kept in sight, inspected, spied upon, directed, law-driven, numbered, enrolled, indoctrinated, preached at, controlled, estimated, valued, censured, commanded, by creatures who have neither the right, nor the wisdom, nor the virtue to do so…. To be governed is to be at every operation, at every transaction, noted, registered, enrolled, taxed, stamped, measured, numbered, assessed, licensed, authorized, admonished, forbidden, reformed, corrected, punished. It is, under the pretext of public utility, and in the name of the general interest, to be placed under contribution, trained, ransomed, exploited, monopolized, extorted, squeezed, mystified, robbed; then, at the slightest resistance, the first word of complaint, to be repressed, fined, despised, harassed, tracked, abused, clubbed, disarmed, choked, imprisoned, judged, condemned, shot, deported, sacrificed, sold, betrayed; and, to crown all, mocked, ridiculed, outraged, dishonoured. That is government; that is its justice; that is its morality. (p. 294)

- J. Edgar Hoover once described the anarchist Emma Goldman (1910) as one of the most dangerous women in America, and she was eventually deported. This was her assessment of the state:

> Just as religion has fettered the human mind, and as property, or the monopoly of things, has subdued and stifled man's needs, so has the State enslaved

his spirit, dictating every phase of conduct. "All government in essence," says Emerson, "is tyranny." It matters not whether it is government by divine right or majority rule. In every instance its aim is the absolute subordination of the individual …

To achieve such an arrangement of life, government, with its unjust, arbitrary, repressive measures, must be done away with. At best it has but imposed one single mode of life upon all, without regard to individual and social variations and needs. In destroying government and statutory laws, Anarchism proposes to rescue the self-respect and independence of the individual from all restraint and invasion by authority. Only in freedom can man grow to his full stature. Only in freedom will he learn to think and move, and give the very best in him. Only in freedom will he realize the true force of the social bonds which knit men together, and which are the true foundation of a normal social life. (pp. 62–67)

References

Birch, D. (2021). *Pandora's Book: 401 Philosophical Questions to Help You Lose Your Mind (with answers)*. Iff Books.

Cicero. (1894) [c. 54 CE]. On the Commonwealth. C. D. Yonge (Trans.), *Cicero's Tusculan Disputations; Also on The Nature of the Gods and on The Commonwealth* (pp. 357–466). Harper & Brothers.

Emerson, R. W. (1985) [1841]. Self-Reliance. In L. Ziff (Ed.), *Ralph Waldo Emerson: Selected Essays*. Penguin Classics.

Goldman, E. (1910). *Anarchism and Other Essays*. Mother Earth Publishing Association.

Hume, D. (1966) [1748]. Of the Original Contract. *Essays: Moral, Political, and Literary*. Oxford University Press.

King, M. L. K. (1986) [1963]. Letter from Birmingham City Jail. In J. M. Washington (Ed.), *A Testament of Hope: The Essential Writings and Speeches of Martin Luther King, Jr.* Harper Collins.

Pasternak, A. (2018). Political Rioting: A Moral Assessment. *Philosophy & Public Affairs*, 46(4), 384–418.

Plato. (1892) [c. 390 BCE]. Crito. B. Jowett (Trans.), *Dialogues of Plato* (pp. 137–157). Oxford University Press.

Proudhon, J. P. (1923). *General Idea of Revolution in the Nineteenth Century*, J. B. Robinson (Trans.). Freedom Press.

Rawls, J. (1971). *A Theory of Justice*. Routledge.

Snyder, L. L. (1976). *Varieties of Nationalism: A Comparative Study*. The Dryden Press.

Thoreau, H. D. (1995) [1849]. *Civil Disobedience*. Penguin Books.

Thunberg, G. (2019). *No One Is Too Small to Make a Difference*. Penguin Books.

Wolff, R. (1998) [1970]. *In Defense of Anarchism*. University of California Press.

Autonomy and Bodily Integrity

> **Key Questions**
>
> - Do we have a right to bodily integrity?
> - Is the right to bodily integrity absolute?
> - Is a person ever be entitled to the body parts of another?
> - Is it ever permissible to interfere with the arrangements and contracts made between consenting adults?
> - Do we own ourselves?
> - Is there a moral limit to markets?

PART I: BODILY INTEGRITY

Activity 1

Recount to the class the following events which took place in California on July 1st, 1949:

Having 'some information' that Richard Antonio Rochin was selling narcotics, three state officers entered his home and forced their way into the bedroom occupied by him and his wife. When asked about two capsules lying on a bedside table, Rochin put them in his mouth. After an unsuccessful struggle to extract them by force, the officers took Rochin to a hospital, where an emetic was forced into

Fact Check

In England and Wales, a police inspector is permitted to carry out non-consensual 'intimate searches' of a person's orifices while that person is in police detention on the condition that there are reasonable grounds for believing his stomach against his will. He vomited two capsules which were found to contain morphine. These were admitted in evidence and he was convicted of violating a state law forbidding possession of morphine.

the person has concealed on him anything that could cause physical harm to himself or others (Police and Criminal Evidence Act 1984). Additionally, under the Mental Health Act 1983, in the interests of their own safety or the safety of others, a person can be non-consensually admitted, detained and treated (with, for example, electroconvulsive therapy) in a hospital for a mental disorder.

- Enquiry Question: Should such methods of procuring evidence be legal?

Development Questions:

○ Given that the police are able to acquire warrants to search your home, should they be similarly permitted to search your body?

○ Would the use of a body scanner have been permissible? Would this constitute a violation of bodily integrity?

○ Is there a qualitative difference between this and strip-searching a person?

○ In response to this case, a California Supreme Court judge said 'a conviction which rests upon evidence of incriminating objects obtained from the body of the accused by physical abuse is as invalid as a conviction which rests upon a verbal confession extracted from him by such abuse.'[1] The US Supreme Court ultimately reversed Rochin's conviction on the grounds that the method of obtaining the evidence rendered it inadmissible. Was this the correct ruling?

Present the following claim by John Thrasher (2019) to the class and discuss the strength of the analogy between us and our bodies and a sovereign and its territory.

> The individual is sovereign with regard to the body like the monarch or assembly is sovereign over its territory. (p. 118)

Have pupils determine, and explain, the relations between these entities below using one of these two operators: ~ (similar to) or ≁ (not similar to) e.g.

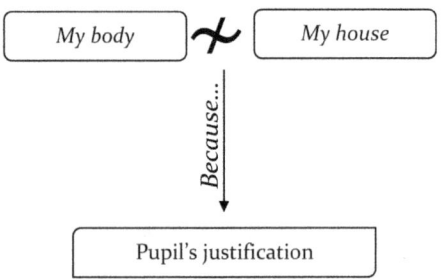

Autonomy and Bodily Integrity

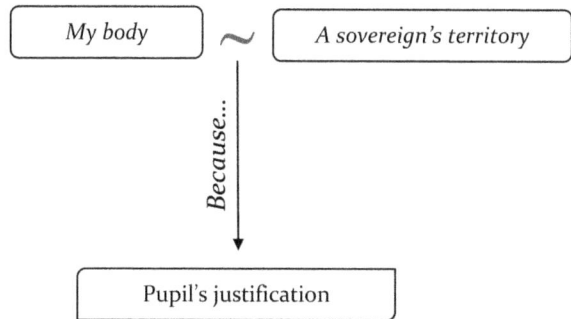

Then have pupils complete both of the following statements and subsequently determine which one they stand in most agreement with:

- *Searching one's body and searching one's home without one's consent are essentially no different because...*
- *Searching one's body and searching one's home without one's consent are fundamentally different because...*

Applying these ideas to concrete scenarios, the task is now for pupils to delineate what they believe ought to be the legal limits of physical interference from the state by drafting an international convention. Forms of physical interference they address might include physical assault, sexual assault, rape, medical experimentation, medical treatment, immunisation, torture and sterilisation.

> **Convention for the Protection of Bodily Integrity**
>
> *To preserve the integrity of the body, it is impermissible, in the absence of consent, and where the individual in question has capacity, for the state to violate the boundaries of a person's body by:*

Activity 2

Present a scenario such as this –

Imagine a country without public services. Leo is a citizen of this country. He is a cleaner who works 13 hour days. Nevertheless, the money he earns isn't enough to pay for adequate housing (he lives in a leaky, cold shack), medicine (he can't afford painkillers required to alleviate his chronic back pain), a healthy diet

Thought Avenue

Would it be permissible for the state to violate one's bodily integrity to protect the interests of another person? Is it ever permissible, for instance, to perform a non-consensual C-section to ensure the survival of the foetus? A reference (his meals largely consist of cheap high-calorie foods such as lard and rice), or an education (he is illiterate), much less enjoy recreational activities. Leo is not alone in his plight. Many people in this country lead abject lives like his.

Aarthi is also a citizen of this country. She inherited her family estate and, through the rent she collects, has more money than she knows how to spend (most of it she pours into other investments). Aarthi is not alone in her privilege. Many people in this country lead affluent lives like hers.

- Enquiry Question (a): Is this situation fair?

- Enquiry Question (b): If this situation is not fair, would it be morally permissible for the state to expropriate a portion (small enough not to impact Aarthi's preferred lifestyle) of Aarthi's wealth (and those similarly privileged) in order to provide housing, education and healthcare to help Leo (and those similarly underprivileged)?

Using the ideas elicited by the discussion, have pupils complete the following:

- *Arguably, it would be morally permissible for the state to expropriate a portion of Aarthi's wealth in order to improve the quality of Leo's life because...*

case for these questions would be the treatment of Angela Carder at George Washington University Hospital in 1987. During her pregnancy, she was diagnosed with cancer. At 26 weeks, her doctors sought a judicial ruling to authorise a C-section in a bid to save the foetus before Carder died, and a lawyer was duly appointed to represent the foetus. Against the wishes of her family and without her express consent, the judge ordered the surgery. The baby only lived for two hours following the operation, and Carder died two days later.

A related thought experiment, one which requires very delicate handling, involves a post-apocalyptic scenario in which there is only one woman left in existence. To ensure the survival of the species, the remaining men urge her to submit to impregnation, but she refuses. Would it be permissible to violate her bodily integrity via intrauterine insemination?

For a less problematic scenario, you might explore these questions in relation to Austria's decision in February 2022 to make Covid-19 vaccinations mandatory for adults. Those who didn't comply faced fines of up to 3,600 euros (the law was suspended after only a month).

Continue with the scenario –

Leo's back pain is not his only health condition. He also suffers from an immune deficiency disorder which means that he is particularly vulnerable to infections and is frequently unwell. There is no medicine that can remedy this condition. To lead a normal healthy life Leo needs a bone marrow transplant, but there are no available marrow donors.

Aarthi is in perfect health. She also happens to be a perfect donor match for Leo. If she were to undergo the painless procedure of having a portion of her marrow extracted she could, without any cost to her health, enable Leo to lead a healthy life.

- Enquiry Question (c): Would it be morally permissible for the state to expropriate a portion (small enough not to impact her health) of the bone marrow of Aarthi in order to enable Leo to lead a healthy life?

Development Questions:

○ If one's answer to question (b) was 'yes', would it be inconsistent to answer 'no' to (c)?

Arguably, it would be morally permissible for the state to expropriate a portion of Aarthi's body in order to improve the quality of Leo's health because...

Ask pupils to plug their ideas from the previous written exercise into this sentence. Do the same principles and ideas expressed therein justify the expropriation of body parts? If so, does that show that if taxation is justifiable, then so is the removal of body parts? If not, what is the source of the incompatibility?

Cécile Fabre (2003) regards the two scenarios as morally analogous and therefore believes that 'the state has a moral power of eminent domain to expropriate, as it were, healthy individuals from some of their body parts [regenerative body parts such as blood and marrow], just as property-owners can be expropriated, against compensation, from their property' (p. 140). She writes –

> [I]f one thinks that the badly off have a moral right, as a matter of justice, to the material resources they need in order to lead a minimally flourishing life, then, in some cases [...] one must be committed to conferring on the sick a moral right that the able-bodied supply them the body parts they need in order to lead such a life.
> Fabre (2006, p. 98)

Discuss this passage. It should be emphasised that Fabre doesn't actually think the state should enforce this moral right of the sick because it would face insurmountable public opposition. It should also be emphasised that the state's enforcement of this moral right need not be a matter of forcibly subjecting individuals to invasive medical

Thought Avenue

Fabre (2003) has written: 'Regular sexual intercourse is one of the things most human beings need in order to lead a decent life ... But if the healthy are under a duty to make available (some of their) body parts to the sick on the grounds that the sick need those body parts in order to lead a decent life, then by the same token, it seems that individuals are under a duty to make themselves available to the sexually deprived whose life is not, for that reason, decent' (p. 141). She believes, however, that her views on body parts do not have this implication. Is she right? Is there a qualitative difference between these violations of bodily integrity?

procedures but penalising, with, say, fines or prison, those who do not comply with the law. Ask pupils to complete the argument schematic below, deciding on which relation (~ or ~̸) they think holds between these two state interventions and therefore whether the state's moral right to my income entails the state's moral right to my body (→ or ↛).

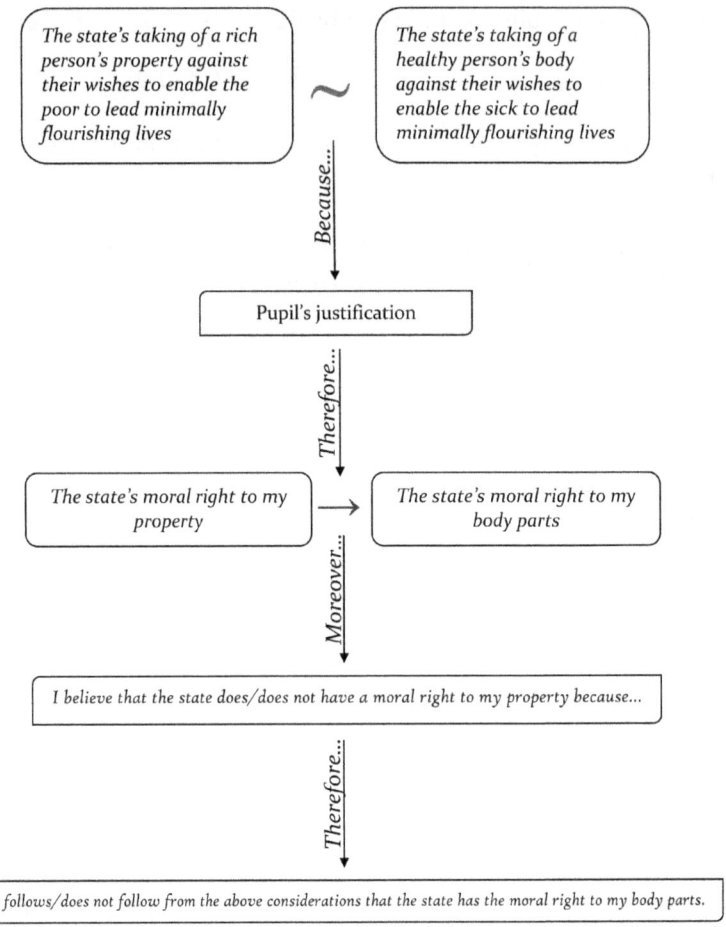

One could well believe that expropriation of body parts is just, but not on the basis that it is analogous to taxation, so to be entirely clear on where they stand pupils should similarly decide on the relation below using either < > as they see fit:

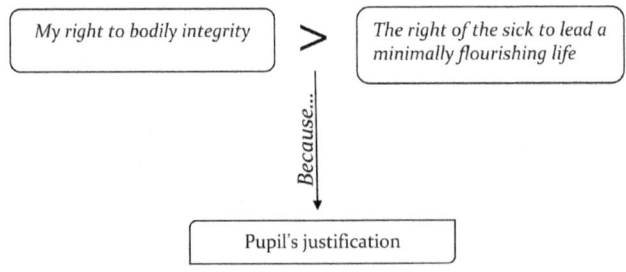

Having completed this, pupils should revisit and, if necessary, revise their Convention on the Protection of Bodily Integrity.

Activity 3

This activity considers whether a paternalistic violation of bodily integrity is permissible. Joel Feinberg (1986), who was opposed to hard paternalism, wrote: 'The life that a person threatens by his own rashness is after all his life; it belongs to him and to no one else. For that reason alone, he must be the one to decide—for better or worse—what is to be done with it in that private realm where the interests of others are not directly involved' (p. 59). Contrariwise, Danny Scoccia (2013) has written:

> Consider a state that attempts to coerce its citizens via fines and short jail sentences to convert to what it insists is the true religion, belief in which is necessary to avoid eternal damnation … [I]f this state's claims about the religion that it favors are true, then the benefit of its paternalism, if successful, will be infinite … Wouldn't it be right for a state to infringe its citizens' autonomy via mildly coercive measures if the expected benefits were infinite? (pp. 89–90)

Concept Check

Paternalism is the interference with the actions of another person in order to safeguard that person's best interests. According to **soft paternalism**, paternalistic interference is only permissible when the individual may not be fully apprised of the facts relevant to their decision (e.g. it is permissible to stop a person about to cross a bridge to inform them that it is liable to collapse; however, once they are aware of this, we cannot then stop them) or their judgment is impaired by an aberrant mental state such as fatigue, drunkenness or psychosis. According to **hard paternalism**, interference is permissible even when the individual is fully informed and unimpaired. This can either be to safeguard their physical and psychological well-being (**welfare paternalism**) or their moral well-being (**moral paternalism**).

He believes this thought experiment shows that the right to autonomy is not absolute. Let's think it through by slightly modifying the scenario:

> *Last year God descended from the heavens to inform the French of His existence. He led every French person on a tour of hell where they saw the likes of Henry Kissinger and Reginald Dyer burning in lakes of fire, desperately imploring the gawking visitors to mend their ways and avoid this dastardly fate. They were also whisked up to heaven to witness its beauty and bliss.*
>
> *Despite God's revelation to them, and His warning that those who do not recognise or honour Him face an eternity with Kissinger, many French people have remained stubbornly secular. The government has pleaded with them to at least take Holy Communion, but they refuse. 'Yes, yes, God exists, we know,' they say, 'but we don't want to think about death and the afterlife. We want to live for the present. Of course, there is always the risk of a premature and unforeseen*

death, but whatever, we'll throw caution to the wind. In the future we may well do as God asked, but for now, we'd rather keep religion out of lives.'

- Enquiry Question (a): To prevent their eternal damnation, would it be permissible for the government to enact laws compelling its citizens to receive Holy Communion?

- Enquiry Question (b): To prevent their eternal damnation, would it be permissible for the government to have the water supply surreptitiously laced with communion wine?

Development Question:

○ If most French people who ascended to heaven were grateful that the state had coerced them into taking communion, would this retrospectively justify paternalistic interference? (Gerald Dworkin calls this 'future-oriented consent', a notion he uses to justify the paternalistic interference with children by their parents.)

To serve as a diagrammatic correlate to their Convention, pupils should now be able to complete the following using a ✓ (with details to outline the circumstances) or ✗ to indicate moral permissibility (the direction of the arrows indicates whether the violation of bodily integrity is one of extraction of insertion). The dashed arrow indicates the state preventing entry, which is addressed in the next activity.

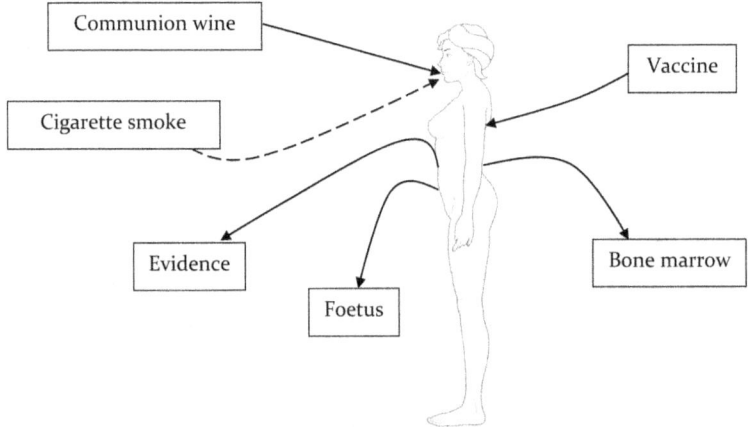

Activity 4

The previous three activities have been concerned with what the state may remove from our bodies. Let's now turn to the paternalistic question of what, if anything, the state may prevent us from putting into them.

Start by presenting this classic example of soft paternalistic interference from J. S. Mill (1910):

> [T]he only purpose for which power can be rightfully exercised over any member of a civilised community, against his will, is to prevent harm to others. His own good, either physical or moral, is not a sufficient warrant. He cannot rightfully be compelled to do or forbear because it will be better for him to do so, because it will make him happier, because, in the opinions of others, to do so would be wise, or even right. These are good reasons for remonstrating with him, or reasoning with him, or persuading him, or entreating him, but not for compelling him, or visiting him with any evil in case he do otherwise …
>
> If either a public officer or any one else saw a person attempting to cross a bridge which had been ascertained to be unsafe, and there were no time to warn him of his danger, they might seize him and turn him back, without any real infringement of his liberty; for liberty consists in doing what one desires, and he does not desire to fall into the river. (pp. 73, 151–152)

Now present a variation –

> *Imagine that Mia knows that the bridge is unsafe but reasons like so: 'Certainly I don't want to die, but I've never died before today, so I think it's unlikely that the bridge will collapse while I cross it.' You explain to her that her reasoning is not very strong. 'You might be right', she says, 'but I really don't see myself having a violent death. I can't see myself as a news item'.*

Have pupils address the following questions:

- Would Mill think it is permissible to stop Mia from crossing the bridge?
- Do *you* think it is permissible to stop Mia from crossing the bridge?

In the scenario, Mia doesn't want to die, but despite knowing the bridge is unsafe, poor reasoning means she is going to act against her own express interests. The paternalist Sarah Conly (2013) would cite such a case as highlighting the problem with Mill's criteria for state interference. She would say that preventing Mia from crossing the bridge is not only permissible, but it is also the right thing to do.

She claims that our capacity to make rational decisions is compromised by cognitive biases, highlighting, for instance, the smoker's bias of time-discounting (disproportionately prioritising present pleasures over future pains) to show that simply being aware of the facts about the dangers of smoking is not sufficient to block paternalistic interference. If the application of those facts to our own decisions is impeded by poor reasoning, then Conly believes that the state can justly interfere in our lives. It would be just, that is to say, for the state to violate our bodily integrity by preventing us from putting cigarette smoke into our bodies. She writes:

> The truth is that we don't reason very well, and in many cases there is no justification for leaving us to struggle with our own inabilities and to suffer the consequences … Typically, people who smoke […] irrationally underestimate the dangers of smoking

to themselves, even while admitting its general danger ... They satisfy the criterion of knowledge as Mill seems to imagine it in the bridge example; they know the facts. They fail to satisfy the criteria of rational choice, however, because of cognitive failures in applying these facts. (pp. 1, 44)

- Enquiry Question: Has Conly made a convincing case for banning cigarettes?

Following this discussion, have pupils complete the following:

Action	Do you do this regularly?	Do you know the likely negative outcome of not doing this regularly?	Do you want those outcomes?	If your sequence of answers is 'No', 'Yes', 'No', does this show that you are not reasoning well about your decisions?	If your sequence of answers is 'No', 'Yes', 'No', should you be coerced into performing this action?
Flossing					
Eating five daily portions of fruit and vegetables					
Getting more than six hours of sleep per day					
Reading					
Exercising					
Significant time away from social media					
Revising adequately for exams					

Make pupils aware that if there is at least once 'Yes' in the final column then they are a hard paternalist. Ask them to complete the following:

Poor reasoning does/does not constitute just grounds for interfering in the decisions of an otherwise well-informed and clear-headed individual because…

They should now revisit the diagram in Activity 3 to indicate their stance on smoking. They should also be in a position to complete the following apotheotic declaration:

It is morally permissible for the state to violate the bodily integrity of a person if and only if…

PART II: AUTONOMY

The last section started to metamorphose from a consideration of bodily integrity to that of autonomy more broadly. We are going to revisit and investigate more closely Mill's claim that 'the only purpose for which power can be rightfully exercised over any member of a civilised community, against his will, is to prevent harm to others'.

Activity 1

Our central question with this activity is whether it is permissible to interfere with the actions carried out by and between consenting adults. Have pupils complete the following table. For welfare paternalists, 'Yes' in the fourth column might be sufficient to answer 'No' in the final column. Likewise the fifth column for moral paternalists.

Activity	Details	Legal status	Does it harm one's physical well-being?	Does it involve morally debasing oneself?	Is it immoral?	Should it be legal?
Snake Handling	Inspired by scripture,* this is a sometimes fatal form of Christian worship that arose in churches in Appalachia in the US. Dozens have died and been maimed by the practice.	West Virginia is the only Appalachian state where it is legal.				

Mutilation	In the late 1990s, an orthopaedic surgeon named Robert Smith carried out below-the-knee amputations on the healthy limbs of two men suffering from Body Dysmorphic Disorder. One of the patients later said, 'By taking my leg away that surgeon has made me complete'.[2] In 2019, Jacob Crimi-Appleby froze the leg of Marius Gustavson at the latter's request so that it would require amputation.	Medical amputation of healthy limbs is not illegal in the UK. Crimi-Appleby was sentenced to three years and eight months in prison for grievous bodily harm.				
Cannibalism	In 2001, Armin Meiwes placed an online ad seeking someone willing to be eaten. Bernd-Jurgen Brandes responded to the ad and travelled to Meiwes's house in the town of Wüstefeld where he was consensually killed. Meiwes froze and gradually ate the body, consuming about forty pounds of it prior to his arrest.	Germany has no laws against cannibalism. Meiwes was convicted of murder and sentenced to life in prison.				

* *'I have given you authority to trample on snakes and scorpions and to overcome all the power of the enemy; nothing will harm you'*, Luke 10:19; *'And these signs will accompany those who believe: In my name, they will drive out demons; they will speak in new tongues; they will pick up snakes with their hands'*, Mark 16:17–18.

> **Thought Avenue**
>
> Libertarian paternalists are those who seek to respect and preserve our autonomy while manipulating the 'choice architecture' to gently nudge us in the right direction. Research shows, for instance, that the layout of food in cafes and shops can affect consumer choice. People are more likely to choose the food that is at eye level, so a nudge towards a healthy diet would involve placing fruit at eye level and salty or sugary snacks on the bottom shelf. People, moreover, are more inclined to opt for an outcome which is presented as having a 20% chance of success rather than an 80% chance of failure, a fact that could be used when, say, encouraging the population to take certain vaccines. Are libertarian paternalists correct that these nudges do not undermine or compromise our autonomy? Is a manipulated choice still a genuine choice?

Activity 2

The aim now is to provide justification for the answers given in the table above. Present pupils the following claims.

> Every Man has a Property in his own Person. This no Body has any Right to but himself.
>
> John Locke (Quoted in Cohen, 1995, p. 209)

> 'To every Individuall in nature is given an individual property by nature, not to be invaded or usurped by any: for everyone as he is himselfe, so he has a self propriety, else could he not be himself … Every man by nature being a King, Priest and Prophet in his owne naturall circuit and compasse.'
>
> Richard Overton (Ibid., p. 209)

> '[E]very man is himself and belongs to himself, and represents his own individuality, not only in form and features, but in thought and feeling.'
>
> Frederick Douglas (Quoted in Thrasher, 2019, p. 116)

While it is uncontroversial to speak of self-love, self-hate, self-control, self-belief, self-knowledge, does it similarly make sense to speak of self-ownership? To probe this question, think of the

> **Thought Avenue**
>
> Should the state authorise and protect slave contracts made between consenting parties? Imagine, for instance, that two people very much wanted a slave, even to the extent that they were willing to risk becoming one themselves. They therefore agreed to toss a coin, signing a contract with the following terms before doing so: 'Whoever loses

implications of owning a particular item and the extent to which they apply to the body:

- **Possession:** Exclusive control of the item entailing no interference without consent.
- **Use:** Personal use of the item.
- **Income:** The power to extract financial value from the item.
- **Liability:** The item can be taken by creditors in lieu of payment.
- **Divestment:** The power to part with the item via gift or sale.

The two aspects of ownership that may pose a problem for self-ownership are divestment and liability. Can we part with the body via gift or sale? Should we allow creditors to take the body in lieu of payment? On this last question, if bailiffs can take our cars, why not, say, our hair (the global market for wigs and extensions was worth $5.8bn in 2021)? If one does bristle at the idea of bailiffs taking our body parts, does this show that our body is not property? On this question of divestment Eike-Henner Kluge (1975) has written, 'What we own—in any full-blooded sense of that term—we can disown, give away, sell, or otherwise dispose of so that it becomes the property of someone else. We cannot do this with our lives. Therefore, whatever the unique relationship this bears to us, it cannot be one of ownership' (p. 119).

> this coin toss will thereafter have a duty to fulfil all the commands of the winner, a duty they cannot release themselves from.' J. S. Mill (1910) believed the state should not allow or honour such contracts: 'The reason for not interfering, unless for the sake of others, with a person's voluntary acts, is consideration for his liberty ... [B]y selling himself for a slave, he abdicates his liberty; he forgoes any future use of it, beyond that single act. He therefore defeats, in his own case, the very purpose which is the justification of allowing him to dispose of himself ... The principle of freedom cannot require that he should be free not to be free. It is not freedom, to be allowed to alienate his freedom'. (pp. 157–158)

Have pupils complete the following using = or ≠ as they see fit:

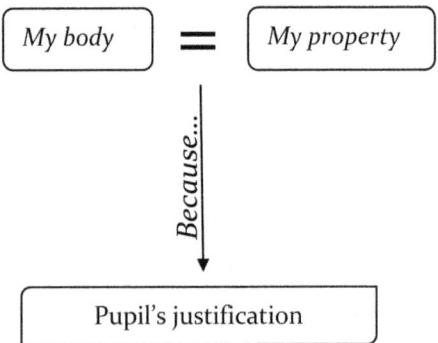

Drawing on these ideas, or the concepts of welfare paternalism, moral paternalism and legal moralism, as they see fit, they should not then complete the following:

I believe that acts which do no harm to non-consenting parties and are carried out by and between consenting and informed adults who have capacity should always/not always be legal because…

Activity 3

To further explore the notion of self-ownership and its relation to autonomy, let's focus on the 'income' dimension of the body. To what extent should the state permit the body to be consensually commodified and marketised? There are at least two possible objections to permitting the body to become part of market exchange:

- It is exploitative (it is not a free exchange because the impoverished condition of one party means that their power to demur is significantly compromised).
- It is degrading because it commodifies that which, due to its profound intrinsic value, should not be commodified.

	Details	Is this exploitative?	Is this degrading?	Should it be legal?	Justification for its legal status
Commercial* surrogacy	Unlike the UK, commercial surrogacy is legal in Ukraine (altruistic surrogacy is legal in the UK and surrogates can be paid to cover 'reasonable expenses') with surrogates earning up to £20,000. It is a popular choice for foreign couples. One surrogate explained her rationale: 'It's hard to find a well-paid job in Ukraine. I wanted to renovate the house and set aside money for my son's university fees – they're very expensive.'[3]				

Sterilisation	Project Prevention is a charity founded by Barbara Harris which pays drug addicts to undergo sterilisation (tubal ligations and vasectomies) to ensure they don't give birth to drug-dependent babies.					
Dwarf tossing	Illegal in Florida and New York, dwarf tossing is a 'bar sport' which involves throwing a person with dwarfism. Governor Mario Cuomo justified his decision to prohibit the practice by saying, 'Any activity which dehumanizes and humiliates these people is degrading to us all'.[4] When a Paris suburb banned dwarf tossing, Manuel Wackenheim, who has dwarfism, sued because he wanted to continue making a living being tossed. France's supreme court of administrative justice upheld the ban, stating that dwarf tossing 'affronted human dignity'. Wackenheim complained to the United Nations Human Rights Committee, but his complaint was rejected.					

Organ sales	Iran is the only country in the world where it is legal to buy and sell kidneys. Nasser Simforoosh, chairman of the kidney transplantation department at the Shahid Labbafinejad Medical Center, has commented on the business: 'Yes, people donate because they need money, but this is a reality all over the world. Instead of doing something illegal to cover their debts, like stealing or smuggling, they are saving a life first. This is not exploitation. The end result is good for the recipient and the donor.'[5] Research into illegal kidney donors in India found that 96% had sold their kidneys to pay off debts, 86% reported a marked deterioration in their health and 79% would not recommend others to do the same.				

* To guide pupils' thinking on this, you might present the following perspectives:

- The 1984 Report of the Committee of Inquiry into Human Fertilisation and Embryology chaired by Mary Warnock, which informed the Surrogacy Arrangements Act 1985, concluded that commercial surrogacy violates the dignity of a woman's sexuality and reproduction: 'It is

Thought Avenue

Is the selling of our body parts any more degrading or exploitative than the selling of our labour? Karl Marx (1986) wrote, '[The worker] feels at home when he is not working, and when he is working inconsistent with human dignity that a woman should use her uterus for financial profit' (Quoted in Satz, 2010, p. 120). The objection is targeted squarely at the commodifying rather than the exploitative nature of the transaction.

- Elizabeth Anderson (1990) develops this perspective by suggesting that one cannot respect a person while also using them to fulfil your own ends. In her own words, commercial surrogacy 'reduces the surrogate mothers from persons worthy of respect and consideration to objects of mere use ... When women's labor is treated as a commodity, the women who perform it are degraded.' (p. 80)

- In her book *Why Some Things Should Not be for Sale: The Moral Limits of Markets*, the philosopher Debra Satz

> he does not feel at home. His labour is therefore not voluntary, but coerced; it is forced labour. It is therefore not the satisfaction of a need; it is merely a means to satisfy needs external to it' (p. 39). In the words of Carole Pateman, the consequence of entry into an employment contract is 'subordination' and a 'diminution' of 'autonomy and self-government'. G. D. H. Cole believed that the servile and undemocratic structure of the workplace precluded genuine political democracy: 'Why are the many nominally supreme but actually powerless? Largely because the circumstances of their lives do not accustom or fit them for power or responsibility. A servile system in industry inevitably reflects itself in political servility' (Quoted in Pateman, 1970, p. 38).

expresses doubts about the claims from Warnock and Anderson. She suggests that one cannot consistently oppose commercial surrogacy on the grounds that it compromises a woman's dignity while not taking issue with women selling their bodies in other ways: 'Why is selling the use of a woman's uterus "undignified", while selling the use of images of her body for a television commercial is not?' (p. 120). Satz makes the further point that it is possible to treat a commodity with respect; to sell one's service does not necessarily degrade one or make one an object of mere use. She cites the example of teaching: 'I think that my teaching talents should be respected, but I don't object to being paid for teaching on such grounds.' (Ibid., p. 120)

- One argument in favour of commercial surrogacy could run as follows:

1. We have absolute right over our property.

2. Whatever I own is my property.

3. I own myself.

4. Therefore, I am my property.

5. Therefore, I have absolute right over myself.

Immanuel Kant (1930), however, rejected this reasoning on a number of levels. Firstly, he disputes premise 3 on a conceptual basis:

1. If x is owned, it is necessarily a thing.

2. If x is an owner, it is necessarily a person.

3. An entity cannot be both a thing and a person (both an object and a subject, that is a contradiction).

4. Therefore, one cannot own oneself for that would make one both owner and owned, both person and thing.

He expresses this argument like so:

> Man cannot dispose over himself because he is not a thing; he is not his own property; to say that he is would be self-contradictory; for in so far as he is a person he is a Subject in whom the ownership of things can be vested, and if he were his own property, he would be a thing over which he could have ownership. But a person cannot be a property and so cannot be a thing which can be owned, for it is impossible to be a person and a thing, the proprietor and the property. (p. 165)

Not only does it conceptually make no sense to claim that we have a right to sell ourselves since we own ourselves, Kant also thinks this position is morally problematic. He believes that we should not treat persons as objects of mere use, a prohibition that applies to both how we treat others and how we treat ourselves. Whether it's your own or another's, debasing and degrading a person's humanity is always wrong. He addresses this point in relation to sex work:

> [T]o allow one's person for profit to be used by another for the satisfaction of sexual desire, to make of oneself an object of demand, is to dispose over oneself as over a thing and to make of oneself a thing on which another satisfies his appetite, just as he satisfies his hunger upon a steak. But since the inclination is directed towards one's sex and not towards one's humanity, it is clear that one thus partially sacrifices one's humanity and thereby runs a moral risk. Human beings are, therefore, not entitled to offer themselves, for profit, as things for the use of others in the satisfaction of their sexual propensities … The underlying moral principle is that man is not his own property and cannot do with his body what he will. The body is part of the self; in its togetherness with the self it constitutes the person … (pp. 165–166)

Activity 4

Time to synthesise and conclude –

There ought to be extensive/some/no legal limits to the behaviour between consenting adults. With respect to degrading acts, I believe that individuals should always/should not always be free to permit their own degradation. I also believe that exploitation does/does not violate one's autonomy. As such, a consensual act where one is fully apprised of the relevant facts is always/not always an autonomous act. It follows from this that all/not all freely entered into market transactions should be legal. The fundamental principle behind my thinking is this ...

Notes

1 https://supreme.justia.com/cases/federal/us/342/165/
2 https://www.theguardian.com/uk/2000/feb/06/theobserver.uknews6
3 https://www.aljazeera.com/features/2018/9/13/ukraines-baby-factories-the-human-cost-of-surrogacy
4 https://www.latimes.com/archives/la-xpm-1990-07-25-mn-1001-story.html
5 https://www.latimes.com/world/middleeast/la-fg-iran-kidney-20171015-story.html#:~:text=%E2%80%9CThis%20is%20not%20exploitation.,organ%20sales%20aim%20to%20prevent.

References

Anderson, E. (1990). Is Women's Labor a Commodity? *Philosophy and Public Affairs.* 19(1), 71–92.
Cohen, G. A. (1995). *Self-Ownership, Freedom, and Equality.* Cambridge University Press.
Conly, S. (2013). *Against Autonomy: Justifying Coercive Paternalism.* Cambridge University Press.
Fabre, C. (2003). Justice and the Compulsory Taking of Body Parts. *Utilitas,* 15(2), 127–150.
Fabre, C. (2006). *Whose Body Is It Anyway? Justice and the Integrity of the Person,* Oxford University Press.
Feinberg, J. (1986). *The Moral Limits of the Criminal Law Volume 3: Harm to Self.* Oxford University Press.
Kant, I. (1930). *Lectures on Ethics* (Trans. L. Infield.). Methuen & Co.
Kluge, E-H. (1975). *The Practice of Death.* Yale University Press.
Marx, K. (1986) [1844]. The Economic and Philosophical Manuscripts of 1944. In J. Elster (Ed.), *Karl Marx: A Reader* (pp. 35–47). Cambridge University Press.
Mill, J. S. (1910) [1859]. On Liberty. *Utilitarianism, Liberty and Representative Government.* J. M. Dent & Sons.
Pateman, C. (1970). *Participation and Democratic Theory.* Cambridge University Press.
Satz, D. (2010). *Why Some Things Should Not Be for Sale: The Moral Limits of Markets.* Oxford University Press.
Scoccia, D. (2013). The Right to Autonomy and the Justification of Hard Paternalism. In C. Coons & M. Weber (Eds.), *Paternalism: Theory and Practice* (pp. 74–93). Cambridge University Press.
Thrasher, J. (2019). Self-Ownership as Personal Sovereignty. *Social Philosophy and Policy,* 36(2), 116–133.

Index

Note: Bold page numbers refer to tables.

ableism 56
abortion law 9
agape 155
ahimsa 99
anarchism 181, 185–186
Anderson, Elizabeth 204
Anscombe, Elizabeth 100
anthropocentrism 72, 75–76, 79
antinatalism 24–25
Aquinas, Thomas 41–2, 70, 156, 166
argument schematics 2, 12, 22, 38, 53, 54, 118, 143, 146, 149, 167, 192
argument trees 12, 15, 62, 88, 134, 136, 149
Aristotle 42, 70
Augustine 31, 41, 75, 174
Aurelius, Marcus 148
Australia, White Australia policy 141–142

Barrington, Mary Rose 45
Basil, Caesarea of 121–122
Belgium, euthanasia laws of 28–29, 30
Benatar, David 24–25
Bentham, Jeremy 75, 155
Bible: 1 John 39, 43; 1 Samuel 31; 2 Corinthians 44; Deuteronomy 170; Exodus 75, 154; Ezekiel 170; Genesis 65–66; Isaiah 65; John 39, 43; Acts 136, 175; Judges 31; Luke 43, 122, 169, 198; Mark 39, 132, 198; Matthew 31, 98, 103, 132–133; Philippians 29, 44; Romans 98, 166, 175

biocentrism 72, 75, 79
Black Lives Matter 169
Braithwaite, John 153, 155
Brittain, Vera 89–90, 102
Browning, Elizabeth 77

Camus, Albert 166
capabilities approach 55
Carens, Joseph 145, 148
Carruthers, Peter 57–58, 69
Che Guevara 99
Chesterton, G. K. 42
Cicero 84, 92, 176
civil disobedience 184–185
Code of Hammurabi, 155
Cole, G. D. H. 204
colonialism 99
Conly, Sarah 195–196
consent, different types of 135, 180, 194
contractualism 57–58
cosmopolitanism 147–148
Crisp, Roger 63
Cyprian, Saint 78, 133

Dalai Lama 96
Darrow, Clarence 64, 170
Davis, Angela 170
Declaration of Geneva 31–32
deep ecology 76, 79
Deleuze, Gilles 5

Descartes, René 69
Devall, Bill 76
Dickens, Charles 169
Donne, John 39
Douglass, Frederick 199
duty, different types of 115

ecocentrism 75, 79
ecofeminism 76, 79
Einstein, Albert 179
Emerson, Ralph Waldo 174, 186
Euripides 44
extensive farming 59

Fabre, Cécile 88, 191
Fanon, Frantz 99
Feinberg, Joel 193
Fleurbaey, Marc 112
Francis of Assisi 122–123
Freud, Sigmund 99–100
Frey, R. G. 58, 69
Fullwinder, Robert 93

Geneva Conventions 85, 102, 108
Golden Rule 15
Goldman, Emma 181, 185
Graves, Robert 97
Guattari, Félix 5

Haag, Ernest van den 156, 165
Hardwig, John 45
Hare, R. M. *see* Golden Rule
Hecht, Jennifer Michael 41
Herbert, George 77
Hippocratic Oath 31
Hobbes, Thomas 127
Homer, *Odyssey* 69
Hume, David 127, 180–181
Hurka, Thomas 91
Huxley, Aldous 97–98

Ignatius of Antioch 43
infanticide 11–12, 16, 45–46
intensive farming 50–51
Iran, capital punishment in 168
Islam, pacifism in 100

Jantzen, Grace 76, 78
Jesus 39, 69, 122, 132–133, 156, 169
Josephus, Flavius 38–39, 42
jus ad bellum 92–93, 98–99

Kaba, Mariame 170–171
Kant, Immanuel 27, 70, 75, 205
Khan, Abdul Ghaffar 100
Kierkegaard, Søren 155–156
King, Martin Luther 98–99, 174

Lenin, Vladimir 99
Leopold, Aldo 76–76
lex talionis 153
libertarianism 131–138
Locke, John 17, 126–127, 130–131, 137, 199

Malcolm X 99
marginal cases, argument from 61–62
Marquis, Don 19–20
martyrdom 43
Marx, Karl 203–204
Masada, siege of 38–40
McKeogh, Colm 91
McMahan, Jeff 20, 45–46, 67, 87, 92–95
Mill, J. S. 34–36, 166, 195, 196, 200
Miller, David 117, 147, 150
Milton, John 78

Naess, Arne 76
Nagel, Thomas 106–107
Netherlands, euthanasia laws of 28
Nietzsche, Friedrich 44, 97
Norcross, Alastair 52–55
Nozick, Robert 132–133, 136–137
Nussbaum, Martha 55, 57, 64

Oberman, Kieran 145–147
Oregon, assisted suicide in 34
organ trade 203
Orwell, George 89–90, 97, 102
Overton, Richard 69, 199

pacifism 84, 96–100
panentheism 78
pantheism 78

passive euthanasia 36–37
Pasternak, Avia 184
Pateman, Carol 204
paternalism, different types of 193, 199
Pearce, David 65
Plato 28, 41, 61, 97, 136, 168, 176
Plutarch 68–69
political rioting 184–185
predation 64–68
prison abolition 169–170
problem of dirty hands 106–107
pronatalism 25
Proudhon, Pierre-Joseph 185
Pythagoras 65, 68, 69

qisas see Iran

Rachels, James 33, 36–37, 118–120, 123–124
Rachels, Stuart 25
Rawls, John 184
realism 84, 100
Refugee Convention 140
Regan, Tom 55
Reiman, Jeffrey 167–168
replaceability 46, 63
rights, different types of 129
Rousseau, Jean-Jacques 147–148
Russell, Bertrand 155
Ryan, Cheney 97

sabr see Islam
Sandel, Michael 131–132
Sartre, Jean-Paul 99
Satz, Debra 204
Schopenhauer, Arthur 25
Schweitzer, Albert 75
Scoccia, Danny 193
Seneca 33, 38–40
Sengupta, Arjun 112
senicide 44–45
sentiocentrism 72, 75, 79
Sessions, George 76
Singer, Peter 25, 46, 56, 63, 112–119, 124
slavery: consensual 199–200; Nat Turner's rebellion 103–104, 106–107; taxation as an instance of 136–137

Socrates 168, 176–178, 180, 183–184
snake handling **197**
speciesism 56
state of nature 127, 129
supreme emergency 105
surrogacy **201**, 203–205

Tännsjö, Torbjörn 25
Taylor, Paul 61
Taylor, Sunaura *see* ableism
theft: taxation as an instance of 134–135; wealth as an instance of 121–123
Thomson, Judith Jarvis 20–22, 57
Thoreau, Henry David 175, 184
Thucydides 84
Thunberg, Greta 184
Tooley, Michael 12–13, 16, 19, 46
Tolstoy, Leo 98–99
torture 167
transhumanism 65
Turner, Nat *see* slavery

Universal Declaration of Human Rights 9, 33, 139, 146, 147, 152, 165, 167, 170
utilitarianism 25, 33, 36

vegetarianism 68–69
Virgil 77

Walzer, Michael 87–88, 93, 105–107, 144, 150
war: Peloponnesian 84; Spanish Civil 97; World, First 97–98; World, Second 89–90, 105, 107
Warnock, Mary 203–204
Warren, Karen J. 76
Warren, Mary Anne 10–11, 13, 16, 19
Wellman, Christopher 142–143
Wittgenstein, Ludwig 42
Wolff, Robert 181–182
Woolf, Virginia 1
Wordsworth, William 77

Zinn, Howard 90–91, 96, 109

For Product Safety Concerns and Information please contact our EU representative GPSR@taylorandfrancis.com
Taylor & Francis Verlag GmbH, Kaufingerstraße 24, 80331 München, Germany

www.ingramcontent.com/pod-product-compliance
Lightning Source LLC
Chambersburg PA
CBHW082059230426
43670CB00017B/2900